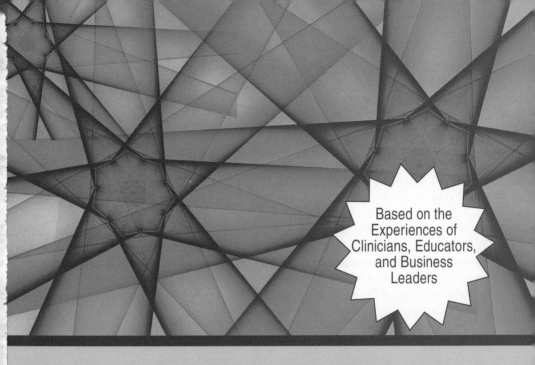

Based on the
Experiences of
Clinicians, Educators,
and Business
Leaders

Mentoring Leaders

The Power of Storytelling for Building Leadership in Health Care and Education

Ellie Gilfoyle, DSc(Hon), FAOTA
Ann Grady, PhD, FAOTA
Cathy Nielson, MPH, FAOTA

With Contributions From Wendy Coster, PhD, OTR/L, FAOTA

D1400530

AOTA PRESS®
The American
Occupational Therapy
Association, Inc.

AOTA Centennial Vision
We envision that occupational therapy is a powerful, widely recognized, science-driven, and evidence-based profession with a globally connected and diverse workforce meeting society's occupational needs.

Mission Statement
The American Occupational Therapy Association advances the quality, availability, use, and support of occupational therapy through standard-setting, advocacy, education, and research on behalf of its members and the public.

AOTA Staff
Frederick P. Somers, *Executive Director*
Christopher M. Bluhm, *Chief Operating Officer*

Chris Davis, *Director, AOTA Press*
Ashley Hofmann, *Development/Production Editor*
Victoria Davis, *Production Editor/Editorial Assistant*
Amy McShane, *Development Consultant*

Beth Ledford, *Director, Marketing*
Emily Zhang, *Technology Marketing Specialist*
Jennifer Folden, *Marketing Specialist*

American Occupational Therapy Association, Inc.
4720 Montgomery Lane
Bethesda, MD 20814
Phone: 301-652-AOTA (2682)
TDD: 800-377-8555
Fax: 301-652-7711
www.aota.org
To order: http://store.aota.org

Disclaimers
This publication is designed to provide accurate and authoritative information in regard to the subject matter covered. It is sold or distributed with the understanding that the publisher is not engaged in rendering legal, accounting, or other professional service. If legal advice or other expert assistance is required, the services of a competent professional person should be sought.
—*From the Declaration of Principles jointly adopted by the American Bar Association and a Committee of Publishers and Associations*

It is the objective of the American Occupational Therapy Association to be a forum for free expression and interchange of ideas. The opinions expressed by the contributors to this work are their own and not necessarily those of the American Occupational Therapy Association.

ISBN: 978-1-56900-319-0

Library of Congress Control Number: 2011901817

Cover Design by Debra Naylor, Debra Naylor Design, Inc., *Washington, DC*
Composition by Maryland Composition, *Laurel, MD*
Printed by Automated Graphic Systems, Inc., *White Plains, MD*

Contents

About the Authors

Elnora "Ellie" Gilfoyle, DSc(Hon), FAOTA

For over 50 years, Ellie has served the profession of occupational therapy and Colorado State University (CSU), and she has been a strong advocate for women and leadership. She has many awards for her accomplishments: In 1996 she was inducted into the Colorado Women's Hall of Fame for her contributions to occupational therapy, higher education, and the advancement of women leaders. At CSU, she holds the rank of professor emeritus. There, she served as full professor and department head of occupational therapy and as a dean of the College of Applied Human Sciences. She was also named provost/academic vice president in 1991. CSU awarded her an honorary doctor of science degree for her scholarly contributions.

Ellie served as president of the American Occupational Therapy Association (AOTA) from 1985 to 1980. In 1984, AOTA honored her with its highest scholastic award, the Eleanor Clarke Slagle Lecture; in 1990, she received the Award of Merit, the highest award for meritorious service; and she was named a Fellow with the first group of inductees. Currently, Ellie is a consultant for leadership, mentoring, and organizational change.

Ann Grady, PhD, FAOTA

Ann most recently taught leadership and interdisciplinary teamwork at the University of Colorado School of Medicine, consulted with the Colorado Department of Education on issues related to community inclusion, and directed the occupational therapy department at The Children's Hospital in Denver. She holds a bachelor's degree in sociology from the College of New Rochelle, a certificate in occupational therapy from Columbia University, a master's degree from the University of Denver, and a doctoral degree in human communications from the University of Denver.

Ann's research interests include the development of leadership in women and the effectiveness of services delivered in context with children and families. Ann has served the profession in several capacities on state and national levels. She is a charter Fellow, former speaker of the Representative Assembly, and past president of AOTA. Ann previously served as vice president of the American Occupational Therapy Foundation (AOTF) and chairperson of its Research Development Committee. She has been recognized by numerous awards, most notably AOTA's Eleanor Clarke Slagle Lecture, the Award of Merit, and AOTF's Meritorious Service Award. Her passion from all her professional work focuses on the inclusion of all people in their community of choice for living, working, and playing.

Cathy Nielson, MPH, FAOTA

Cathy is Professor Emeritus, Division of Occupational Science in the Department of Allied Health Sciences, School of Medicine at the University of North Carolina–Chapel Hill (UNC–CH). She was on the faculty at UNC–CH for 23 years, serving as the director of the Division of Occupational Science until her retirement in 2007. During her tenure at UNC–CH, she also served as the director of the Division of Rehabilitation Psychology and Counseling, special projects assistant to the chairperson of allied health, and in roles on numerous UNC–CH committees. Cathy has a bachelor of science degree in occupational therapy from the Medical College of Georgia (MCG), where she was recognized in 1992 as a Distinguished Alumni of the MCG School of Allied Health. She has a master of public health degree in health policy and administration from the School of Public Health, UNC–CH. She is a recipient of a UNC–CH Distinguished Teaching Award for Post Baccalaureate Instruction and is a member of the university's Academy of Distinguished Teaching Scholars.

Cathy has been active in professional activities as a past vice-speaker of the AOTA Representative Assembly and member of the AOTA Executive Board. She was named a Fellow in 1994, having previously received the North Carolina Occupational Therapy Association's Suzanne C. Scullin Award for outstanding contributions to the profession of occupational therapy in North Carolina. She was the catalyst mentor for 2 years in the AOTA–AOTF Leadership Fellowship Program.

Currently, Cathy is the chief operating officer of Mountain BizWorks in Asheville, North Carolina.

Wendy Coster, PhD, OTR/L, FAOTA

Wendy came to the Leadership Fellowship Program with many years of academic leadership and mentoring experience. She has been a faculty member at Boston University College of Health and Rehabilitation Sciences—Sargent College since 1986 and has served as chairperson of the Department of Occupational Therapy since 1997. She also served as Interim Chair of the Department of Physical and Athletic Training for 3 years. Her experience has given her a deep appreciation of the many challenges faced by professional program directors and faculty trying to ensure delivery of effective educational programs while also working toward their personal leadership and scholarship goals and responding to institutional demands.

Wendy has an active research program that focuses on the development of improved measures activity, participation, and environment for children, youth, and adults with disabilities. She has mentored numerous doctoral students, most of whom now hold faculty positions in occupational therapy programs around the country. Among her many honors and awards are the 2007 Eleanor Clarke Slagle Lecture, AOTF's A. Jean Ayres Research Award, membership in the AOTF Academy of Research, and the Sargent College Award of Merit. Wendy has authored and co-authored numerous articles and grant proposals and is the consummate leader, teacher, mentor, and friend to many in the profession. She served as catalyst mentor for the first and fourth Leadership Circles.

Acknowledgments

An acknowledgments section provides an opportunity for us to reflect and identify all the persons who have contributed to our endeavors. Our writing has been a collaborative effort, and in that same spirit we have integrated our experiences, readings, and teachings from so many. We deeply appreciate you all — the mentors and mentees who have taught us so much; the many organizations who have sponsored mentoring programs, the brilliant authors who have educated us with their writings, our families and friends who encouraged us to continue, and others to whom we are grateful.

First and foremost we want to thank Amy Burgess, CEO, and Julie Manhard, President, of The Mentoring Company,™ for the creation of the innovative mentoring program, Mentoring Circles®. Their belief in the power of mentoring with stories to promote positive forward movement and discovery of solutions for both mentors and mentees has inspired us to delve into mentoring as a learning relationship.

Second, we thank the 30-plus mentors with whom we have worked to provide mentoring programs and the over 500 mentees who have participated. From these experiences during the past two decades, we have gained knowledge about leadership, cultures, organizations, life, and the power of mentoring for learning.

Next, we want to express our appreciation to the American Occupational Therapy Foundation and the American Occupational Therapy Association for their belief in mentoring as a process to develop a leadership community within the occupational therapy profession. These organizations have been supportive sponsors of the mentoring programs discussed in Chapter 4 of this book. Special thanks to Martha Kirkland, Ruth Ann Watkins, Chuck Christiansen, Mindy Hecker, Maureen Peterson, Carolyn Baum, Diana Ramsey, and Penny Moyers Cleveland for their commitment to leadership and mentoring as an effective process to develop leadership in the profession.

All the authors in our reference listings have contributed to our intellectual growth and our curiosity to learn more; our sincere appreciation to all of you. A particular note of thanks goes to Lois Zachery for her writings about mentoring — you have been an inspiration. Appreciation to James Kouzes and Barry Posner who have provided us with the knowledge that leadership is both a science and an art. From their work we have learned a leadership language, discovered leadership as relationships, and acquired awareness that leadership is an activity that belongs to everyone. Stephen Denning, Jack Maguire, Annette Simmons, Lori Silverman, and others have informed us with their pioneer work about storytelling in organizations. We are grateful for their creativity and discovery of the power of stories. Finally, a special thanks goes to Frank Dance and Carl Larsen for their teachings and writings about communication.

Mentoring Leaders: The Power of Storytelling for Building Leadership in Health Care and Education

A special thanks goes to our colleagues in the universities and facilities where we have worked—our daily work with you has been a major influence on our development as leaders, and our relationships with you have inspired many of our stories. We want to thank our family and friends who have helped us with ideas and who have believed in us even when we didn't believe in ourselves. You have been faithful facilitators and patient supporters of our efforts. *Mentoring Leaders* is a tribute to you.

Stories, Figures, Tables, Boxes, and Appendixes

Mentoring Leaders: The Power of Storytelling for Building Leadership in Health Care and Education

Chapter 5. Introduction to the Workbook

Chapter 6. Self-Reflection and Growth

Chapter 7. Community Building

Chapter 8. Enacting Leadership Practices

Chapter 9. Building Followership

Chapter 10. Leading for the Future

Introduction

Composing our book has been an art of integration. Ideas shared throughout the chapters have not resulted from a straight path to life's achievements but were instead created like a quilt of many parts, discovered over time and collectively pieced together to make a whole. Everything in this text originated in a frame of mind centered in leadership. This book is a result of our varied life experiences in which our commitment to leadership has been continually refocused, redefined, and relearned. Mentoring experiences and research studies with various professionals and parent leaders greatly influenced the emerging ideas and concepts shared in this book. The writings in the book's chapters have emerged as *our story* about building leadership and catalyzing social change through storytelling and mentoring.

As we continued to learn and experience leadership we became cognizant of the power of narrative and voice. We discovered that finding voice through stories and mentoring had something to offer in our pursuit to better understand the process of mentoring leadership. As a result, we began to focus our own learning and studies on mentoring and storytelling. What emerged was the power of integrating stories in mentoring relationships to build a person's leadership capacity.

The cornerstone to linking leadership, mentoring, and storytelling is communication. The ideas presented here are a starting point for developing transformational leadership, not a prescription on how to be a leader for change.

Why Read This book?

We believe that readers of this book will learn about building their own leadership capacity to perform leadership for our changing times. The text will help readers learn about the power and effectiveness of mentoring with stories to mobilize individual leadership performances and create a leadership culture within organizations.

Mentoring Leaders is not just another book about how to become a transformational leader, nor is it a book about leadership or mentoring or a collection of stories; rather, it is a book that links leadership, mentoring, and the use of stories to develop leaders and build a leadership culture. In this book we present leadership as a communication activity of human relationships intended to transfer knowledge, facilitate desired actions to achieve goals, and assist others in discovering their leadership voice for the purpose of social change.

Who Should Read This Book?

This book is designed to provide anyone performing leadership or in a mentoring relationship (mentor or mentee) with knowledge about being a leader, mentor, mentee, and storyteller. While reading the text, readers may notice emphasis on roles and activities of occupational therapy faculty, but the text applies to various professional positions. Additionally, the content presented can be applied to a wide scope of roles, including managers, leaders, administrators, mentors, teachers, health care providers, students, and others. The ideas, beliefs, principles, values, and concepts in this book apply to nearly all individuals and group leadership activities.

The dynamic perspective of leadership that has guided the book's construction has varied implications for readers. Each of us have multiple and varying roles during our lives; therefore, messages gleaned from this text will most likely be perceived via the perspective of the role for which readers identify themselves and the roles sought in the future.

For the health care or education professional, our message is simply that relevant, real-time experiences can create the best path for learning and discovery. Sharing these experiences through stories and mentoring is a powerful tool for discovering the leader within and facilitating the discovery of learning in others (The Mentoring Company, 2008). Reflecting on experiences and applying the learning to current situations results in creative ideas and solutions for action.

The material centers on the value of learning relationships as a gift of knowledge. For mentees, the gift comes from listening and integrating the messages with previous life experiences and cultures. For mentors, the gift comes from listening to an inner voice while reflecting on past experiences. Mentoring is an interactive process that creates common ground between mentors and mentees.

For those who identify themselves primarily as student or scholar or educator, the implications are centered on learning and knowledge transfer. A person cannot understand the discovery or transfer of knowledge without considering effective behaviors for sharing the information. Mentoring with stories is a proven and effective method for sharing and discovery of knowledge and the leader within (The Mentoring Company, 2002).

For leaders and managers, our message has its foundation in the belief that one cannot understand organizational phenomena without considering its culture as both the cause of and as a way of explaining phenomena (Schein, 2010). Leadership is culture managed so people can thrive, learn, and feel valued. We discuss organizational culture as the product of shared meanings and beliefs among groups. We believe that an effective process for discussing, understanding, and building culture is active participation in mentoring programs.

Although implications for readers may differ on the basis of an individual's self-identity or leadership role, the message remains the same: Leadership belongs to everyone, and effective leadership learning results from mentoring relationships built through positive communication and stories. Facts inform, but stories inspire (Simmons, 2002).

How Is This Book Organized?

The book has two parts. "Part I. Mentoring Leaders" provides readers with knowledge about mentoring with stories to build leadership practices and promote a culture of leadership within organizations. The material in these chapters prepares readers to receive mentoring from the stories in "Part II. Mentoring Through Stories — The Workbook."

Part I first presents leadership and communication (Chapter 1), followed by the history and concepts about mentoring (Chapter 2). Chapter 3 focuses on stories and storytelling, illustrating the power of narrative and voice. Part I concludes by providing evaluative data on the outcomes of participation in an innovation mentorship program using stories, Mentoring Circles® (Chapter 4). Each chapter in this section begins with a "table chat" — a short story introducing the chapter's purpose and learning objectives.

To further stimulate learning and to underscore the importance of storytelling, we have integrated stories into the content of Part I. We believe that using stories and storytelling in mentoring relationships is an effective activity for building individual leadership practices and leadership cultures, and we reflect this belief in the construction of this text.

Part II is a workbook that includes stories of mentors with questions and activities to guide readers in reflecting and discovering the knowledge being transferred in story form. Most importantly, these stories provide readers with examples that have been effective in several mentoring programs designed to facilitate leadership learning and create a leadership culture. (To honor confidentiality and maintain anonymity, names and situations have been changed.) Stories are followed with reflective questions for readers to enhance learning. Within some stories, the mentor mentions books and articles that have been effective for learning. We encourage readers to refer to these publications.

Finally, notice the image of a kaleidoscope opening each chapter throughout the book. A kaleidoscope is an art form, and here it represents the art of leadership, symbolizing the importance of connections and relationships in building leadership capacity. A kaleidoscope image results from its moving parts that connect with each other. The image constantly changes but always intersects and symbolizes our path to linking leadership, communication, storytelling, and mentoring.

We invite readers to immerse themselves in our writings and stories, to learn from our experiences, to commit to the mentoring process, and find their voice as leaders. The change and growth achieved will be transformative — a catalyst for developing individual leadership practices and creating a sustainable leadership culture.

References

The Mentoring Company. (2002). *Measurable results*. Retrieved January 24, 2011, from http://mentoringcircles.com/results.html

The Mentoring Company. (2008). *Mentor orientation manual*. Loveland, CO: Author.

Schein, E. H. (2010). *Organizational culture and leadership*. San Francisco: Jossey-Bass.

Simmons, A. (2002). *The story factor*. Cambridge, MA: Perseus.

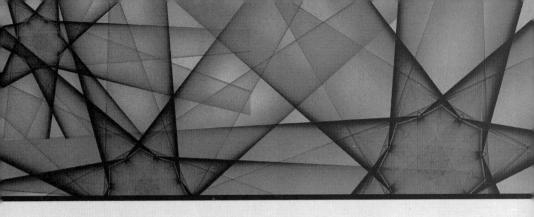

Part I. Mentoring Leaders

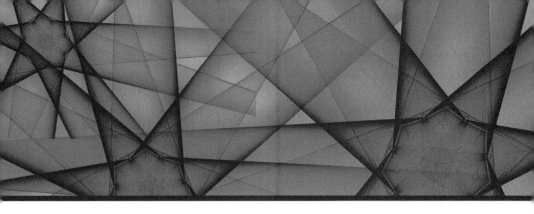

Chapter 1.
Leadership and Communication

Table Chats

Is there a better way to start a creative project than by gathering with colleagues on a beautiful Colorado fall day, with its perfect blue sky, fall colors, and clear mountain air? It was just that kind of day when we gathered around a cozy table to plan our book on leading and mentoring. Each of us had unique experiences to bring to the project from our studies on leadership and communication and our roles as mentors and facilitators with mentoring programs.

Relationships between leadership and communication became an important topic, emerging as the cornerstone for our writings. Of particular importance was the way leadership connects leaders and followers and provides leaders with a means for developing their visioning and the ways in which they influence others to participate.

As we began to shape the content for our book, communication became core to the ideas we developed. Chapter 1 lays the groundwork for exploring the linkages among leadership, communication, mentoring, and storytelling. The stories illustrate leadership practices and the importance of finding voice and narrative and provide a framework to distinguish leadership from management.

Introduction

Storytelling and listening, mentoring, and leadership practices are inextricably linked through the development and use of specific functions of human communication. According to Hackman and Johnson (1991), development and use of *voice* as a component of leadership reflect the view that leadership is best understood as a product of human communication. They propose that "leadership is human (symbolic) communication which modifies attitudes and behavior of others in order to meet group goals and needs" (p. 11).

Leadership competence increases with communication competence. Leadership shares all the features of human communication in the sense that leaders use symbols to create reality with the language they choose, stories they tell, and rituals they create. Leaders use spoken and unspoken language to communicate about the past and present and as foundation for describing a vision for a desirable future. Leaders use symbols to describe a journey toward the future and enroll others in the process. Leadership, like communication, is a continuous, dynamic, ever-changing process by which information and meaning are transacted through the uniquely human use of symbols.

Leadership effectiveness depends upon development of skills in the three areas of communication function described by Dance and Larson (1976):

1. Linking with human beings and their environment, or the *connecting* aspect of leadership;
2. Developing higher mental processes as a result of symbol usage, or the *visioning* aspect of leadership; and
3. Regulating behavior of self and others, or the *influencing* aspect of leadership.

Connecting

Linking with others through communication is a critical skill, because listening and processing verbal and nonverbal messages about events, norms, culture, and individual concerns inherent to the group or organization characterize relationships between leaders and individuals and the environment in which they serve. The relationships required to establish trust, create a successful and satisfying environment, and develop effective work groups and teams are served by the linking function of communication.

Linking with others requires (1) monitoring the environment, (2) creating a trusting climate, and (3) team-building. The ability of a leader to use information and meaning gleaned from linking with persons and their environments to create and articulate a meaningful vision for the future comes from the leader's cognitive ability to create and use symbols.

Envisioning

Envisioning involves creating new agendas and visions from previously existing elements. For example, in the 2011 State of the Union Address, President Barack Obama used the past "element" of Sputnik to create an agenda for investing in new innovations and a vision of America's ability to move forward and achieve greatness (Obama, 2011).

Influencing

With relationships based in trust and credibility established between leaders and constituents (Kouzes & Posner, 1993) and direction articulated through communication of vision, the function of regulating behavior and bringing others along is accomplished through mutual agreement among leaders and followers to adhere to the mission and values set forth and adopted by the group. *Regulation* means influencing others by developing credibility and power, using effective verbal and nonverbal communication, creating positive expectations, managing change, gaining compliance, and engaging in negotiation (Hackman & Johnson, 1991).

The discussions on leadership and communication, as presented in this chapter, are not definitive. Rather we present our perspective on linking of leadership and communication, which we believe is best developed through a mentoring approach using storytelling. Selected theories and concepts from the literature are integrated into our view of leadership—a type of leadership resulting from mentorship programs that promote discovery of self as leader, facilitate leadership readiness and performance, and contribute to building a leadership culture.

Leadership

In a report on leadership and higher education, Astin and Astin (2000) stated, "We believe that effective leadership is an essential ingredient of positive social change. No society can continue to evolve without it, no family or neighborhood holds together in its absence, and no institution prospers when it is unavailable" (p. iv). In Astin and Astin's experience, the power of leaders and leadership is associated with other expressions of the human spirit or hope, commitment, energy, and passion. The capacity to lead is rooted in virtually any individual and in every community. Leadership practice in our communities, informal organizations, and corporations frequently emerges because ordinary people are challenged to find their voice in the interest of promoting social justice, opportunity, fairness, and inclusion or bringing an organization together to inspire a vision for a desirable future for its members and society.

Development and use of voice for employing the linking, mental processing, and regulating functions of communication are essential for acting upon opportunities for leadership practice, particularly the challenges that call upon the leader to address issues of values and change. *Finding voice,* as identified by Helgesen (1990), reflects ways in which communication functions can facilitate leadership through speaking, listening, organizing, visioning, modeling, instructing, influencing, and persuading. The idea of finding voice for leading change resonated with many women in the leadership development study conducted by Grady (1999). Although the women in the study represent a specific group of leaders (mothers of children with disabilities), their leadership lessons have tremendous relevance for all leaders, and their stories give voice and substance to leadership concepts.

Grady (1999) found a notable emergence of leadership among the women in her study. Motivated by the success of the civil rights movement, the women's rights movement, and the fledgling disability rights movement, the mothers began finding their voices to speak for justice for their children. Their children were often marginalized by society because of their differences and frequently excluded from community, education, and health programs available to typically developing children. Local and national leaders emerged from the group, finding their voices and focusing on justice for their children. As one woman said,

> I think leadership has much to do with finding your own voice, being confident in your own voice, enough so you can quiet your voice, and allow your presence to amplify other people's voices. I do the same thing when I speak, or when I'm going to take on the board at the agency, as I do when I have a question about my kid's IEP [individualized education program]. I call five people and say, "This is what I'm going to do, and kind of pump myself up to do it. So that's having my voice heard individually, but my voice is also subject to other people's voices, and what I've been learning over the past year is how to ask questions, and how not to say, "Oh, you'll be fine" or "You're great," but to just listen and help people talk louder and clearer. (p. 90)

A Framework for Leadership: The Leadership Practices

Kouzes and Posner (2007) described *leadership* as "the art of mobilizing others to want to struggle for shared aspirations" (p. 30). They emphasized that the key to effective leadership rests with the words *want to* in the definition. Leadership is best understood as meaning-making through its practice in a community. The innovative work by Kouzes and Posner introduced such groundbreaking ideas as leadership belonging to everyone, it being performance and behaviors, and it having its foundation in human relationships.

From their study of leaders in a wide variety of situations, Kouzes and Posner (2007) identified five essential leadership practices:

1. Challenging the process,
2. Inspiring a shared vision,
3. Enabling others to act,
4. Modeling the way, and
5. Encouraging the heart.

In the sections that follow, each of these practices are discussed and illustrated with stories from Grady's (1999) study as well as in Part II of this book.

Challenging the Process

Change is key to challenging a process. Leaders seek and accept challenging opportunities to test their abilities and to find opportunities for change and innovation.

Experimenting, clarifying values, and taking risks are part of this practice. Leaders seek to continue the quest, despite opposition or setbacks.

In Story 1.1, Anita, whose son Kevin was born with Down syndrome, tells about tackling barriers to Kevin receiving a typical educational program. She began challenging the system to change, thus developing her own leadership potential. She has since become a leader for statewide change in education for children with disabilities.

Story 1.1. Anita Challenges the Process

I believe I have fallen into leadership. My leadership beginnings have been very situational; the decisions to do things in a different way have created situations that were somewhat innovative and allowed me to be seen as competent. It's always taken me aback the way people see me as a leader, because I don't know that I have always seen myself that way.

The experiences that have led me to leadership have just happened. I think the biggest one, when Kevin was about 6 months old, [was when] we were told that he had to receive services at a particular school. I knew it wasn't right for our family. When I had to go there it set me back in the whole grief spiral every week. I had to find something else.

It meant going to people and saying there really needs to be something else because this doesn't work. Not taking what they offered for me was very empowering. When they said, "Well, actually there are a couple of other choices," and so we went to another center and that fit—it felt better.

And then after awhile, we looked even further and went to yet another school, and then after that we thought, "This was great, but why can't Kevin go to preschool in our neighborhood?" I was constantly pushing that system. And so for us, I do think that is where the leadership came [from]. It was taking the risk to say, "This doesn't feel right." Trusting myself, always trusting.

And in those days it was much harder, because I felt very guilty, very worried about how I would be seen and judged as a parent. It was turning our family upside-down. So, I think, again, [it was about] being unwilling to fit the norm for children with disabilities, but being willing to do something different than what we were told we should do. Even though in those days it felt very uncomfortable and I felt guilty [and] very judged and thought, "People aren't going to think I'm a good mom, but I've got to do it anyway."

I think the second leadership event was when we were trying to get Kevin in kindergarten and we were all over the places they told us that kids with Down syndrome would go after preschool. I looked at those and I knew that—again, it was that gut feeling—that these weren't right. But I wanted to make that change in a nonadversarial way. I really wanted to bring people along, and I didn't want to do it in anger.

And looking back, it was an exhausting experience. I probably visited over 15 different schools and settings. In the process, I did take Kevin's teacher, who was a public school teacher and I think not much of risk-taker herself, and really invested her into the process. She took two personal days and went and observed schools.

We did make the decision to do a typical school, which was again totally out of the realm of what people were doing at the time. Most kids with Down syndrome were going to special

(Continued)

Story 1.1. Cont.

programs, not neighborhood schools. I think that was when all of a sudden it becomes clear that we were in control; we can be in control and do it in partnership when people buy in. So for me, that was where I really did become passionate about family choice, which is doing what works for families in a partnership, in a positive way.

[Kevin's] teacher from preschool said that it had been an exciting process for her and that she wished more parents would push to do things differently. I started feeling less paranoid and less judged, realizing there was a way to create change. Sometimes it's easier to say, "I'm not able to do it your way. Will you come along with me and help us do this differently?"

Because we had made some changes that were unusual changes at the time, and we had made them in a nonadversarial way, I wanted to share that with other parents. You can do it. It's hard, but it's doable. So at that point, I was becoming a leader, and I began to be seen as doing things a little bit differently. I was seen as a leader challenging the system and making changes.

Heifetz (1994) believes that leadership takes place every day, rather than emanating from the traits of a few, or existing as a rare event or once-in-a-lifetime opportunity. He stresses that when a person faces a conflict or encounters a gap among competing values and one's lifestyle, a person will face the challenge to learn new ways. Effective leaders engage others to face the challenge, adjust their values, seek new ways, and develop new habits of behavior.

Inspiring Shared Vision

Seeing possibilities is key to envisioning the future. Leaders look to the future to propose what is possible and, through their passion, engage others in pursuing the dream, working together, and sharing success. Leaders help others see how their own dreams can be realized through a common vision, such as in Story 1.2. Ellen was a parent leader and consultant for the Colorado Health Care Program for Children. In her story, she reflected on differences between management and leadership; in doing so, she talks about inspiring a shared vision.

Story 1.2. Ellen Inspires a Shared Vision

There are [those] who will tell you what to do. Now I think my view of leadership is real different. I mean, when I think about leaders I think about people who have the ability to inspire—who have the ability to get people to do things that are right because of their actions. Because of how they live their life on a day-to-day basis, or how they actually carry out certain things in a certain arena. Not necessarily someone who's in charge. Not necessarily someone whose job is where we want to go.

But really, it's interesting, because I've almost reached a point in my life [that] when I find out who the main man is, I totally overlook that person and start looking for where the inspiration comes from. To me, that's leadership.

Enabling Others to Act

Through an atmosphere of mutual trust and respect, leaders empower others to contribute their best. Collaboration is essential for enabling involvement of followers in empowered relationships and provides opportunities for future leaders to emerge.

Lou Shannon (Story 1.3) was a legendary physical therapist whose career at The Children's Hospital in Denver, Colorado, spanned more than 40 years. When she suddenly died, an outpouring of stories illustrated her many contributions to the lives of children and staff alike. The story comes from Jane Sweeny, a therapist in Gig Harbor, Washington, and speaks to the leadership practice of enabling others to act. In the story, Lou enabled Jane to clarify her purpose and move forward with her project by listening with respect and support. She helped her initiate her plan by organizing some of the details. Since hearing this story, many people who knew Lou are "passing it on" by asking how they can help others to act.

Modeling the Way

Leaders consistently act on standards and values, adhering to values and acting accordingly, responding openly and honestly, and encouraging followers to consistently meet interval goals and continue on the path to a vision. Leadership by modeling the way reminds others of the values that guide individual or collective decisions about social actions. Finding voice that inspires and guides emerging leaders is essential for modeling the way. Leader credibility, characterized by a straightforward, honest leader who does what she says she will do, is another essential aspect of modeling for others.

Jean (Story 1.4) is the director of the Blue Grass Technology Access Center in Lexington, Kentucky. She talks about how her values motivated her to take on a leadership role in a way that was comfortable for her and provided a model for others to enact their leadership.

Story 1.3. Lou Shannon—Enabling Others to Act

Lou was certainly a wonderful mentor and support to me with my master's research data collection at Denver Children's Hospital. She treated me like I was a VIP from the NIH [National Institutes of Health]! I was not used to such high levels of support—it was wonderful!

As if it happened yesterday, I remember entering her office for the first time to tell her about my master's research and see if any of the children with cerebral palsy could be subjects. Before I could start my carefully rehearsed abstract of the research, she greeted me with, "How can I help you?" This led to a tour of the available clinic spaces and a sign-up roster for 3 days of data collection.

I use the "How can I help you?" greeting with all of my advising appointments with my students and often think of Lou with her many gifts to us.

Story 1.4. Jean's Values

I always thought about leadership as the person in charge, the person who's going to lead the way, the director—that's pretty much been my thoughts [sic] in the past of leadership. I never thought of myself as a leader. I never wanted to be that person in charge. I like to take on missions and go after them, but leadership has a lot of responsibilities. One of the things, when we started Blue Grass, I knew right off the bat [was] that I did not want to be the person in charge. But I've learned to look at it differently because with every situation, [being] the director of a center means that you have to have the financial interests, and those were the things I never wanted to take on. But I accept that I have taken some leadership in getting technology accessible to people who need it and to take on the funding arena that is the area that I've chosen as my focus.

I guess getting the center started is the best experience I've had. We knew bringing technology to folks who needed it was not a one-shot issue. It was going to be continuous, and there was constant need for keeping up with the information and sharing it with other families. My values guided the way we developed and delivered programs to families and modeled to the community.

The situation I was in at the time when we got the center started influenced the outcomes. I was a single mom [and had] two kids. We had to take from the system, and that was something that I was always taught—that you don't just take, you give back. And so pursuing the center was a way that I could give back to other people, not just take . . . a way to stand up and say, "This is something you can do, something you can try."

I think more of that value of being able to share. And I think that something that's wrong with the system is that we within the country, within the welfare system, . . . we never give recipients a chance to give back . . . we put them in situations that make them totally dependent and never [give] them that chance, and that's especially true with people with disabilities. I think that the best part about the center as a whole is that there are always opportunities for people to come in and volunteer and start giving back.

Encouraging the Heart

Leaders encourage others to expand their leadership by visibly recognizing and celebrating accomplishments and promoting balance as part of the work process. Encouraging the heart gives formal and informal recognition to colleague and client accomplishments. The key is *meaningful* recognition and feedback that speak to the heart and build a spirit of community.

In Ellen's story (Story 1.5), Ellen relates how she learned that encouraging the heart is a leadership practice with multiple resonating benefits by working with one client.

Story 1.5. Ellen—Encouraging the Heart

This story actually has to do with my relationship with one person. I think in some ways there has been a ripple effect. I met Maria when her son, Jesus, was a baby. He had been at Denver Health for a year, and he had come home and [was] referred to our program.

I went out to see Maria and what I found was this very feisty and determined woman who spoke very little English, but had spent a year in the hospital with her son. What English she was speaking, she was speaking because she had to learn it being in the hospital. And Maria is a pretty quick study. But I remember coming in there and feeling very bad [and] in some ways very sorry for her.

I felt sorry for her because she didn't speak English, and I wondered how was she going to get this baby where he needed to go without some of the skills she would need to communicate with doctors and make her needs and wants known. I sat there and I thought to myself, "This woman is pretty much going to be told what to do."

[That visit] led to another visit and another visit and pretty soon Maria was coming into the center. There was this kind of instant glimmer between the two of us. There was something about her that I loved. It was her sense of humor, I think. Here was a woman who had been through this whole year of hell—what I would have considered hell. I don't think she did. And she had this sense of humor about her, and we just instantly clicked.

I found myself pushing her. Mentoring her. "Maria, do this. Maria, have you thought about doing this? Maria, can you imagine if you did that? If you went to school to learn English?" And I remember sitting and telling her, "You have so much to offer."

And then I remember she came to me one day, and she said, "Ellen, I really need to get a job," and we hired her as an interpreter. She understood English very well. She just didn't speak it very well.

Our program happened at a time to be looking for more people who were bilingual, because we were serving a lot of Spanish-speaking, monolingual-Spanish-speaking families. And I said, "We'll hire you." And so she came to work for us and I just started to see the blooming of this bud—kind of like you see a rose, you know? It's closed and then it starts opening, slowly but surely.

And then people said, "Maria, you'd be great for this and we need Hispanics." We started an organization for Spanish-speaking parents, and ultimately I hired her to work for Healthy Tomorrows.

But I saw that this woman was starting to bloom. I saw her having the same effect on others that I had had on her. So I would have to say that watching others bloom has probably been the experience that changed me from a point in my life where I strived for recognition. If I did something good, I wanted the recognition for it. It really made me reach a turning point where I [realized] that . . . someone else could be recognized for something. I could take as much satisfaction in Maria's recognition and others as I would ever take in my own.

Even now . . . she and I are still presenting individualized education program training in Spanish, and there are times when I think to myself, "If anybody asks me to do one more thing, I can't do anymore. Unless it involves Maria—I will do anything with Maria."

Like Kouzes and Posner, Donald Clifton, the founder of Strengths Psychology, spent decades asking leaders about what they do best as a leader (Rath & Conchie, 2008). Believing that a focus on weaknesses was a wrong approach for leadership development, Clifton began searching for leaders' self-identified strengths, not their shortcomings.

In collaboration with Gallup, the Strength Finder survey was developed and administered extensively, and most recently reported by Rath and Conchie (2008). Their research revealed that what "great leaders have in common is that each truly knows his or her strengths and can call upon the right strength at the right time" (p. 13). As a result of their studies, the Gallup survey team did not produce a specific list of leader characteristics; rather, in keeping with more contemporary ideas on leadership, they focused on recognizing leadership strengths. The report includes three key factors to consider: "(1) The most effective leaders are always investing in strengths, (2) the most effective leaders surround themselves with the right people and then maximize their team, and (3) the most effective leaders understand their followers needs" (pp. 2–3). The extensive research conducted by Kouzes and Posner (2007) and by Gallup (Rath & Conchie, 2008) adds credibility to their findings and approach to identifying an individual's leadership practices and strengths.

Crucibles of Leadership

Bennis and Thomas (2007) have searched for ideas that account for why some people become leaders in formal or informal situations. They concluded that one of the most reliable indicators and predictors of true leadership is a person's ability to find meaning in negative events and learn from even the most trying circumstances. Being able to conquer adversity and emerge stronger and more committed than ever are characteristics of effective leaders.

The authors termed these formative experiences "crucibles" of leadership. A *crucible* is a transformative experience or point of deep reflection on values, actions, assumptions, judgments, and direction through which a person comes to a new or altered sense of identity. "Crucibles rupture the status quo and create opposing forces between the new and the familiar" (Bennis & Thomas, 2007, p. 22).

The experiences are not necessarily violent or obviously traumatic to an observer. When told as a story, the person can express how and why life changed from relative balance to imbalance at some specific time. The point may be trauma, loss of a loved one, loss of function, instances of exclusion and prejudice, or a rapid change in job function or expectations.

Grady (1999) observed a notable emergence of community and organizational leadership among mothers of children with disabilities or special health and education needs. Disability was excluding their children from typical educational settings and access to appropriate health care. Some of the women created organizations for change, others took significant positions in policymaking organizations, and others became a voice for change in their community. Some of the women referred to having a child with special needs as a defining event in their lives and subsequent leadership development. The combination of having a child who differed from their expectations, coupled with resistance and prejudice encountered in their communities, was a call to action for them.

A *defining opportunity* is an event or experience that changes a person's life course in a significant way. The event or experience may occur in an instant or over a period of time. The time is characterized not by its length but by recognition that it was a turning point and that life has changed in some significant way. As a turning point that alters life in a positive way, the event is identified as an opportunity by the person involved, regardless of whether the experience appears optimal or desirable at the time (Grady, 1999).

In Stories 1.6 and 1.7, each woman faces an adverse event and emerges a confident and effective leader. From a defining opportunity Jackie created the Alliance for Technology Access, a national organization for individuals with disabilities to improve their lives by using assistive technology for everyday living. For another woman, her Native American culture's notion of a life path guided her response to adversity that came with her daughter's disability, and she went on to become an influential leader in the tribe and held a position rarely given to a woman.

Story 1.6. Jackie Finds Opportunity

There is that opportunity that is a defining opportunity . . . where you say, is it going to bury me, or is it not? Are we going to give up and live with sadness, or not? Or are we going to do something different and explore a different life than we had thought about?

Judith's birth—not her birth, but her disability acquired when she was 8 months old—did that for me. When she became disabled during a surgery, it was a very important moment to decide what our new relationship was going to be with this new child that we had. I think that it wasn't easy, and it didn't all happen in one step, but [going] though a process of opening your mind, head, and heart to the parameters of other ways of thinking and another experience offers itself as another way to go. I have always felt that was true. Once you open your thinking, you begin to open your life to new possibilities.

You know, I've always wanted to have a meaningful life. I don't ever remember thinking that my life didn't have some [meaning]. I don't know if it had purpose, but life for me meant doing something of value—having more than my own selfish needs in mind for my life.

So these thoughts were all there at that moment that said, "Well, you asked for it, you got it. This is one of those moments when you can do something worthy." I have to say, it must be something in my family's makeup, too. It's funny because I think my dad has that in him—sort of an unwillingness to live with the way things are.

Story 1.7. Finding the Positive

I always felt [and] we were always taught that you look for the positive in whatever happens in life. You know, I don't care if it's the worst situation that you've ever experienced. You look for that something positive in it, and you focus on that. Because we believe you don't want to get stuck on your path. And so if something is negative and you dwell on it, it holds you there. And it not only has an effect on you, but it has a ripple effect on everybody else. So you have to keep moving on. I think I got a little bit more assertive, starting with my daughter.

Leaders who learn from adversity tend to acquire four essential skills (Bennis & Thomas, 2007). They tend to engage others in dialogue about the situation in the interest of developing shared meaning so they can go forward together. They develop and use a compelling voice on the basis of the integrity of agreed upon values. They profit from being suspended outside their familiar zone and instead in a vulnerable place where they must build a new structure to move forward with others.

Most important, they develop an adaptive capacity, which includes an ability to grasp the context of the situation and its value to constituents, and hardiness, which supports perseverance and hope. Leaders who love learning—the aspect of learning that allows them to grow and learn from changing circumstances—find meaning in events that initially seem negative. For some, the event affords them the opportunity for transformational leadership experiment.

In Story 1.8, the therapist employed each of Bennis and Thomas's (2007) essential skills to bring about a dramatic change in her practice that strengthened her professional identity and elevated her effectiveness as both a therapist and leader.

The findings from Thomas's (2008) study of crucibles in leadership development are validated in a classic study of leaders and managers by Zaleznik (1977), who differentiates between managers and leaders according to both their function and their focus He refers to people who are *once-born* as those for whom adjustments to life have been relatively straightforward developmental experiences. Their sense of self comes from being in harmony with the environment, including people in the environment. These people perceive life as a series of orderly events, much like their own experiences.

People who are *twice-born* have life experiences that are marked by struggles to achieve a sense of order. Leaders who deal primarily with change are twice-born. Their sense of self comes from being separate from others and their environment. They develop their self-concept following a defining or life-changing experience from which they withdraw and re-enter, prepared to deal with the more circular and less predictable progressions of change. As a result, leaders are often in pursuit of opportunities to *change* the status quo, while managers focus on *maintaining* the status quo (see Story 1.9.).

Throughout the leadership–management literature and research, there is overlap, fusion, and confusion surrounding concepts and functions of management and

---

Story 1.8. Ann—A Change in Practice

As an occupational therapist directing the program at The Children's Hospital in Denver, I experienced a significant program change imposed from outside our organization. The re-authorization of the Education of All Handicapped Children Act (1975), later codified as the Individuals with Disabilities Education Act (1997), mandated that intervention for infants and toddlers be conducted in the child's own environment. Hands-on hospital or clinic-based therapy would not be reimbursed from the newly available funds. Along with the legislative details from law came verbal criticism of the kind of clinic-based developmental programs currently provided by our staff.

We had invested a considerable amount of time and money learning and expanding developmental approaches for the children. I was personally invested in researching, teaching, writing, and speaking about neurodevelopmental therapy. I had become identified as an expert in this area and built my professional concept of who I was and what I had to contribute on this body of knowledge. Now, with the change, my beliefs, commitments, and organization were under attack! I was angry and uncertain about the next steps to take, especially with my own staff and colleagues in the community.

Time for reflection, dialogue, and clarification of values helped turn the tide. Clearly, many parents supported the change in practice and had indeed lobbied for the new legislation. Exploring my professional values I recognized the idea that functional activities are best taught where they will be used.

How had I forgotten that important principle? And I have long believed that parents know what's best for their family and many of them liked the new idea. Some staff members were already practicing in the new mode [in the child's home] through a grant program. As early adopters, these therapists gave testimony to the fact that it was possible to practice in the child's environment, although different. Important components from the old approaches could be incorporated in effective ways.

I began to change my objections and turn toward the actions we needed to take. Clearly, creativity, which used to drive my former program development, was needed. What fun it could be. Using the therapists now experienced with the new ideas, and parents who [liked] it, we began giving presentations to our staff and at community gatherings.

My reputation as a neurodevelopmental therapist was somewhat jeopardized at first, but my identification as an occupational therapist was enhanced, and that felt good. Opportunities to create something new abounded, and that surprising outcome would feed my soul once more. Clearly, there's more work to be done toward including people with disabilities in everyday living—an opportunity for leadership practice.

---

leadership (Kouzes & Posner, 1993, 1999, 2007; Rath & Conchie, 2008). However, an increase in developing a "science of management," along with continuing development of leadership concepts, supports differentiation between the nature and functions of leadership and management (Bennis & Thomas, 2007).

According to Zaleznik (1989), leaders are measured by their ability to anticipate the future and lead the process of change to achieve a desirable future. Leadership is concerned with purpose and distribution of power to influence direction. Managers are measured by how well they get people to go along with the organiza-

Story 1.9. Florence—A Thrice-Born Leader

When Florence, the director of Parents Helping Parents (PHP), heard the concept of once-born managers and twice-born leaders, she said,

I must be *thrice born,* once as a person of color, once as a woman, and once as a parent of a child with a disability. I couldn't stand seeing people not treated right. That's why I hated hazing; I hated the racial stuff and a lot of other things like that.

Now, here I have to fight again. I fought as a woman. I fought as a Black person. Now, with special needs, and then pretty soon it's going to be aging. I'll be one of the Gray Panthers next. As a parent, I thought these kids ought to have every opportunity to do whatever it is that they can do, and people need to be giving these challenged kids a chance.

And then it turns out that being a good leader is one of the things you learn, like which dragons to slay and which battles to choose to fight, and that's the thing that saves your energy for the things that you need to do. It also, I think, assists other people to know that you have a sense of judgment.

Growing up as a highly achieving student, I was once not given the high grade I earned because "Black children, especially girls, do not make such high grades." As a nurse, I was qualified but passed over for supervisor because "we don't have any Black supervisors here."

For my son with Down syndrome, I saw the same excluding practices in place for people with disabilities and thought, "Oh no, here we go again." The day the community pool designated special hours for children with disabilities was the day I called upon leadership practices learned when I was a student and treated differently because of race or gender. To resolve the special pool problem, I connected with other parents and developed an inclusive swim program that satisfied everyone.

When I think about leadership and leaders, two things come to mind quickly, and they almost seem like opposites. The one is the fire in the belly for leadership, which I differentiate from the irritation in the gut for solving your own personal problems. There are many people who get excited about solving their own problems because, like I say, they get an irritation in the gut about something that has happened to them.

But as a leader, you have to go to another level of fire in the belly in order to think beyond yourself. This to me is what leadership is about. When you get beyond your problem and thinking about changing one particular thing to thinking *systems change* and everybody else who has been affected, you get the fire in the belly for leadership.

Resolving the pool incident didn't change the world or bring about world peace, but it did change the perception of disability for our community and a few people with disabilities in the community. Perhaps that's how being twice born as a leader helped me focus on the values driving my actions as a leader.

tion's expectations. Management focuses on a rational assessment of situations and systematic selection of goals and purposes through strategic planning, marshaling and assignment of resources, organizational design, and efficient staffing.

Transactional and Transformational Leadership

The possibilities for transformation and change through the *leadership* process distinguish leadership from the more transactional process of *management*, which is aimed at achieving established goals by either redefining or clarifying roles, responsibilities, and task assignments. In times of stability, routine management is effective for maintaining the status quo, but in times of change, or when change needs to be instigated, leaders must emerge to create, or manage change (Bennis & Nanus, 1997). According to Bennis and Nanus, individuals pursuing leadership development need to include the following commitments and actions in their development plan:

1. Make a commitment to change and lifelong learning.
2. Develop an ability to embrace error. Successful leaders learn from their mistakes.
3. Adopt a willingness to encourage dissent and engage in creative resolution. Followers who are encouraged to raise issues or disagree tend to become leaders.
4. Engage in "reflective backtalk" with a trusted colleague, coach, or mentor with whom ideas can be critiqued in advance and organized for presentation.
5. Be vulnerable to others when they present a different and better idea for your plan. Your vision and plan will be improved, and the contributors will feel included in the process.
6. Generate a bias toward action with a clear and accountable plan for change.
7. Constantly improve ability to generate and sustain trust.

Burns's (1978) classic work describing transformational and transactional leadership remains relevant to current leadership study, particularly as we discuss leadership and mentoring. Burns moved leadership scholars from a focus on leader characteristics to a more comprehensive discussion of leadership practices and their distinctive functions. This important contribution changed concepts of leader–follower relationships to encompass the transformation of a person when a leader focused on what was important to followers. When leaders focus on what the followers seek, they join the leader to create the change they both desire. Transformation acts as a foundation for leadership thinking and is the cornerstone for mentoring.

The study of leadership, according to Burns (1978), is central to the structure and processes of human development and political action. De Pree (1989) concurred and stated that leadership is a process, much the same as the process of becoming a fully developed person.

Burns (1978) described leadership as being part of the dynamics of conflict and power, linked to collective purpose, and measured by actual social change. He identified two basic types of leadership:

1. *Transactional leadership,* in which leaders (or managers) engage followers in action on the basis of exchange, usually comprised of rewards or punishments, and
2. *Transformational leadership,* in which leaders recognize an existing need, motive, or demand of a potential follower and seek to satisfy higher needs by fully engaging the person as a follower.

Burns described transformation and transactional leadership in terms that support the difference between leadership as a process of relationships and management as execution of distinct skills. The interactions between leaders and followers take on these two fundamentally different forms.

Bass (1990) proposed that transformational leadership augments the effects of exchange relationships characterized by transactional leadership in order to influence the efforts, satisfaction, and effectiveness of followers. The result is a relationship of mutual stimulation and elevation.

Transactional Leadership

Transactional leadership involves the exchange of valued things. Exchange may be economic, political, or psychological in nature. Each person is aware of the resources held by the other person, and their common, although perhaps temporary, connection. Transactional leadership is comprised of exchanging promises or actions between leaders and followers, often on the basis of self-interests such as increased performance for increased pay or additional responsibility in exchange for increased pay. Transactional leadership tends to be associated with maintaining the status quo or moving along with the tide, and it is characteristic of management approaches to change.

Transformational Leadership

Transformational leadership occurs when one or more persons engage with others in such a way that leaders and followers raise one another to higher levels of motivation and morality. Thus, effective mentors are transformational leaders. Their purposes, which might have started out separate but related, become, in the case of transactional leadership, fused. Power bases are linked not as counterweights but as mutual support for common purpose.

Various names are used for such leadership, such as *elevating, mobilizing, inspiring, exalting, uplifting, exhorting,* and *evangelizing.* The relationship between leaders and followers can be moralistic, but transforming leadership ultimately becomes moral in that it raises the level of human conduct and ethical aspirations of both the leader and the led, and thus has a transforming effect on both (Burns, 1978).

Transformational leadership, unlike naked power wielding, is inseparable from followers' needs and goals. The essence of the leader–follower relationship is the interaction of persons with different levels of motivation and power potential, including skill, in pursuit of a common purpose. Transformational leadership is related to initiating actions and changing the course of events. A transformational leader recognizes the higher-level needs of followers in order to engage the person in achieving a greater good.

Transformational leadership links leaders and followers in a relationship characterized by power, as well as mutual needs, aspirations, and values, and is termed *moral leadership* by Burns (1978). Moral leadership includes an element of choice on the part of followers. As you will read in the following chapters, mentoring with stories is a process that promotes choice on the part of a mentee. In this concept of leadership, *choice* means that followers have knowledge of alternative leaders and programs and capacity to choose among the alternatives. Leaders take responsibility for their commitments by providing the means to bring about promised change. Moral leadership emerges from and returns to the fundamental wants, needs, aspirations, and values of the followers. Moral leadership is the kind of leadership that can produce the type of social change that satisfies followers' needs.

Transformational leaders raise consciousness by articulation and role modeling of values and vision (Astin & Astin, 2000). In the transformative process, the leader knows and honors the important function of communication, inspiring himself or herself and others with visual images. The spoken and written word, in addition to leader's actions, is what influences others, not commanding or directing followers to action.

When Chemers (1997) summarized the earlier work of Bass (1990) on transformational and transactional leadership, he observed that transformational leadership includes the leader's charisma as seen by a follower; inspirational motivation, which elicits commitment; and intellectual stimulation, or new ways of thinking. Transactional leadership factors include possible rewards to reinforce a positive interaction, and negative actions to respond when something goes wrong in the leader–follower interaction.

Managing and Leading: Finding Your Voice

This chapter has presented some of the classic theories on leadership and management. In distinguishing between leadership and management, classic theories often imply that the two cannot or should not co-exist in the same person. In reality, most situations demand both leadership and management at the same levels of competence and a single person must meet dual demands. Story 1.10 demonstrates both the distinctions and interrelationships between leadership and management from a mentor's point of view.

The last story (Story 1.11) exemplifies how finding one's leadership voice, communicated through storytelling, is one of the most powerful tools for leadership development and one of a leader's most effective means of leading. Raising a child with Down syndrome as well as leading others to create change required her to simultaneously manage meeting the needs of her child while leading for others. To do so, she found her voice.

Story 1.10. Leadership and Management on the Oregon Trail

I was trying to think of a way to capture my ideas about the relationship between leadership and management when I remembered the game *Oregon Trail*. This was one of the early computer learning games, and it simulated a journey following the pioneers west who traveled the Oregon Trail in the 1800s. The game involved the players in various activities, including selecting the year of travel and the route; deciding which wagon team leader to throw your lot in with; purchasing supplies; and dealing with various unexpected events along the way, such as fording rivers, foraging for food, meeting up with strangers, or being bitten by rattlesnakes. As I thought about it, it seemed to me that the Oregon Trail was a perfect analogy for the challenges faced by leaders or managers.

The wagon train group came together around a common goal: the promise of a better life somewhere out west. However, within the group, people were at different places with respect to that goal. Some focused on a better life for their families, and others just wanted the adventure. Some were escaping lives that had not gone well, and others were simply doing what they had been told. The dynamics were complex, and things would get tense more than once. The group had to find a way to defuse the tension and recapture its focus if it was going to go on successfully.

The group always traveled with a wagon train leader. The leader knew the trail; knew where the travelers wanted to go; and made decisions about how best to get to the destination, given the conditions. This involved not only selecting the best route but also carefully monitoring the health and well-being of the group. For example, if the leader didn't stop at the right time for a real rest, perhaps with a deer roast and dancing to fiddle music, morale would flag. There might be a rebellion, or too many people would take sick to keep the train moving forward.

However, the leader had little to do with getting the wagons ready to travel. This task was left to the manager in each small group, who was in charge of buying needed provisions, from wagons to rifles to food. Although it seemed to be a very straightforward task, the manager also needed to have a clear vision of what might lay ahead so that he could be well prepared. The first time playing the game, we all died of scurvy because our manager forgot to buy pickles to provide Vitamin C. The next time, we starved because we were so focused on moving ahead that we didn't stop often enough to hunt for game.

Although the wagon team leader had considerable experience, things happened that required on-the-spot decisions. For example, a normally fordable river had become a raging torrent due to storms in the mountains. What to do? Would it be safe to wait a few days to see if the water subsided, or would that delay mean the group might hit winter weather while crossing the Rockies? Should a risky crossing be tried? How many wagons might be lost, along with crucial supplies? Would the group be able to move on without them? Once the decision was made, the wagon managers had to figure out what individual plan was most likely to be successful. If a wagon was lost, they had to improvise to make the best use of what remained.

As I thought about the Oregon Trail, I thought it was a perfect illustration of the delicate balance between the leader and manager roles. The leader needs to hold the vision of the group and make decisions that will help make that vision a reality, but the leader depends on the manager to keep the team healthy so that they can continue their trek forward on the trail. The trick in being a program or department director is that the leader and the manager are the same person, and so the roles are often blended. I find that it requires a delicate balancing act and a shifting back and forth from the leader side of me to the manager side.

The leader side must always be checking to be sure that the wagon train—the program or department—is on the right trail. The trail markers are not always clear, so considerable time and attention must be spent on this important task. Sometimes leaders might have to exercise their authority to decide how best to respond to changing conditions that only he or she fully understands. The leader also has to remember that although everyone in the group has the same general vision or goal, they approach it from different places and different things are going to matter to them.

At the same time, the manager side has to make sure that the day-to-day decisions are made in a way that will provide the structure to make the vision happen, keeping the wagon train healthy and moving forward. The manager has to make sure there are enough supplies, that those who need some help get it, and that everyone knows what his or her task is.

If the manager doesn't pay enough attention to important details, the group might die of scurvy—or the program or department will descend into chaos. If the leader doesn't keep the group's eyes on the vision, they will lose the passion that set them on the trail in the first place. They might just give it up, turn again each other, or wander away into the wilderness.

Story 1.11. Finding My Leadership Voice

I have a very strong belief that on the whole, people are only going to participate or buy into something in which they feel like they have had part in forming, so that is where I kind of get this *voice* concept. I think until most people really buy into it some way as part of them, they are not going to come along with me.

I think that what I discovered through the whole thing is that I really do like to present and to tell stories. I do think people learn through stories. It was fun to share the stories . . . I'm very impressed with the power of stories.

One of the ways that I came to be a leader . . . was through the birth of a child who had Down syndrome, a very different experience for me. And so the leadership started out of a very personal situation and then grew to a passion for other children, other families, and other disabilities—a very broad[ly] based vision about quality of life. But one of the ways you interpret all that globalness to the stranger on the street or the stranger next door is by talking about a particular story about a particular person and helping them to grow. So, I would say that storytelling is really an important way of helping others catch the vision.

Conclusion

Readers of the next chapters will discover the power of stories and storytelling as valuable tools for a mentor to use in the mentoring process. In learning about mentoring and storytelling, readers may find it helpful to review Story 10.1 as an illustration of the linking of leadership, communication, mentoring, and storytelling. We hope the story above helps readers differentiate the roles of leadership and management and make the theories applicable to their own situations. As Bennis and Nanus (1997) put it, "Leaders are people who do the right thing; mangers are people who do things right" (p. 32). With many positions within organizations and communities, people need to perform both roles of leadership and management.

The following chapters feature more stories that speak to the inextricable link between leadership and communication. Storytelling is a powerful tool for mentoring leaders and building a leadership culture. In the history of leadership thought such as Burns's transformational leadership, Bennis's and Thomas's crucibles of leadership, and Kouzes' and Posner's leadership practices, there have been significant ideas that have relevance for understanding the links among leadership, communication, mentoring, and storytelling.

References

Astin, A. W., & Astin, H. S. (2000). *Leadership reconsidered: Engaging higher education in social change*. Battle Creek, MI: Kellogg Foundation.

Bass, B. (1990). From transactional to transformational leadership: Learning to share the vision. *Organizational Dynamics, 18*, 19–31.

Bennis, W., & Nanus, B. (1997). *Leaders: The strategies for taking charge* (2nd ed.). New York: HarperBusiness.

Bennis, W. G., & Thomas, R. J. (2007). *Leading for a lifetime: How defining moments shape the leaders of today and tomorrow*. Boston: Harvard Business School Press.

Burns, J. M. (1978). *Leadership*. New York: Harper & Row.

Chemers, M. M. (1997). *An integrative theory of leadership*. Mahwah, NJ: Lawrence Erlbaum.

Dance, F. E. X., & Larson, C. E. (1976). *The functions of human communication: A theoretical approach*. New York: Holt, Rinehart & Winston.

De Pree, M. (1989). *Leadership is an art*. New York: Doubleday.

Grady, A. P. (1999). *Voices for change: Development of leadership practices in women*. Unpublished doctoral dissertation, University of Denver, Denver.

Hackman, M. Z., & Johnson, C. E. (1991). *Leadership: A communication perspective*. Prospect Heights, IL: Waveland Press.

Heifetz, R. A. (1994). *Leadership without easy answers*. Cambridge, MA: Belknap Press/Harvard University Press.

Helgesen, S. (1990). *The female advantage: Women's ways of leadership*. New York: Doubleday Currency.

Kouzes, J. M., & Posner, B. Z. (1993). *Credibility: How leaders gain and lose it, why people demand it*. San Francisco: Jossey-Bass.

Kouzes, J. M., & Posner, B. Z. (1999). *Encouraging the heart: A leader's guide to rewarding and recognizing others*. San Francisco: Jossey-Bass.

Kouzes, J. M., & Posner, B. Z. (2007). *The leadership challenge: How to keep getting extraordinary things done in organizations* (4th ed.). San Francisco: Jossey-Bass.

Obama, B. (2011). *State of the union.* Retrieved January 31, 2011, from http://www.whitehouse.gov/state-of-the-union-2011

Rath, T., & Conchie, B. (2008). *Strengths-based leadership.* New York: Gallup Press.

Thomas, R. J. (2008). *Crucibles of leadership: How to learn from experience to become a great leader.* Boston: Harvard Business Press.

Zaleznik, A. (1977). Managers and leaders: Are they different? *Harvard Business Review, 55,* 67–78.

Zaleznik, A. (1989). Real work. *Harvard Business Review, 67,* 57–64.

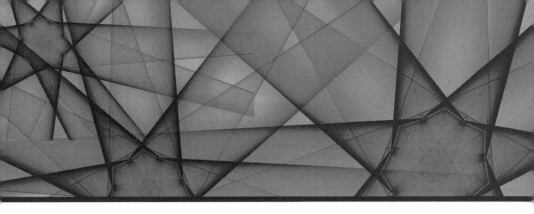

Chapter 2.
The Nature of Mentoring

Table Chats

As we shared thoughts and reflections about our own leadership development, we realized that over the years many people had a profound impact on what we learned, believed, and valued. These were our mentors! We became intrigued about the concept of mentoring and how it influenced our thoughts, ideas, and actions. We realized that, like leadership, mentoring is a communication process that served as the foundation for our leadership development. From the literature we learned that contemporary mentoring had its roots in antiquity, but no universally accepted definition of *mentoring* exists, and the nature of its practices is varied. Our experiences with mentoring taught us that the cornerstone for all mentoring programs is a relationship based on learning. As we shared our various experiences with mentoring, we became aware of the power of stories and the storytelling–listening process as effective mentoring tools that made learning personal for us. We hope that this chapter leads readers to appreciate that successful, sustainable leadership performance is grounded in the vitality of strong mentoring relationships.

Introduction

At its core, mentoring is about learning and relationships. Communication between mentor and mentee is the foundation on which learning relationships are built and the development of leadership thrives. Mentoring lifts a person's hopes and raises a person's performance and productivity to higher standards. Mentoring inspires people to get from where they are to where they want to be or where they have never been.

The vitality of mentoring rests on the bedrock of clear and consistent communication. Mentoring, like leading, is a communication process to influence thoughts, voice, and discovery of ideas and action. To influence others, there is no better communication tool than storytelling. Storytelling and listening are compelling forces for leadership development.

In this chapter, we review mentoring history, describe its concepts and practices, and discuss the relationship of mentoring and learning. Additionally, mentoring within organizations is addressed. Throughout the chapter, the power of stories and the storytelling–listening process as effective mentoring are explored.

History

Although the roots of mentoring practices have been lost in history, we know the word *mentor* was inspired by a character in Homer's *The Odyssey*, Mentor (Zachary, 2000). In the story, Mentor is a long-time friend of the hero, Odysseus. When Odysseus leaves his family to fight in the Trojan War, he entrusts Mentor with guardianship of his son, Telemachus. Because Mentor is not an effective teacher, Athena, the goddess of wisdom, takes on his appearance to guide Telemachus in his times of challenge and difficulty. "Thus, Mentor is both male and female, mortal and immortal—an androgynous demigod, half here, half not there. Wisdom personified" (Daloz, 1999, p. 20). The seeds of contemporary mentoring were planted in this ancient story.

From these historic beginnings, the word *mentor* has been used to define a loyal and trusted counselor and teacher; *mentoring* has been defined as the practice of educating a mentee with knowledge to live in the world (Daloz, 1999). The integration of Athena as Mentor illustrates the significance of mentoring connections, learning, and wisdom.

The concept of mentoring relationships and partnerships has historic beginnings in Greek literature with stories of famous mentor–protégé partners such as Socrates and Plato, Plato and Aristotle, and Aristotle and Alexander the Great. Throughout history, mentoring systems have included the disciple traditions practiced in Hinduism and Buddhism, discipleships practiced in Judaism and Christianity, and the apprentices of the medieval guild system.

The mentor–mentee relationship has a deep rich history, especially assisting young professionals in health, education, legal, and corporate fields. Contemporary mentoring practices in organizations began to emerge in the 1930s but soon lost its favor as a means to develop workers and aspiring professionals, possibly as a result of the declining economy. The renaissance of mentoring via the feminist movement and desire for diversity in the workplace significantly influenced organizations to sponsor mentoring programs.

In the 1970s, mentoring regained prominence in our culture; in fact, mentoring became a national movement. January was named *National Mentoring Month,* and *The National Mentoring Partnership* was recognized as a valuable professional organization. Since the 1970s, mentoring practices have become widespread, giving birth to an abundance of literature about mentors and mentoring.

Many individuals and groups offering services to children, youth, and adults in a variety of industries, including health care, education, the arts, and profit and nonprofit organizations embrace current mentoring practices. In modern times, the concept of mentoring partnerships is frequently mentioned, but the reality is that its practices have been more hierarchical than collaborative, with a mentor being the expert and a mentee the novice.

Mentoring practices during the 1970s and 1980s focused on teaching or training, with research on mentoring surfacing in the 1980s (Kram, 2004). Kram reported that the studies in the 1980s primarily focused on a mentor's roles and the benefits of mentoring relationships. In the 1990s, learning and discovery emerged as the basis for mentoring practices, curriculum, and research. In our 21st century, there is a pressing need to have additional research studies that focus on outcomes and cost benefits of mentoring programs. Chapter 4 of this book discusses findings of a 3-year study designed to identify leadership outcomes resulting from participation in Mentoring Circles®, a group mentorship program.

Today's mentor is not expected to be the consummate teacher, as portrayed in ancient literature. Rather, the modern mentor is considered to be a partner in a vibrant, evolving learning relationship focused on sharing and discovery of knowledge to build upon the mentees' capacities. Each mentee brings unique past experiences, knowledge, and culture to the learning relationship. As a partner, the mentor honors and respects the unique self of the mentee. In this context, mentoring prospers.

Defining Mentoring Practices

No single, universally accepted definition of *mentoring practice* exists; instead there are multiple definitions, depending on the purpose and model being practiced (Zachary, 2005). As mentoring gained popularity in organizations, its practices have adapted to meet recognized needs and to take advantage of available technology. Today, the classic one-to-one, mentor–mentee relationship is only one type of mentoring practice in an ever-expanding list of choices.

Mentoring can be informal or formal; self-directed or assigned; held face-to-face or over distances; and consist of mentor and one mentee, or of a mentor and group of mentees. Mentoring practices described in the literature are summarized in this chapter to provide an overview about the concept of mentoring and an increasing awareness of available options. For more comprehensive and detailed information, readers are encouraged to read the original writings of the authors cited in this chapter.

Informal Mentoring

Informal mentoring is an "intense relationship, lasting several years, in which a senior person oversees the career and psychosocial development of a junior person" (Douglas, 1997, p. 76). It has existed for centuries and is now seen in forms such as a doctoral candidate and dissertation advisor, a health care professional and intern or resident, a master craftsman and apprentice, or a manager and subordinate. These relationships naturally occur in the work environment and encompass mentoring, coaching, role modeling, and supervising.

Prior to the 1970s, informal mentoring in organizations was available to high-potential professionals with other developmental activities, primarily training, rotating jobs, and some career coaching (Douglas, 1997). Today, informal mentoring relationships are self-directed, developing on their own between partners (Rosenbach, 1993). Frequently a person may not know she or he has been identified as a mentor.

Formal Mentoring

Formal mentoring refers to assigned relationships and is usually associated with organizational mentoring programs. Designed to promote professional development, formal mentoring has established goals, schedules, curriculum, and evaluation. Formal mentoring is not intended to create the type of relationship or partnership experienced in informal mentoring programs, and the goals, objectives, and processes are different as well. For example, formal mentoring programs are designed to meet goals and objectives of the organization and to be part of its overall professional development offerings. Informal mentoring has a one-to-one relationship, centering on the goals or objectives of the individual.

Formal mentoring within organizations was first reported in the early 1930s when the Jewel Tea Company initiated a program with new managerial employees when it assigned a senior manager to serve as a mentor to new hires (Douglas, 1997). The practice did not gain popularity until the late 1970s. It then faded away again, re-emerging yet again in the 1990s. Douglas (1997) cites the increasing number of women and minorities hired for management positions, affirmative action programs, and advances in knowledge about adult learning as factors contributing to the development of formal mentoring programs. During the 1990s, formal mentoring programs grew in popularity, due in part to the positive reports about informal mentoring and the importance of professional career development programs.

Douglas (1997) reports on research that suggests that formal mentoring focuses on organizational goals with some emphasis on the social relationship aspect of the mentoring process, but informal mentoring centers on the goals of an individual and the relationship between mentor and mentee. As presented in this book, effective formal mentoring programs can focus on the goals of the organization or the individual as well as emphasize relationships and learning.

Onsite and Long-Distance Mentoring

Onsite and long-distance mentoring are options for both informal and formal programs. It no longer is imperative that mentoring be a face-to-face, onsite narrative exchange. Technology has opened up many avenues for long-distance or virtual mentoring to take place, such as via telephone, video conferencing, online chats, and e-mail.

The keys to success for distance mentoring are to (1) establish relationships, (2) develop goals and objectives for learning, (3) agree to ground rules, (4) establish commitments to participate, and (5) establish a means for human connections to take place (Zachary, 2000).

Another important factor for success are the people involved in discussing and determining what confidentiality means for the group (The Mentoring Company, 2008a). We believe that distance mentoring programs that include more than two people and meet by telephone or video conferencing do best when a facilitator monitors and guides the conversations.

One-to-One and Group Mentoring

One-to-one mentoring and group mentoring are both popular professional development programs in organizations. Contemporary mentoring includes both the classic one-to-one relationship and the newly recognized group mentoring programs.

Prior to the 1980s, literature about mentoring was limited to the one-to-one model, which was designed to offer information and insight from the mentor to another person. The main purpose for one-to-one mentoring programs was to assist another to climb the organization's ladder by better understanding the organization's systems and people. The information was a one-way street, traveling from the mentor to the protégé or mentee; it was likened to "grooming."

The hierarchical positioning of the mentor–mentee relationship can be negatively viewed because it is elitist in nature. Hall (1999) proposed that a downside of the grooming, one-to-one model is the *cloning effect* in which the mentee thinks and acts like the mentor. This cloning effect can contribute to static growth. When the mentor–mentee relationship is strong and the mentor assists the mentee to discover his or her own strengths and style, the model can be successful. One-to-one mentoring continues to be a popular model within organizations.

Group mentoring models allow learning from a group of people, rather than from just a single mentor. Swoboda and Millar (1986) introduced network mentoring, which operates with more than two persons and relies on the recognition of each member as equal within a group setting. There is not a selected mentor; rather, the group members mentor each other. Network mentoring provides opportunities for visibility, constructive criticism, shared power, and differing perspectives that add to one's learning (Haring, 1993). Listening to ideas from a group about others' personal issues and concerns with relevant, real-time experiences promotes the mentee's own problem solving.

One-to-One Mentoring

In *Creating a Mentoring Culture*, Lois Zachary (2005) defines *one-to-one mentoring* as two persons meeting to engage in a learning relationship. Within the one-to-one model, she proposes three variations: (1) reverse mentoring, (2) peer mentoring, and (3) supervisory mentoring.

Reverse mentoring

Reverse mentoring is an exchange process between a more senior person who has history with and knowledge about a corporation's culture and political systems and a younger employee who brings technological expertise and a perspective of the younger generation's work styles and ethics (Zachary, 2005). Through the exchange, the senior person acquires technological knowledge and an understanding of the new generation entering the workforce. The younger employee acquires knowledge about corporate culture and how to navigate the political system. Zachary (2005) reports that reverse mentoring connects people who may be separated by hierarchical and generation barriers, and it also builds a more connected workplace.

Peer mentoring

Peer mentoring takes place with two persons who are at the same level or hold the same title within an organization (Zachary, 2005). Some situations lend themselves to effective peer mentoring, such as faculty members learning about teaching a course, nurses learning about new ward procedures, or new employees becoming familiar with an organization (Zachary, 2005). A particular advantage of peer mentoring is the absence of intimidation that may occur in a hierarchical relationship.

Supervisory mentoring

Supervisory mentoring is an informal relationship between supervisor and supervisee to facilitate the learning needed for job performance (Zachary, 2005). This model has difficulties and pitfalls, because the process could interfere with the chain of command within supervisory responsibilities for training, overseeing performance, and evaluation. To be effective, both supervisor and supervisee need to manage the supervisor–mentor and supervisee–mentee roles (Zachary, 2005).

Group Mentoring

Group mentoring is a relationship among two or more persons and includes three types: (1) facilitated group mentoring, (2) peer mentoring groups, and (3) team mentoring (Zachary, 2005). *Facilitated group mentoring* is structured facilitation that creates a learning group with a mentor, mentees, and a facilitator. Group mentoring is a cost-effective use of training funds.

When compared to other models, our experiences suggest group mentoring led by a facilitator produces stronger and more knowledgeable teams within an organization. The richness of mentoring experiences multiplies as each participant brings personal experiences to the conversation. Zachary (2005) stresses the critical role of a facilitator, including ensuring that everyone in the group can participate and that agreed-upon confidentiality and ground rules are honored.

Other responsibilities for the facilitator include asking questions that expand the conversation, keeping the narrative meaningful, providing feedback, sharing personal experiences when appropriate, and serving as a sounding board (Zachary, 2005). A facilitator should be a person outside the organization who has had experience with mentoring practices as both a mentor and a mentee.

Peer mentoring groups

Similar to group mentoring, *peer mentoring groups* is a model in which a group of employees who are at the same level in the hierarchy and who share similar learning interests or needs mentor each other. The group is self-directed and self-managed.

Many senior-level executives prefer this model because it gives these leaders a sounding board consisting of people at their own level with similar responsibilities and an opportunity to test ideas and receive feedback. Peer groups can be a safe haven for preparing significant personal and organizational policies and transitions (Zachary, 2005). At times when a facilitated group mentoring program comes to closure, participants may select to continue to meet as a peer mentoring or team mentoring group.

Team mentoring

Team mentoring is a method for facilitating learning relationships among an intact team or unit (Zachary, 2005). Individuals making up the team actively engage in reaching mutual goals and planning the mentoring process. Team members must support and learn from each other's experience.

Team mentoring is most effective when an outside facilitator is selected to work with the team. For example, a major hurdle for team mentoring is developing trusting relationships and promoting an environment where members can feel safe to be vulnerable and not competitive. Because of the importance of building a trusting mentoring climate for team members, it is highly recommended that a facilitator from outside the organization be assigned the responsibility of facilitating the mentoring process.

Mentoring board of directors

Mentoring board of directors is an emerging informal mentoring model that integrates elements of one-to-one and group mentoring described earlier. This model operates similarly to an advisory board and can function as a group or in individual meetings. The mentee determines his or her learning needs, invites experts in the areas needed for learning, and manages individual or group meetings to assist with achieving learning goals. The board of directors model is a valuable strategy for assisting individuals with their career planning and execution (Zachary, 2005).

An Innovative Facilitated Group Mentoring Program

Mentoring Circles, developed by Amy Burgess, CEO of The Mentoring Company, is a unique structure and process that integrates components of facilitated group mentoring, peer mentoring, team mentoring, and onsite and distance mentoring offerings.

The Mentoring Company (2008a) defines *mentoring* as "discovery and learning that occurs through the transfer of knowledge, insight, and skills based on trusting relationships over a sustained period of time" (p. 2). The power of The Mentoring Company's methodology is its egalitarian focus rather than the hierarchical practice of advice giving, teaching, or parenting (The Mentoring Company, 2008b). A primary principle for the Mentoring Circles' process is to avoid giving advice and instead provide the opportunity for self-discovery and reflection (see Story 2.1).

The circle program has a copyrighted process that involves a mutually supportive group of people who use storytelling to foster safe, trusting communities to transfer best leadership practice. The foundation for the process and activities is the use of stories to promote learning. Storytelling is not an esoteric appendage; it is the heart of what Mentoring Circles are all about. It is the narrative that gives voice to leadership learning.

Within Mentoring Circles, the primary role for the mentor is to share stories of relevant personal experiences instead of imparting knowledge or giving advice. A mentor acts as leader, guide, change agent, coordinator, and facilitator of learning. The mentor is a group member who collaborates with the circle's facilitator to promote collaborative problem solving and active participation. The concept of a storytelling mentor replaces the classic mentor as "sage on the stage" to "guide on the side" (Rosenbach, 1993, p. 3).

The various types of mentoring programs provide individuals and organizations various options for a structure that could achieve desired goals and be best suited to the organization's culture. They offer choice, but a common, underlying theme exists for all mentoring programs: empowering individuals through learning-centered relationships.

Story 2.1. Mentoring Circles

When asked about the value of Mentoring Circles, a mentee replied, "The most valuable part of my Mentoring Circles was the opportunity to enjoy learning once again. I think sharing our real-time challenges and listening to our mentor's stories gave me the opportunity to listen and put myself in that place; it was like a discovery process. I really liked the opportunity to have quiet reflection time after the mentor's story. I could think about what I heard and begin to apply some of the ideas to my own situations. I wasn't required to prove what I learned to anyone; it was all for me—truly a gift. Learning like this is fun!"

Another mentee said, "The major value of the program has been the sharing of experiences and the wonderful ideas people have presented for dealing with various leadership issues. I really liked the time to reflect and apply what I had just heard to my own situations. Listening to the stories by our mentor and other stories of participants has helped me put my own experience into perspective and to see that these experiences have made me grow and become even better at what I love to do."

Mentoring and Learning

Learning is the cornerstone of all mentoring programs. At its best, mentoring is more than transferring knowledge from mentor to mentee; it includes critical reflection, transformation of ideas and thought, and application of ideas to creative actions.

Critical Reflection

Critical reflection is introspective dialogue carried on in thought and narrative form. Reflection is an essential element for self-discovery and learning. Successful mentors reflect on their experiences and capture the richness for developing and telling stories. Successful mentees reflect on what they hear from the mentor, integrating relevant ideas with their own experiences and challenges.

Craft Knowledge

The power of stories and the storytelling–listening process are effective mentoring tools. When mentoring stories share real time and personal experiences and are accompanied by analysis and reflection, they become "craft knowledge." According to Roland Barth (2001, as cited in McCay, 2003), *craft knowledge* is the critical lessons learned that informs our practices and promotes discovery and learning. It "emerges when we use our stories to discover deeper meanings or truths about our experiences" (McCay, 2003, p. 70).

Shared stories go beyond informing; rather, stories inspire collaborative learning between mentor and mentee. Collaboration in learning is creative work influenced by storytelling about past experiences that culminate in self-reflection and discovery of ideas for action for current situations. "Everything that happens to you is your teacher . . . The secret is to learn to sit at the feet of your own life and be taught by it" (Berends, 1990, p. 5).

Applied Learning

Mentoring facilitates learning in context, such as when people interact, share challenges, discover solutions, and solve real-time problems. Learning in context is applied learning that facilitates discovery of ideas for action. In an *applied learning* paradigm, the main agent is the mentee or learner, not the mentor or facilitator. Applied learning facilitates transformation of self to acquire the personal capacity to face challenges and change with vitality and conviction. It is essential for developing leadership practices needed to resolve complex problems that face organizations (Knowles, 1980). As such, applied learning is the foremost purpose, core process, and desired outcome of mentoring.

Mentoring experiences grounded in an applied learning paradigm become a powerful learning relationship for both the mentor and mentee and are the essence of mentorship. Mentorship encompasses mentoring as its practice, mentor and mentee as its people, storytelling–listening as its communication tool, and applied learning as its outcome.

Adult Learning Theory

Mentorship is grounded not only in an applied learning paradigm but also in the concepts of adult learning theory. Research indicates that one of the ways adults best learn and retain knowledge is by consciously reflecting and acting on their learning (Knowles, Holton, & Swanson, 1998). Adult learning principles must be considered in the process of integrating learning with mentoring. Zachary (2005) discusses three adult learning models relevant to mentorship practices: (1) self-directed learning, (2) experiential or action learning, and (3) transformational learning.

Self-directed learning is a process with the mentee assuming responsibility and being accountable for his or her learning. *Experiential or action learning* is applied learning or taking in information, reflecting on it, and then acting. *Transformational learning* is a three-step continuum that includes (1) self-reflection, (2) awareness, and (3) understanding. Combining the models with the concepts of challenging thoughts, supporting ideas, and visioning play a critical role in facilitating learning (Zachary, 2000).

In his book *Leading and Learning*, Brill (2008) suggests that adults learn not only from their own experiences but also from their formal and informal conversations with other adults. He stresses the value of organizations providing systems and protocols that promote community learning because group learning promotes higher levels of achievement and more positive relationships than those found with individual learning situations.

Adult learning theory, developed by Knowles (1980) and Knowles et al. (1998), can guide developing and implementing mentorship programs. Principles of adult learning theory include

★ Adults best learn when they are involved and actively participate in their own learning.
★ Adults best learn when the conversation is relevant and in real time, and there is a specific need.
★ Adults best learn and retain knowledge by consciously reflecting on their learning.
★ Adults must know why they need to learn something before undertaking the effort to learn it.
★ Adults have a self-concept of being responsible for their own decisions.
★ Life's reservoir of experience is a primary learning resource; life experiences of others enrich the learning process.
★ Adult learners have an inherent need for immediacy of application.
★ Adults respond best to learning when they are internally motivated to learn.

Mentorship programs that use stories and integrate the principles of adult learning theory can successfully help adults achieve a sense of their personal power, leadership strengths, and self-worth. The storytelling–mentoring process unites and empowers people to conquer adversity. As introduced in Chapter 1, finding meaning in negative circumstances and learning from those experiences are "crucibles" of leadership. The storytelling–mentoring process can be a transformative experience and lead to breakthroughs for the mentor; mentee; and, ultimately, the workplace.

Mentorship Within Organizations

An organization's culture that includes the value of mentorship programs increases employee engagement and helps them face challenges and change. Organizations are constantly experiencing change—change is inevitable, but growth is optional. A powerful option for promoting growth is the promotion of mentorship as part of an organization's investment in employees' learning. Recent literature stresses the value and cost-effectiveness for an organization investing in its employees' growth, thus promoting employee engagement. Engaged employees are more committed, are more inclined to stay, and tend to "go the extra mile" for the organization (Rieger, 2006).

Evidence suggests that formal mentorship programs are vital for employee engagement because these programs convey the message that employees are valued (Fullan, 2002). Reports indicate that only 1% of those who have no mentor are able to achieve real engagement with their employer, whereas 66% who report having someone at work who encourages their development are classified as *engaged*, leaving 33% who are *not engaged* and 1% who are *actively disengaged* (Robison, 2006).

The major objectives of formal mentorship in organizations include (1) meeting employees' professional development needs, (2) facilitating networking, (3) providing challenges and support to employees identified as top talent, (4) facilitating committed organizational change, (5) increasing diversity of senior management, (6) decreasing turnover, and (7) and increasing retention rates (Douglas, 1997).

In addition to supporting and retaining employees, many organizations have discovered that mentorship programs benefit their recruitment and on-boarding efforts for potential talented employees (Robison, 2006). Wagner and Hart (2007) argue that sponsoring mentoring programs is important for an organization's future, including it as one of their six elements of great management.

In the 1990s, organizations began to invest in learning. Organizational learning became imperative in order to develop employees, compete in the corporate world, and attain industry results. Learning (Senge, 1990) became a fixture in organizational life, and organizations began investing in it (Zachary, 2005).

In *The Fifth Discipline*, Senge (1990, 2006) discusses his five learning disciplines: (1) *personal mastery* (clarifying and deepening one's personal vision, personal growth, and learning), (2) *mental models* (deeply ingrained assumptions and images of how we see and make sense of the world around us), (3) *shared vision* (pictures or images that people in an organization carry in their heads and hearts and the skill of interrupting others' pictures of the future), (4) *team learning* (process of aligning and developing the capacity of a group to create the results wanted by the team), and (5) *systems thinking* (having a perspective about the organization's systems and reflecting on one's own assumptions and ways of operating in the organization's systems).

Senge (1990) states, "Organizations learn only through individuals who learn. Individual learning does not guarantee organizational learning. But without it no organizational learning occurs" (p. 139). Our work supports the premise that mentorship is an effective process for a learning organization to achieve Senge's five disciplines.

Many organizations have defined and offered formal mentoring based on their informal mentoring programs described earlier in the chapter. As previously noted, clear differences exist between formal and informal mentoring processes, so it is inappropriate to base one on the other. Douglas (1997) suggests blurring definitions and offerings has led to confusion and resistance to formal mentoring programs. She proposes that the concepts and definitions of formal mentoring be based on the activities being implemented, roles of the people, and developing relationships.

Benefits of formal mentoring include accelerated learning about the organization, expanded and diverse perspectives, increased tacit organizational knowledge, additional insights about other business units, improved skills in specific areas, job or work satisfaction, and increased retention rates (Zachary, 2005). Rosenbach (1993) believes organizational benefits of mentoring include smoothly functioning leadership teams and clear lines of leader succession that ensure continuation of the organization's values and culture.

Formal mentorship programs help new employees adapt to and integrate within the organization's culture more quickly (Zachary, 2005). In her review of literature, Douglas (1997) reported that formal mentoring programs accelerate positive integration of diverse populations within an organization: "Affirmative-action initiatives and organizational goals to increase diversity within middle- and senior-management levels have used formal mentoring programs to accelerate the movement of minorities and women into senior-management positions and meet organizational timetables" (p. 65).

Formal mentoring not only helps top talent; it also improves the performance of everybody else. De Long, Gabarro, and Lees (2008) emphasize the importance of building mentoring programs not just for "A" players (top talent) but also for "B" players (the solid citizens who make up 70% of an organization). According to De Long et al., an organization's B players are its heart and soul; these employees stay longer, have motivation to succeed, and are committed to the organization.

De Long et al.'s (2008) research found the majority of professional service organizations focus on A players and ignore the heart and soul of their organization. Zachary (2005) reiterates this sentiment, arguing, "Mentoring humanizes the workplace by building relationships of head, heart, and soul" (p. 9). Employee engagement increases in those organizations committed to a core value of opportunities for all employees' development. Findings from De Long et al.'s research support the value for organizations to offer formal mentoring programs for both A and B employees.

Diversity

In the 1970s and 1980s, as a result of an increasingly diverse workforce, organizations began to face challenges and changes including sexual harassment as well as employees' lack of understanding about the differences among ethnic and gender cultures. Additionally, organizations faced generational issues among employees due to different generations working together, each with its own values, motivating factors, and job performance factors (Zemke, Raines, & Flipczak, 2000). Although organizations recruited and hired a more diverse workforce, many would leave the workplace within a few years (Heim & Golent, 1993; Murphy & Heim, 2003). Retention of a diverse workforce became a major challenge for organizations.

Murphy and Heim (2003) found that workplace interaction is the most significant difference between men and women in an organization. Their findings stress that women value relationships more than men do. Further, their research across generations of men and women (e.g., Gen-Xers, Baby Boomers, mature workers) found that women of differing ethnic and generation cultures all value relationships as an important factor for career development.

Managers realized that gender and generational diversity were significant cultural demographic variables that had important implications for workplace engagement and retention (Klenke, 1996). Professional development programs to address sexual harassment, supervision of diverse populations, and understanding and respect for cultural difference were offered. As Douglas (1997) reported, the increasing number of women and minorities hired for management positions, affirmative action programs, and advances in knowledge about different cultures and how adults learn contributed to the development of mentoring programs within organizations.

In our work with various organizations, we have discovered that a key component of group mentorship programs with diverse populations is the use of storytelling. As a mentoring tool, stories transcend culture, giving the story listener the opportunity to integrate messages from the story with his or her own experiences, beliefs, and culture (see Story 2.2).

The human dimension of an organization is its most valuable resource. Organizations that value their people and implement formal organizational mentorship programs as part of the culture realize benefits and build strong leadership communities. According to Drucker (2002), organizational learning programs are essential for continued growth: "In a traditional workforce, the worker serves the system; in a knowledge workforce, the system must serve the worker" (p. 7). Mentorship serves the worker.

Structuring Organizational Mentoring Practices

Implementing mentoring practices requires support from the organization. According to Rosenbach (1993), "A culture of transformational leadership stimulates mentoring ... [it] can be a powerful force to empower followers to be leaders" (p.

Story 2.2. Group Mentoring

I was surprised to get an invitation to join a mentoring program whose curriculum was based in leadership. I'm from India and have just finished my doctoral studies. I have been working as a software engineer for the organization for 3 years.

At first I questioned what I would get out of the time spent with the group; after all, the majority of the group was made up of older workers who represented the past at our company. They didn't have anything in common with me, and I knew much more about programming and technology than they did.

Well, I couldn't have been more surprised. Our group's mentor told stories about real-time happenings and shared what she did, her feelings, and her learning. I was amazed how I could identify with her stories and how much I could take from them and integrate her messages with my day-to-day work demands. Also, we had a chance to bring our problems or issues to the group and receive mentoring from the mentor and others in the group.

I got a lot from listening to others in the group. After a few months, I felt comfortable to bring my issues to the group and soon realized that my problems were like theirs and they could help me problem-solve. I may not value the same things at work that the older members do, and they may not know as much about new technologies, but we each have something to offer each other.

Our mentor will always be a mentor for me and our group has become a great network. Although our program has ended, we still meet together on a regular basis, sometimes just to socialize, and sometimes to help each other. I feel the company has invested in me and I am committed to stay, maybe become a leader as well.

---

149). Organizational support and a learning-centered culture are the underpinnings to successful mentorship programs. Likewise, from our work, we have discovered mentorship to be an effective tool for acquiring both knowledge of self and building a leadership culture within an organization (see Chapter 4, "Outcomes of an Effective Mentoring Program").

Understanding the phases of mentoring relationships that are being built within the mentorship programs is essential for structuring programs that will meet desired goals and purposes. Zachary (2005) suggests four dynamic phases necessary for building mentoring relationships:

1. *Preparing:* Includes self-preparation and relationship preparation;
2. *Negotiating:* Identification of learning goals, success criteria and measurement, delineation of mutual responsibility, accountability, protocols for addressing stumbling blocks, consensual mentoring agreement and work plan;
3. *Enabling:* Time for learning and development, building of networks, and sharing stories and best practices; and
4. *Coming to closure:* Opportunity for mentors and mentees to process and evaluate learning and move on.

As reported by Douglas (1997), literature about formal organization mentoring programs cites five major phases for implementation:

1. *Goal-setting:* Identification and prioritization of program goals,
2. *Initiation:* Selection and matching of mentor and mentees,
3. *Cultivation:* Building the partnership of mentor and mentee,
4. *Separation:* Relationship shifts from mentor–mentee to colleague, and
5. *Redefinition:* Review and renew roles and responsibilities of mentor and mentee.

Douglas (1997) also reported on a model developed by Gray (1986) that proposes four phases to the developmental relationship in a mentoring partnership:

1. Identification and matching of mentor and mentees;
2. Training of mentors, mentees, and support staff;
3. Monitoring the mentoring process and redefining if needed; and
4. Evaluation of results and implementing modifications needed.

Gray (1986) suggests a model to understand the nature of formal mentoring relationships. It has five levels in which a mentee progresses from a state of reliance on the mentor to relative autonomy. The beginning phase involves the mentor transmitting realities of the organization, including its culture and values, with the goal of helping the mentee become socialized. With further development, mentees are guided to develop their own work style and continue to seek assistance from the mentors.

Although different characteristics of phases and models for implementing effective mentoring programs exist, they typically cluster around five themes: (1) organizational support and culture; (2) identifying purpose; (3) goals and objectives; (4) thoughtful selection and matching of mentors and mentees; and (5) educating participants about the process, continual monitoring of progress, evaluation, and planning for next steps.

Building a Leadership Culture

Leadership begins with knowledge of self. Bennis and Nanus (1995) argue that knowing oneself is the cornerstone of the ability to lead and the place to start on the journey of leadership. A major premise for our book is the value of mentorship for discovery of self and the leader within.

Murray (2001) describes leadership development as one of the primary motives for mentoring. Shea (1994) strongly reinforces the mentoring–leadership link by stating that "all the things that mentoring is good at bringing forth—adaptability, creativity, imagination, a sense of balance and proportion, vision, insight, the utility of our feelings, intuition, caring for others, a sense of sharing and helping . . . are the capacities that successful, proactive leaders need in abundance" (p. 77). Mentoring is acknowledged as a highly effective approach to leadership development (Andrews & Wallis, 1999; Daloz, 1999; Murray, 2001; Pellegrini, 2009; Shea, 1994; Stone, 2004).

Culture creates a sense of identity and reflects the essence of an organization. Culture ties people together, giving meaning and purpose to their day-to-day lives. *Corporate culture* concerns the conditions and forms in which meaning and value are configured and communicated (Deal & Kennedy, 2000). Culture is the soul of an organization, a social energy that moves people to action.

Just as leadership starts with knowledge of self, a culture of leadership begins with the people of an organization. As leadership develops and filters throughout an organization, a leadership culture is built. An employee who had been with a large corporation for 30 years (Story 2.3) shares the following about her organization's culture.

Leaders create and transform culture, but culture in turn creates future generations of leaders (Schein, 2010). Preservation of culture depends upon human capacity for learning and transmitting knowledge to succeeding generations. Valuing the human dimension as the organization's most important resource is the core of a leadership culture.

A leadership culture empowers people, breaks down the barriers of hierarchy, and distributes leadership throughout the organization. In a leadership culture, leaders position themselves among the group, not above it (Reicher, Haslam, &

Story 2.3. Culture

I have always loved my work and was very proud of my corporation's culture, especially the emphasis on the value of the human dimension. About a year ago we acquired another large company and the merger began with a big bang!

The culture of the other company seemed to value the bottom line over the people. We didn't like working with each other; there seemed to be a lack of trust. We all complained behind closed doors, and our productivity began to lessen. The management that was put into place didn't seem to know what to do to help us become one company and create our culture together.

Those of us who have been around for years began sharing our stories of the past, and actually began to grieve the loss of our past. It was apparent that our new organization didn't have any stories to tell. It was then that I realized the power of our stories to help us identify our organization and learn from our past. How sad it was to not have any stories to tell together.

A group of us decided to talk with our bosses and suggest we do something about building a new culture. We could even tell stories about the process of becoming one corporation and create some new stories. Or, we could share stores about our past with the other group and they could share with us. Hopefully, trust would build, [and] we could learn to laugh together and even grieve our losses. Realizing the need to share experiences through real-time stories was a defining opportunity for us to build a new culture. Maybe that will help us have passion for our work once again.

Platow, 2007). Leadership culture includes leadership performance as part of the organization's strategies, and development of leaders as part of its mission and vision. Invisible qualities (e.g., values, style, character, informal rules, way of doing things) are grounded in leadership and the development of leaders. Mentorship programs have been effective for developing leaders and distributing leadership throughout the organization.

Leadership culture facilitates a dynamic, integrated process of learned behaviors, attitudes, thoughts, and values by which women and men communicate and relate. A leadership culture does not regulate a person's behavior according to set standards; rather, it influences interactions in regard to the people and context of the situation. The soul of a leadership culture rests in the people of the organization and their relationships.

Organizational culture that is managed with leadership as its core can expect high morale and quality performance from its people; it will be, in the best sense, a cultured organization of leaders (Kilmann, 1985; Schein, 2010). Mentorship programs designed to develop a person's leadership practices can influence the formation, transformation, and preservation of a culture centered in leadership.

Summary

Recent literature about leadership learning suggests that formal organizational mentoring programs are effective ways to augment leadership growth and build human capital. The various mentoring practices presented in this chapter offer options for organizations to select the method best suited to its needs and goals. Although the methods may vary, a common underlying theme for organizational mentoring programs exists: empowering people through learning-centered programs.

Synergy between mentoring and learning takes place when people interact, share challenges, and discover solutions. Learning through mentoring is applied learning that is specific to situations, facilitates collective knowledge, and promotes relevant solutions and actions. Mentoring, storytelling, learning, and communication are the essential ingredients for developing contemporary leadership practices to deal with the complex problems of today's organizations. Mentoring practices grounded in storytelling, adult learning theories, and an applied learning paradigm are the essence of the concept of mentorship introduced in this chapter.

Strong leadership throughout an organization is critical for its sustained growth and success. Successful, sustained leadership performance has its foundation in the vitality of an organization's culture that is centered in the concepts of leadership. Leadership is intertwined with culture formation, transformation, and preservation (Schein, 2010). Culture provides meaning, direction, and motivation that move the organization forward, or, if a dysfunctional culture, it can drive the organization to destruction (Deal & Kennedy, 2000; Kilmann, 1985). Leadership and culture are so central to understanding an organization and making it effective that the creation of a leadership culture should be a supreme goal for organizations.

References

Andrews, M., & Wallis, M. (1999). Mentorship in nursing: A literature review. *Journal of Advanced Nursing, 29,* 210–207.

Barth, R. S. (2001). *Learning by heart.* San Francisco: Jossey-Bass.

Bennis, W., & Nanus, B. (1995). *Leaders: The strategies for taking charge.* New York: Harper & Row.

Berends, P. B. (1990). *Coming to life: Traveling the spiritual path in everyday life.* San Francisco: Harper & Row.

Brill, F. (2008). *Leading and learning.* Portland, ME: Stenhouse.

Daloz, L. A. (1999). *Mentor: Guiding the journey of adult learners.* San Francisco: Jossey-Bass.

Deal, T., & Kennedy, A. (2000). *Corporate cultures: The rites and rituals of corporate life.* New York: Perseus.

De Long, T., Gabarro, J., & Lees, R. (2008, January 1). Why mentoring matters in a hypercompetitive world. *Harvard Business Review.* Retrieved January 31, 2011, from http://hbr.org/2008/01/why-mentoring-matters-in-a-hypercompetitive-world/ar/1

Douglas, C. A. (1997). *Formal mentoring programs in organizations.* Retrieved January 31, 2011, from http://www.ccl.org/leadership/pdf/research/FormalMentoringPrograms.pdf

Drucker, P. F. (2002). They're not employees, they're people. *Harvard Business Review.* Retrieved January 31, 2011, from http://www.peowebhr.com/Newsreleases/Harvard%20Business%20Review.pdf

Fullan, M. (2002). Moral purpose writ large. *The School Administrator, 59,* 14–16.

Gray, W. A. (1986). Components for developing a successful formal mentoring program in business, the professions, education, and other settings. In W. A. Gray & M. M. Gray (Eds.), *Proceedings of the first international conference on mentoring* (pp. 15–22). Vancouver, BC: International Association on Mentoring.

Hall, C. (1999). *Network mentoring thrives in a higher academic setting.* Unpublished doctoral dissertation, Creighton University, Omaha, NE.

Haring, M. (1993). Mentoring for research: Examining alternative models. In *Research mentoring and training in communication sciences and disorders: Proceedings of a national conference.* Rockville, MD: American Speech–Language–Hearing Foundation.

Heim, P., & Golent, S. (1993). *Hardball for women: Winning at the game of business.* New York: Plume.

Kilmann, R. (1985). Corporate culture. *Psychology Today, 11*(4), 63–68.

Klenke, K. (1996). *Women and leadership.* New York: Springer.

Knowles, M. S. (1980). *The modern practice of adult education: From pedagogy to andragogy.* Chicago: Follett.

Knowles, M. S., Holton, E. F., & Swanson, R. A. (1998). *The adult learner: The definition classic in adult education and human resource development* (5th ed.). Woburn, MA: Butterworth-Heinemann.

Kram, K. (2004). The making of a mentor [Foreword]. In D. Clutterbuck & G. Lane (Eds.), *The situational mentor: An international review of competencies and capabilities in mentoring* (pp. xi–xiv). Burlington, VT: Gower.

McCay, E. (2003). Tell your stories—And never forget. *National Staff Development Council, 24,* 68–70.

The Mentoring Company. (2008a). *Mentee manual.* Loveland, CO: Author.

The Mentoring Company. (2008b). *Mentor orientation manual.* Loveland, CO: Author.

Murphy, S., & Heim, P. (2003). *In the company of women*. New York: Tarcher/Putnam.

Murray, M. (2001). *Beyond the myths and magic of mentoring*. San Francisco: Jossey-Bass.

Pellegrini, V. D. (2009). Mentoring: Our obligation . . . Our heritage. *Journal of Bone and Joint Surgery, 91*, 2511–2519. doi:10.2106/JBJS.I.00954

Reicher, S., Haslam, S., & Platow, M. (2007, August/September). The new psychology of leadership. *Scientific American Mind*, pp. 22–29.

Rieger, T. (2006). Engaging customers—All day, every day. *Gallup Management Journal*. Retrieved January 31, 2011, from http://gmj.gallup.com/content/24475/engaging-customers-all-day-every-day.aspx

Robison, J. (2006). A Caterpillar dealer unearths employee engagement. *Gallup Management Journal*. Retrieved January 31, 2011, from http://gmj.gallup.com/content/24874/Caterpillar-Dealer-Unearths-Employee-Engagement.aspx

Rosenbach, W. (1993). Mentoring: Empowering followers to be leaders. In W. E. Rosenbach & L. Taylor (Eds.), *Contemporary issues in leadership* (pp. 141–151). Boulder, CO: Westview Press.

Schein, E. H. (2010). *Organizational culture and leadership*. San Francisco: Jossey-Bass.

Senge, P. M. (1990). *The fifth discipline: The art and practice of the learning organization*. New York: Currency.

Senge, P. M. (2006). *The fifth discipline: The art and practice of the learning organization* (rev. ed.). New York: Doubleday.

Shea, G. F. (1994). *Mentoring: Helping employees reach their full potential*. New York: American Management Association.

Stone, F. (2004). *The mentoring advantage: Creating the next generation of leaders*. Chicago: Dearborn Trade Publishing.

Swoboda, M., & Millar, S. (1986). Networking—Mentoring: Career strategy of women in academic administration. *Journal of the National Association of Women Deans and Counselors, 49*, 3–11.

Wagner, R., & Hart, J. K. (2007). The sixth element of great managing: Why are mentors such a powerful influence on their protégés? *Gallup Management Journal, 10*, 11.

Zachary, L. J. (2000). *The mentor's guide*. San Francisco: Jossey-Bass.

Zachary, L. J. (2005). *Creating a mentoring culture: The organization's guide*. San Francisco: Jossey-Bass.

Zemke, R., Raines, C., & Flipczak, B. (2000). *Generations at work: Managing the clash of veterans, Boomers, Xers, and Nexters in your workplace*. New York: American Management Association.

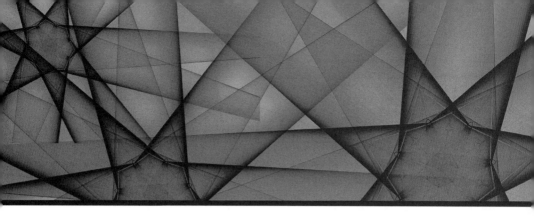

Chapter 3.
The Power of Stories

Table Chats

During our table chats, we discovered that we were mentoring each other and having fun doing so! As we reflected on our mentoring relationships, we shared experiences from our roles as mentors, mentees, and facilitators of mentoring groups. A common theme that emerged was the power of stories and storytelling to enhance learning. From the literature, we learned that storytelling is nothing new; it is timeless. We also realized that, like leadership and mentoring, storytelling is a compelling communication activity that is central to our life and work. As mentors, stories and storytelling gave us opportunities to relive our past experiences and learn from them. As mentees, we could listen and assimilate a story's message into our own framework, transferring the knowledge and wisdom to ourselves. As facilitators of group mentoring programs in a variety of organizations, we learned that mentoring stories allow people to actively participate, to think and discover their own creative alternative for action to resolve conflict, solve problems, and address challenges and opportunities. Key lessons that emerged are (1) organizations that value storytelling and stories achieve positive outcomes to align their human resources with their mission, vision, and values, and (2) sharing stories in a mentoring relationship is the cornerstone for building a leadership culture.

Introduction

Stories are an integral part of our own humanity; as Pink (2006) puts it, "We are our stories" (p. 115). Stories born of real-life experiences form the fabric of our personal and social memory. People desire emotional connections, and stories give context to unite.

Sharing stories and experiences taps into an ancient practice — the power of social discourse — and taps into an ancient art form — people sharing of themselves and pursuing meaning in their lives. Storytelling is narrative art. From Greek mythology, Egyptian hieroglyphics, parables of *The Bible*, and days of the shaman around the fire, stories have entertained; taught; recorded history; and conveyed beliefs, values, truths, rules, and tales (Guber, 2007).

Throughout history, stories have been the basic tool of the human mind for the purpose of understanding, relating, and passing on the legends of one's culture. "There have been great societies who have not used the wheel, but there have been no societies that did not tell stories" (Pink, 2006, p. 106). Storytelling has always been a tool for learning, providing a means of conveying "meaningful learning from person to person, generation to generation, culture to culture" (McCay, 2003, p. 68).

Technology-advanced cultures, operating in a wireless Internet world, still reflect people's need for narrative. In today's world, connecting with others through narrative has been losing its luster; the need to connect remains supreme. The popularity of blogs reinforces the human need for reflection, and sharing and reading stories on electronic forums enlarge the audience of story sharing and connections. Storytelling is a compelling communication method that bridges the gap between our digital culture and the need to connect with others.

The power of storytelling is receiving attention in the literature, particularly articles and books discussing the impact stories can have in the workplace. Current literature is rich with concepts about the power of stories and the vital role of a storyteller in today's organizations, schools, hospitals, clinics, and corporations (Denning, 2005; Silverman, 2006). "As a modern shaman, the visionary business leader taps into the human yearning to be part of a worthy cause" (Guber, 2007, p. 59). Storytelling and story listening are central to every phase of organizational management and leadership (Guber, 2007).

Sharing relevant experiences enables us to grasp ideas in an enjoyable, nonthreatening manner, transcending cultures and generations, thus making stories a powerful tool for mentoring in culturally or generationally diverse contexts. Maguire (1998) stresses that the purpose for sharing a story is not to entertain, nor teach; rather, it is to engage others in an experience so they can reflect on the message and discover new knowledge to inspire their own forward movement.

Stories and Storytelling

What Is a Story?

A *story* is a true or fictional narrative account that weaves detail, character, and event into a meaningful and memorable tale that is vivid and emotionally stimulating (The

Mentoring Company, 2008). Storytelling is compelling narrative—the essence of influence, entertainment, communication, understanding, and sharing of self. Whether written or oral, stories have different forms, such as tales of personal experiences and dreams, folklore, recordings of events and history, or journalistic accounts.

Regardless of its type, purpose, presentation, or outcome, a story can best be understood as a painting rather than a photograph because its content, like the medium of a painting, becomes a transmission of meaning and perception for the receiver, rather than fact or conviction (Maguire, 1998). Our brain has an internal "story syntax" that helps us understand our world as a configuration of experiences, not a set of logical propositions (Pink, 2006).

Personal stories can convey the dynamics of a particular culture or point in history (see Story 3.1). Personal stories provide continuity in the lives of a teller and a listener by sharing experiences of where we have been, what we have done, how we have felt, and lessons we have learned. Our life experiences, understanding of events, and thinking and feeling are organized in story form. Not only does the content of a story have impact, but the social discourse of storytelling and listening also creates an effect (Brown, Denning, Groh, & Prusak, 2005). Stories are conversation, not just information (Brown et al., 2005).

Stories differ from information in that they elicit the listener's belief. Simmons (2001) argues that people have all the information they can assimilate; they "are up to their eyeballs" in information. What most of us want more than just facts is to trust and believe in the information we are receiving. Simmons suggests that "it is faith that moves mountains, not facts … Once people make your story *their* story, you have tapped into the powerful force of faith" (p. 3).

Denning (2005) submits that storytelling supplements logical, analytical thinking by enabling a listener to imagine new perspectives and solutions. "Abstract analysis is easier to understand when seen through the lens of a well-chosen story"

Story 3.1. Growing Pains

Q-U-A-R-A-N-T-I-N-E read the large block letters painted on a square of bright red cardboard. The doctor attached the sign to the house near the front door. *"Scarletina,"* he said, "is not as serious as scarlet fever." When the four of us came down with a fever, mother called the doctor to make a house call.

We wondered aloud if Dad would be able to go back to work after he crossed the quarantine line when he walked home for lunch. I remember no complaints from the neighbors, because Dad continued to come and go each day. That was testimony to Dad's capable image. Whatever his action, it was the right thing to do.

However, the library books could not cross a quarantine line. We kids had borrowed 10 library books before that red sign was on display. We were required to buy those books at 10 cents each. The scary contagious scarletina of the 1930s was no doubt the beginning of our home library. (McConnell, 1999, p. 16)

Story 3.2. Coyote and Another One

Two coyotes were crossing a farmer's field. Both coyotes were strangers to each other, for they had never met. Just as they were about to introduce themselves they heard the farmer yell, "There's a coyote in the field!"

The first coyote turned to the other and told him to run! They both started to run for the trees when they heard the farmer yell, "And there goes another one!"

Finally, both coyotes made it to the cover of the trees and they started to introduce themselves. "I never saw you before. I am Wanderer, and I am a coyote like you."

The other coyote looked at him oddly and said, "I am Sleek, but I am not a coyote like you."

"Yes, you are," said Wanderer.

"Oh no, I am not," replied Sleek.

"Look, my friend, you are confused. You have ears like mine, you have a tail like mine, our fur is the same, our snouts are the same, everything is the same. You are just like me, and we are both coyotes," Wanderer tried to explain.

"Listen, let's run across the field again, and you will see," challenged Sleek. So off they ran. First went Wanderer and again the farmer yelled, "There goes that damn coyote." Then Sleek took afoot, and the Farmer yelled, "And there goes another one again!"

When the two coyotes reached the other side on the field, they ducked into the woods. Wanderer turned to Sleek and said, "There! Didn't you hear the farmer? He called us both coyotes."

Sleek looked disappointed with his new confused friend, and said, "Yes, I heard the farmer. He called you a coyote, but I am 'another one.'"

(Denning, 2005, p. xvii). Analysis of information may lead to facts, but a story helps people get inside an idea so they can live, understand, and feel the information. Stories and storytelling do not replace facts, logic, or analytical thinking; rather, they complement rational knowledge by enabling our minds to imagine new ideas (Denning, 2005).

Stories weave experience and emotion into a compelling narrative. The power of a story to deliver a convincing and memorable message for a person to receive is illustrated by the following Native American tale, *Coyote and Another One* (Story 3.2), as told by Charles Philip Whitedog (1996).

Story 3.2 illustrates importance of not allowing another person to define who you are. Folklore stories such as the one presented in Story 3.2 instill values. Likewise, real-life stories can demonstrate values through expression of personal experiences. Stories about personal experiences do not tell people what to do, but they can powerfully influence how people think, choose, and function.

Storytelling is knowledge sharing. Knowledge shared by stories is both direct and implied; consequently, narrative plays an important and vital role in transmitting knowledge to others. To illustrate, the following brief story example shows how a story effectively transfers information that becomes implicit knowledge for the listener:

> When I started my occupational therapy career, I had a child, age 2, and I was 7 months pregnant with my second. My husband and I knew we were facing some big challenges. For one, I knew the school position I was taking would be stressful. I couldn't add the stress of driving to work, so we decided we would commute together by public transportation to our work rather than drive the hour to the city.

From the brief story we can identify many facts, some overtly said and others merely implied. The narrator

* ★ Is married,
* ★ Has a college degree and is a licensed therapist,
* ★ Is beginning a new career.
* ★ Will be a therapist in an urban school,
* ★ Anticipates that being a therapist is a stressful job,
* ★ Has a lot of stress in her life,
* ★ Communicates with her husband about their challenges,
* ★ Is facing great challenges,
* ★ Expects a second baby in a few months,
* ★ Will need to have child care,
* ★ Sees driving a car as adding stress to her life,
* ★ Lives in a area that has public transportation,
* ★ Will commute to the city with her husband, and
* ★ Will have a couple of hours each day to be with her husband to talk and share.

Notice that the narrative explanation is much shorter than the list of propositions or implied knowledge contained in the story. In the example, the conversational story is a richer and more condensed way to express ideas or knowledge; it is more interesting to read and easier to understand and remember than the list of facts.

Part of the power of a story comes from its capacity to create a context for our mind to understand and embrace the explicit ideas being transferred and ultimately received as tacit knowledge.

Tacit Knowledge

Knowledge that is labeled *tacit* is the wisdom hidden within a story (The Mentoring Company, 2008). For a storyteller to be effective in transferring tacit knowledge, the story needs to ring true—not in a scientific or logical sense; rather, the story's elements need to be rational, sensible, and credible (Denning, 2005). Brown et al. (2005) propose four attributes as the cornerstone of an effective story:

1. *Endurance:* A story's message that has lasting impact. Situations may change, but the story remains the same.

Story 3.3. From Our Cherokee Ancestors

A wise and elderly Cherokee grandfather is teaching his grandson about life. "A fight is going on inside me," he said to the boy. "It is a terrible fight, and it is between two wolves. One wolf is evil—he is anger, envy, sorrow, regret, greed, arrogance, self-pity, guilt, resentment, inferiority, lies, false pride, superiority, and ego. The other wolf is good—she is joy, peace, love, hope, serenity, humility, kindness, benevolence, empathy, generosity, truth, compassion, and faith."

The wise Cherokee elder added, "This same fight is going on inside you—and inside every other person, too."

The grandson thought about it for a minute, and then asked, "Which wolf will win?"

The wise Cherokee elder simply replied, "The one you feed."

---

2. *Salience:* The punch a story has—its wit and emotional power.
3. *Sense-making:* A story's explanatory power and truth to one's own notion of how things are done.
4. *Comfort level:* Does the story feel right?

The folklore story in Story 3.3 illustrates the four attributes, plus the power of narrative in conveying tacit knowledge, the wisdom that is hidden within the tale. Story 3:3 not only illustrates the wisdom hidden within a story, but it also emphasizes storytelling as a timeless method for transferring a message that becomes tacit knowledge for a receiver. The journey of sharing information that is transformed into tacit knowledge requires storytelling. The point at which tacit knowledge is received as wisdom is the essence of story listening.

Stories and Mentoring

The concepts discussed about stories and storytelling are relevant for mentoring, but mentoring stories also have some unique aspects.

What Are Mentoring Stories?

A *mentoring story* is a narrative account that weaves detail, character, and emotional content with a personal event or leadership experiences. Most notably, a mentoring story includes outcomes and key lessons that are woven into the story (The Mentoring Company, 2008).

The purpose of using stories for mentoring is to engage another person in a mentor's own experience, to guide discovery of tacit knowledge, and to develop a trusting relationship (Denning, 2005). Mentors' stories help others make sense of and creatively reframe their own dilemmas, challenges, and opportunities. "Because stories are more vivid, engaging, entertaining, and easily related to personal experience than rules or directives, the research would predict they would be more memorable, be given more weight, and be more likely to guide behavior" (Swap, Leonard, Shields, & Abrams, 2001, p. 103).

As living case studies, stories tap into skills, express underlying emotions, and connect facts and feelings (Shea, 1994; Stone, 2004). Stories bring the mentor and mentee together in a unique relationship grounded in shared context, experience, and emotion. Thus, the context for a story and the mentor's key lessons are crucial factors for mentoring to be effective.

Sharing Knowledge

The goal of a mentoring relationship is to transfer knowledge from mentor to the mentee. As a mentor crafts a story, it is imperative that he or she listens to oneself. As a mentor listens, he or she needs to imagine how the mentee may respond and visualize the experience of the story and consider the best circumstances for another person to listen (Maguire, 1998).

In a mentoring relationship, a story shared is innovative and empowering. Maguire (1998) proposes that people have many different ways to talk with each other, such as mechanical back-and-forth conversations, giving advice, asking or answering questions, lecturing, teaching, gossiping, chattering, and so on. These methods of talk are not effective for accomplishing the purpose and goal of mentoring—they are merely *talk*. Storytelling, in contrast, is an effective and innovative alternative to those forms of talking.

Although the mind of the mentee may be the target, the heart is the bull's eye. A challenge for mentors is to enter the heart of their mentees. To reach the heart, a mentor must create a story from a place of complete authenticity, sharing his or her own heart. Sharing of oneself through the mentor's story promotes an identity about the mentor, encourages understanding, builds trusting relationships, and prompts action (Guber, 2007). According to Simmons (2001), personal stories let others see "who we are better than any other form of communication" (p. 10).

Authenticity

Mentoring stories shared from a place of *authenticity*—something real, valid, and true—become powerful tools for building trusting relationships (Denning, 2005). An effective, powerful story must convey some sort of truth that resonates with the reader. Gruber (2007) submits that there are four kinds of truth in effective stories:

1. Truth of the teller or authenticity,
2. Truth for the listener or expectations fulfilled,
3. Truth in the moment or context respected, and
4. Truth to the mission or story created and devoted to a cause beyond self.

Story 3.4 was shared with a mentoring group and illustrates Guber's four types of truths.

Maguire (1998) questions what "truth" in a personal story means. He believes that storytellers must be true to themselves and the experiences being shared. However, it

Story 3.4. Authenticity

Every once in a while there is a moment when a value of principle that has hovered just outside your awareness becomes clear. You realize that it has always been there guiding you, but until now you hadn't quite put it into words. After that moment, it never slips out of your mind again.

This happened to me several years ago during one of many discussions with my long-time collaborator and friend. We were talking about next steps in our research to develop outcome measures, and he was discussing current trends in the field. His argument was essentially that we would need to tailor our work more to "fit" the current reimbursement climate and give the payers what they were asking for.

For me, his argument was a business position focused on what would sell, not necessarily what would benefit the recipients of the services. I found myself struggling against his position and, finally, was able to put my response into words. Simply put, I believe the U.S. approach to health care is fundamentally wrong and that many of the current problems stem from the fact that health is treated as a business, not a social service. I did not want to cater to and support that system in my work—and I said so to my friend.

It was good to have clarified this value for myself; however, the right response was still not clear to me. Should I refuse altogether to do work that might be used in our current health system? That would be one way to adhere to my principles. However, it would jeopardize my very important relationship with my friend and wouldn't necessarily get him to change his view. The alternative that occurred to me was to honor the knowledge and skills I possessed to do something different and try to alter the system. Could I apply that knowledge and try to change the system, or at least provide an alternative?

With more reflection after that moment of clarity, I came to realize that I am a subversive, not a radical. A *subversive* works from within to change the process in such a way that the system does not realize what is happening, whereas a *radical* steps outside the system altogether. I think of this as being a *positive subversive.*

A new outcomes instrument has the potential to be applied in thousands of assessment situations and to affect both research and clinical results. This feels like an awesome responsibility. Trying to remain authentic in my researcher role means trying to keep the ethic of caring in the foreground, so it guides all the decisions that have to be made in the course of developing a new tool so that I can be an effective subversive.

I used to worry about displaying those aspects of myself that were not quite what everyone else in a group was displaying. Over the years, I have come to recognize that my authentic self has achieved much more success than any pretense I adopted to try to conform. There is something about authenticity that is far more compelling than any act.

is imperative to acknowledge that truth is based on the mentor's own perceptions and interpretations, not necessarily on factual reality. Mentors craft their story to share their experiences and feelings about a topic or challenges pertinent to the listener; however, great mentors must be flexible enough to drop the script and improvise when the situation or context calls for it (Guber, 2007). The content of a mentor's story may be its foundation, but the context in which the story is being told is its cornerstone. Context efficiently conveys specifics, implies values, depicts emotions, and suggests actions; in short, mentoring stories thoroughly immerse the mentee in a detailed level of understanding on which the mentee can immediately reflect and begin to translate into their own context and use.

There are times when a story is appropriate for a mentoring situation, and certain times when it is not. Storytelling flexibility in mentoring situations can honor the truths of effective stories proposed by Gruber, but the original purpose or mission for telling the story remains absolute.

Story 3.5 provides an opportunity to think about the authentic self, as shared by the storyteller to a group of people participating in a mentoring program designed to enhance business development, specifically in marketing and sales.

Story 3.5. Marketing Authenticity

Jackie asked me to share a story about what I did to sell and/or market mentoring programs in the organizations where I was contracted to facilitate group mentoring programs. When she asked me, my first response was "sure," as I thought it would be easy to create the story!

I started thinking about it and soon realized I didn't know what I did to sell. In fact, I don't think I sold mentoring programs; they just seemed to sell themselves. So, did I sell? I don't know if I did selling, but I did something that resulted in additional mentoring programs being offered.

As I was thinking about what I did, one thing became very clear: I realized that I am not a salesperson. In fact, if I tried to be a salesperson, I would be an imposter! So my real challenge was to honor who I am. I admit this was a scary and difficult process to discover the real me, but it has proven to be rewarding.

Since I didn't know what I did that resulted in an organization contracting additional mentoring programs, I chose to review those times when I felt effective in a process that resulted in additional mentoring programs. I started the process by recognizing the strategies or actions that resulted in more programs. I realized that my actions were a reflection of my best qualities or my strengths. I even listed them so I could remember to share them with you in this story!

My strengths are my positive, futuristic self who enjoys people and relationships. Also I am strategic and visionary. I thought about this and learned that my strengths are my rechargeable power supply!

My next step was to think about how my strengths influenced my actions. So what is it I did to use my strategic strength? [The] first step was discovering what the organization wanted, or their goals, and identify[ing] how mentoring programs could benefit them. I found myself culling through the goals and values of the organization and then think[ing] about the most strategic path to facilitate the achievement of the organization's goal.

(Continued)

Story 3.5 Cont.

The second strategy was using my strengths with relationships to get to know my contacts in the organization. From these persons, I learned a lot about the needs of the organization and the people in it. Because I have passion for the mentoring process, it was easy to find a good match for what mentoring could do to move the organization forward. The best part of enrolling others is getting to maximize my strengths and be the best of who I am.

As a positive person, I truly see the glass as half-full. I always find ways to celebrate every achievement, and I rarely get dragged down. I'm enthusiastic and energetic, and I get my greatest joy by encouraging people. This strength really helps with my relationships with my mentors and mentees.

[I am] futuristic. I find myself saying such things as "Did you ever think about . . . ? I wonder if we could . . . ? Let's figure out what we can do. . ." I'm always looking for ideas and options, for ways not to be mired by the status quo. Usually I find myself suggesting a mentoring program for the issues and challenges I hear about.

What have I learned from reflecting on how I have been able to expand mentoring programs in organizations?

★ My retrospective analysis has been critical in my developing a positive view of the traditional aspect of selling as a process of enrollment.

★ Enrollment is a dynamic process that results from successful mentoring programs; the programs sell themselves.

★ Be myself; don't try to be someone I'm not.

★ Accept my strengths and use these strengths as components of my abilities.

★ Using my strengths is the foundation to being true to who I am [and] my values and principles. Being true to self is leadership integrity.

Choice

When used as a mentoring tool, stories offer the mentee *choice* — power, right, or liberty to choose — in receiving the story's message. An engaging story allows listeners or mentees to add their own knowledge or information compared to what is explicitly stated.

As mentees listen they can choose to assimilate a mentor's story into their own framework, transferring the knowledge and wisdom to self.

Organizations and Storytelling

Organizations must continually communicate their missions, visions of the future, workplace strategies, and values and align their people with them (Denning, 2001). As we move from the information age to what Pink (2006) calls the *conceptual age,* an age of *conceptual thinking,* that is, identifying patterns and connections among situations in which communicating and connecting people at all levels of an organization are fundamental. Storytelling becomes a valuable skill and essential dimension for organizational communication.

In the emerging conceptual age, organizations need to focus on building relationships, promoting creativity, using imagination and emotional intelligence, and depending more on tacit knowledge rather than technical manuals (Pink, 2006). Moving into the conceptual age requires organizations to forge relationships and emphasize and understand subtleties of human interactions.

Pink (2006) suggests that most of our experiences, thinking processes, and acquired knowledge are organized in stories, arguing that stories are central to how we think. Our present and future workplaces should include activities to create compelling narratives and use those stories for knowledge acquisition, empowerment of people, promotion of leadership practices, and sharing the organization's traditions and values (Silverman, 2006).

It is now common to have different generations and diverse cultures working together. Because an organization's human dimension is its most valued resource, stories become a compelling narrative to engage and build trusting relationships among diverse employees. Organizations that value storytelling and stories within their culture achieve positive outcomes to align their human resources with their mission, vision, and values (Silverman, 2006). As a result, storytelling takes on new and important emphasis for leadership. As Alan Kay, a Hewlett–Packard executive puts it, "Scratch the surface in a typical boardroom, and we're all just cavemen with briefcases, hungry for a wise person to tell us stories" (Pink, 2006).

Characteristics of a great leader in today's organizations are the same qualities of an effective storyteller: integrity, honesty, being true to one's self, and being open to share beliefs and emotions (Guber, 2007). People in organizations have lessons about life and leadership to share with others, and story sharing is a powerful practice to transfer their lessons to colleagues. Leaders, like mentors, can use stories about personal experiences to turn visions into goals and, ultimately, into results (Guber, 2007).

Leaders of organizations have discovered that storytelling is an effective way to deliver a common message and instill understanding for their employees, members, or audience. Silverman (2006) argues for the importance for organizations to formalize the storytelling process, having leaders practice telling stories and giving them tools to become effective storytellers in communicating strategic information.

Incorporating storytelling training into development programs to build leadership practices has beneficial outcomes for an organization. Several corporations have discovered how stories can affect business practices. IBM promotes storytelling and conducts research about its possibilities; Xerox discovered that its repair employees better learned to fix machines by sharing stories rather than training manuals; 3M gives top executives storytelling instruction; and NASA and the World Bank have used storytelling in their knowledge management initiatives (Pink, 2006).

Hewlett–Packard and Miller–Coors have active mentoring programs that use storytelling to promote leadership performance, networking, on-boarding programs, employee engagement, and retention. Using stories in mentoring programs promotes engaged employees and helps organizations retain top talent because employees learn from relevant experiences shared by the mentor and feel support-ed by the organization's investment in them (Silverman, 2006).

A senior vice president at a large corporation reported positive results in its metrics to measure progress: "Story has increased communication effectiveness. All indicators on our four buckets of measures are going in the right direction. Costs have significantly decreased—about $15 to $20 million a year in terms of costs of goods. There's decreased absenteeism and improved employee engagement scores. Employees feel they're part of the business and are on equal footing with manage-ment" (Silverman, 2006, p. 60).

Stories and storytelling have an important and just place in people's everyday work lives. From interviews within several organizations, Silverman (2006) reports that leveraging stories through an organization's leadership has considerable ben-efits (p. 60), including improving financial aspects, building committed teams, im-proving project management, and promoting change.

Pink (2006) asserts that stories mean big money to business. He reports per-suasion (e.g., counseling, marketing, consulting) accounts for 25% of the U.S. gross domestic product. If the use of story is a component of just half of these persuasive efforts, Pink proposed that the use of stories is worth about $1 trillion a year in the U.S. economy. No wonder organizations are espousing the value of storytelling!

Sharing a Vision

Sharing a vision is critical for transforming organizations and communities (Kouzes & Posner, 2007). A vision presented as a story rather than a traditional vision state-ment is a more dynamic and meaningful tool to create shared meaning and forward thinking (Lewis, 2000). Lewis promotes the development of an organization's vi-sion by involving employees in the creation of stories about the future, arguing, "For a vision to create shared meaning it must project people into the future so they can readily see it in action and imagine themselves as part of it. A vision story's use of dynamic, vivid imagery and colorful narrative description of events, actions, and experiences helps this experience occur" (p. 96).

The imagery and examples contained in a story promote identification and understanding of future directions, compared to abstractions and generalizations found in typical organizational vision statements. A vision story shows people "the future in such detail that it produces a type of virtual experience of it, thereby facili-tating a form of vicarious learning" (Lewis, 2000, p. 98). Appreciation of the future and what it can become for the people involved promotes personalization of a vi-sion and expectations for performance.

Stories about an organization's past and present also provide grounding for its people to move forward. Stories about the past provide history and informa-tion about an organization's behavior. In their book about corporate cultures, Deal and Kennedy (2000) emphasize that storytellers help pass on traditions and values of the corporate culture; they hold rich tales and artifacts that shed light on an organization's culture. "The tales that storytellers tell, like myths in a tribal setting, explain and give meaning to the workaday world" (p. 87).

Shared "tribal knowledge" is a powerful motivator for understanding the organization's culture and behaviors. Stories about the system and legends of an organization provide guidance about what is required to move ahead.

Organizational Storytelling

In addition to stories of the past, there are other categories for organizational storytelling. Brown et al. (2005) suggests several categories, including stories about the people of an organization and stories about the organization's work or projects.

A story about another person gives the listener needed information to develop trust in others. Stories about work or projects give lessons about what is going on within the organization and what makes it work. All people have stories about themselves that communicate a person's identity. Stories about the organization itself communicate what the organization is about and they help people make sense of their place of work.

The Transformative Co-Journey

With the use of stories, mentoring becomes a transformative journey for mentor and mentees as well as their organizations or cultures. Telling and listening to stories create interconnectedness with common skills needed to participate in the mentoring process. The co-journey affects others in the mentor and mentee's environments because the work produces change in the individuals and their relationships with other colleagues, coworkers, superiors, and subordinates. As the individuals grow and enact change, the culture evolves to support both mentoring and leadership (Mavrinac, 2005).

The critical self-reflection prompted by writing and listening to a story is at the heart of the transformative journey. In writing a story, the mentor engages in a process of reflective autoethnography to share feelings, thoughts, and life experiences with mentees who in turn reflect on the story to generalize and apply learning to their own life experience (Gurvitch, Carson, & Beale, 2008).

The mentee benefits from the mentor's reflection because the story creates greater closeness, stronger rapport, and enhanced communication that bolsters the mentee's confidence, positioning him or her to actively engage in learning (Chan, 2008; Zachary, 2005). Mentors' level of self-reflection compels them to examine the facts of their stories and promotes their awareness of unconscious assumptions, checking them for accuracy. A mentor's self-awareness converts to self-understanding as assumptions are confronted. The cycle of self-reflection leading to self-awareness and then to self-understanding that organically evolves through the mentoring process for both mentor and mentee is fundamental to transformative learning (Zachary, 2005).

Story 3.6. Transformative Journey

Our last circle. An ending and like all endings, although we've anticipated and planned for it, the reality is both a little celebratory and a little sad. Ends are also beginnings, and we share the responsibility of ensuring that what we've learned is reinvested in our colleagues, our profession, and ourselves.

Every one of us, the past 9 months, has brought transformation in how we know ourselves, how we think and feel, and how we act. For me, personally, the journey has occurred at a transitional point in my life and will be one of those pivotal professional experiences that serve as a reference point for the rest of my career. This is the ultimate gift of having been the catalyst mentor—at this point of transition, having the privilege of revisiting my career and being able to put mistakes to rest, understand[ing] and appreciat[ing] my strengths, honor[ing] my university community and history, enjoy[ing] the accomplishments of that community, and respect[ing] my role in achieving those accomplishments.

What I hope this last story does is contribute to our closure by sharing some of my learning and acknowledging your role in my transformation. I also hope that the story is part of your beginning, as you see from my story the power, the benefits, the gifts of being a mentor and take that role on as you continue your journey.

A year ago I thought that this mentoring journey was primarily about *you*—what you would learn, how you would change. Now I know that it has been about *us*—we've learned from each other, from individual stories and comments [as well as] from the collective intelligence that has grown from our shared experience and commitment to each other, our circle, and our process.

In Story 3.6, the mentor of a Mentoring Circles® program discusses her transformative journey and the role that the mentees have played in her growth.

The shared experience, a product of mutual reflection on the story, establishes a partnership on the basis of open communication. The partnership is reciprocal as both the mentor and mentee equally engage in and learn from the story. The mentor gains the satisfaction from his or her knowledge and experience and, more importantly, is reaffirmed and energized by the review, often generating new perspectives and approaches in his or her own leadership practice.

Beyond gaining knowledge, mentees should recognize their role in a mentor's learning. They are not simply a grateful receiver of the mentor's knowledge but an active contributor to the mentor's learning (Zachary, 2009).

Finally, the transformation is a function of the mutual trust that must be established early in the relationship in order for the learning partnership to develop. As the mentor shares intimate details within his or her stories and mentees expose their vulnerability by acknowledging their needs, discussing confidentiality, and establishing clear boundaries for the relationship (The Mentoring Company, 2008), they must overtly establish trust. "Mentoring requires leadership and courage, on the part of the mentee to engage in this new relationship, and the same for the mentor who must be willing to open up his or her life. It takes courage to be mentored and still more to mentor, and for both a commitment to an adventure in personal leadership, learning, and growing" (Stone, 2004, p. vii).

To be engaged in such an adventure is not merely learning a new skill set but rather is transforming one's view of self and awareness of one's potential to lead and effect significant change. It is the leadership and courage that support and emerge from story-based mentoring that directs change at all levels. As the partners are individually transformed, their expectations for cultural and organizational change increase and their capacity to generate such change expands.

Summary

"Telling stories changes the way you manage. You become a different kind of leader — you create an environment where people are receptive to change and new ideas" (Armstrong, 1992, p. 10). Storytelling is creative conversation or a narrative method that puts together a personal tale about experiences relevant for an individual's everyday work or activities (Simmons, 2001). The purpose of a mentoring story is to transfer the knowledge of the mentor to mentees so they can discover ideas and actions that are best for them. Sharing stories in a mentoring relationship is the keystone for building a leadership culture within an organization.

Story listeners perceive the narrative art of a story in their own image, integrating the message with their own life experiences and cultures. The strength of a mentoring story comes from its capacity to create a framework for our mind to understand and embrace the explicit ideas being transferred and ultimately received as tacit knowledge.

Stories help us bridge the gap of different generations and cultures that work together. The real value of stories and storytelling for organizational mentoring programs is the mutual creation that involves interaction and understanding with the storyteller and listeners. Mentoring stories are real accounts of the mentor's experiences and actions, their feelings, outcomes of actions, and key learning (The Mentoring Company, 2008) and are an innovative and effective way to share a message that has a lasting impact.

References

Armstrong, D. (1992). *Managing by storying around: A new method of leadership*. New York: Doubleday Currency.

Brown, J. S., Denning, S., Groh, K., & Prusak, L. (2005). *Storytelling in organizations*. Burlington, MA: Elsevier/Butterworth-Heinemann.

Chan, A. W. (2008). Mentoring ethnic minority, predoctoral students: An analysis of key mentor practices. *Mentoring and Tutoring: Partnership in Learning, 16*, 263–277. doi: 10.1080/13611260802231633

Deal, T. E., & Kennedy, A. (2000). *Corporate cultures: The rites and rituals of corporate life*. Cambridge, MA: Perseus.

Mentoring Leaders: The Power of Storytelling for Building Leadership in Health Care and Education

Denning, S. (2001). *The springboard: How storytelling ignites action in knowledge-era organizations.* Boston: Butterworth-Heinemann.

Denning, S. (2005). *The leader's guide to storytelling.* San Francisco: Jossey-Bass.

Guber, P. (2007, December). The four truths of the storyteller. *Harvard Business Review,* pp. 53–59.

Gurvitch, R., Carson, R. L., & Beale, A. (2008). Being a protégé: An autoethnographic view of three teacher education doctoral programs. *Mentoring and Tutoring: Partnership in Learning, 16,* 246–262. doi:10.1080/13611260802231625

Kouzes, J. M., & Posner, B. Z. (2007). *The leadership challenge* (4th ed.). San Francisco: Jossey-Bass.

Lewis, I. M. (2000). Vision revisited: Telling the story of the future. *Journal of Applied Behavioral Science, 36,* 91–107.

Maguire, J. (1998). *The power of personal storytelling.* New York: Tarcher/Putnam.

Mavrinac, M. A. (2005) Transformational leadership: Peer mentoring as a values-based learning process. *Libraries and the Academy, 5,* 391–404.

McCay, E. (2003). Tell your stories—And never forget. *National Staff Development Council, 24,* 68–70.

McConnell, L. (1999). *A basic pattern: Memories of an ordinary life.* Arvada, CO: Author.

The Mentoring Company. (2008). *Mentor orientation manual.* Loveland, CO: Author.

Pink, D. H. (2006). *A whole new mind: Why right-brainers will rule the future.* New York: Riverhead.

Shea, G. F. (1994). *Mentoring: Helping employees reach their full potential.* New York: American Management Association.

Silverman, L. (2006). *Wake me up when the data is over.* San Francisco: Jossey-Bass.

Simmons, A. (2001). *The story factor.* Cambridge, MA: Perseus.

Stone, F. (2004). *The mentoring advantage: Creating the next generation of leaders.* Chicago: Dearborn Trade.

Swap, W., Leonard, D., Shields, M., & Abrams, L. (2001). Using mentoring and storytelling to transfer knowledge in the workplace. *Journal of Management Information Systems, 18,* 95–114.

Whitedog, C. P. (1996). *Coyote and another one.* Retrieved January 24, 2011, from http://www.ilhawaii.net/~stony/lore58.html

Zachary, L. J. (2005). *Creating a mentoring culture.* San Francisco: Jossey-Bass.

Zachary, L. J. (2009). *The mentee's guide.* San Francisco: Jossey-Bass.

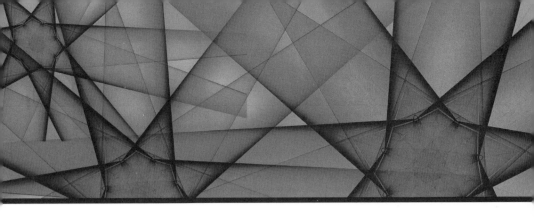

Chapter 4.
Outcomes of an Effective
Mentoring Program

Table Chats

Sharing our experiences and probing the literature were basic for our quest to write about mentoring and leadership, but what became apparent was the importance of knowing the outcomes of mentoring programs. We knew we needed evidence of what mentoring with stories could do for those who participated. The American Occupational Therapy Association (AOTA), the American Occupational Therapy Foundation (AOTF), and The Mentoring Company™ (TMC) partnered to sponsor a leadership fellowship that included outcomes measurement of a group mentoring program. The ultimate goal of the project was to build a leadership community. This chapter presents the details of the measurement process and leadership outcomes from quantitative and qualitative data collection. Our objective in sharing the data and outcomes is twofold: (1) to demonstrate the value of mentoring with stories to build an individual's leadership capacity and a leadership culture in organizations and (2) to stimulate readers' thinking for applying the knowledge they gain to building their leadership capacity and creating a leadership culture within the workplace.

Introduction

Recognizing the importance of leadership for the future of professions and organizations, AOTA and AOTF partnered to develop a leadership culture among its membership. An essential part of a leadership culture is positive social change, as discussed in Chapter 1. "No society can continue without [leadership], no family or neighborhood holds together in its absence, and no institution prospers when it is unavailable" (Astin & Astin, 2000, p. iv).

Knowing that ongoing, positive social change is essential for the future of the profession, AOTA and AOTF determined that it was important to develop a leadership culture among faculty and academic administrators, because they influence students—future professionals of the occupational therapy community.

Faculty set standards for curriculum, provide role modeling and mentoring for leadership learning, and influence leadership through their research and scholarship. In 2007, AOTA and AOTF decided that the most efficient and effective means to reach a critical mass was through group mentoring programs focused on leadership. Building a community of educational leaders with a mindset that leadership was an essential activity that will move the profession forward was a desired outcome for these group mentoring programs.

TMC was contracted by AOTA and AOTF to implement group mentorship programs because of its successful record with group mentoring programs designed to promote the discovery of self as a leader, facilitate leadership readiness and performance, and build a leadership culture. A pilot program was initiated in 2007, followed by three programs offered in 2008, 2009, and 2010. A brief description of the Mentoring Circles program appears in Chapter 3 of this book. For more detailed information about the Mentoring Circles program, readers are encouraged to explore mentoringcircles.com.

To document the power of mentorship programs that link leadership and communication with mentoring and storytelling, this chapter presents both quantitative and qualitative data from evaluation processes of the Mentoring Circles programs sponsored by AOTF and AOTA. Each mentoring group met together for a 2-day launch and again 9 months later for a 2-day closing. Between the launch and closing, the participants met for 14 2-hour group mentoring sessions, which were held via telephone conference twice monthly for 7 months. Curriculum for the group mentoring programs was grounded in the theme *Building a Leadership Community*.

Data Collection

Quantitative and qualitative measures were implemented to measure the outcomes of participating in the Mentoring Circles program. A standardized instrument, The Leadership Practices Inventory (LPI), developed by Kouzes and Posner (2003), was administered as a pre–post survey, with surveys being given before and after the program. The LPI has a high degree of reliability and validity; thus, the data is believable. Word data were collected from a formative evaluation questionnaire that consisted of nine open-ended questions created by AOTF and AOTA personnel. Questions are displayed in Appendix 4.A.

Quantitative Data

The LPI was administered to 72 persons who participated in 4 different circles: The 2007 circle had 17 mentees, the two circles offered in 2008 and 2009 had 18 mentees in each, and the 2010 circle had 19 mentees. Circle participants included occupational therapy faculty and administrators in higher education. The standardized LPI provides an assessment of self as compared to an assessment by others. Participants selected 8 persons to provide an assessment of their leadership practices. Persons selected represented a wide range of colleagues (e.g., boss, peers, direct reports). Following the initial assessment, each participant received a report with the data and analysis about their leadership preferences with five leadership practices as first defined by Kouzes and Posner (1995):

1. Model the way.
2. Inspire a shared vision.
3. Challenge the process.
4. Enable others to act.
5. Encourage the heart.

For both the self-assessment and assessment from others, the LPI includes 30 statements that represent leadership behaviors—6 behavior statements for each of the 5 practices. The numerical rating assigned to each statement represents frequency of performance, from 1 (or *almost never*) to 10 (or *almost always*). Data were compiled and tabulated by a computer program developed for analyzing the LPI. Each participant received a 13-page report that compared his or her self-assessment with the assessments of others. Participants received an opportunity to have an individual telephone conference with the circle facilitator regarding their report findings.

In addition to LPI data, participants completed an online survey designed to identify their leadership strengths. The underlying philosophy of the Mentoring Circles program is based on the value of focusing on a person's strengths, so the outstanding work of the Gallup organization to develop a measurement tool to identify a person's strengths was chosen to use in the programs. The online surveys, Strength Finder 2.0 (Rath, 2007), was administered with the 2007 group, and Strengths Based Leadership (Rath & Conchie, 2008) was used for the 2008, 2009, and 2010 groups.

The surveys are based on Gallup's 40-year study (Rath, 2007) of human strengths, and both provided participants with an in-depth analysis of their top-five leadership strengths as well as ideas for using strengths to lead others. The 34 strengths identified by Gallup "naturally cluster into 4 domains of leadership strengths based on a statistical factor analysis" (Rath & Conchie, 2008, p. 24). The leadership domains identified include (1) executing, (2) influencing, (3) relationship building, and (4) strategic thinking. Strengths and domains of the circle participants are displayed in Appendix 4.B.

Qualitative Data

Word data from the written evaluation questionnaires, completed by 62 persons, were analyzed to measure outcomes or impact of the leadership Mentoring Circle programs. Qualitative data from written responses to the 9 questions (Appendix 4.A) were separately reviewed by 3 persons to identify emerging themes or categories. Following review and discussions, 5 categories together with subcategories emerged as outcomes of circle mentorship programs: (1) leadership readiness and performance, (2) transformation of self-engagement, (3) retention and leadership endeavors, (4) collaboration and trust, and (5) circle methodology. Appendix 4.C lists the subcategories for each of these areas.

Outcomes

Following closure of the group mentoring programs, 63 of the 72 participants selected to participate with the post assessments. Reasons for those who did not participate were various factors (e.g., job changes, illness, major difficulties at work, personal crises). A report illustrating pre–post comparison scores for both self-assessment and assessment by others was given to each participant. Numerical data from pre–post assessments provide a measurement regarding changes in each of the 5 leadership practices. Gains in leadership practices and behaviors represent both participants' self-assessment and how others perceive the frequency of leadership performance on 30 behavior statements, 6 for each of the 5 leadership practices practices.

Group averages for each group and pre-post comparisons and point gains for each of the 5 practices are displayed on Tables 4.1, 4.2, 4.3, and 4.4. The ceiling or top possible score was 60. In general, scores with the 4 groups was in the mid-40s, which is considered to be in the moderate to high range (Kouzes & Posner, 2007). Because of the high degree of reliability and validity of the LPI, positive gains in all 5 practices for both self-assessment and assessment by others may be considered a result of participating in the leadership mentoring program.

Pre–post results from the LPI displayed positive gains in all 5 leadership practices, in both self-assessments and assessments by others. Because leadership begins with knowledge of self, gains in self-assessment ratings are noteworthy. Performing behaviors more frequently indicated a gain in one's self-confidence, the foundation for leadership performance.

Learning about leadership practices and behaviors also had affected the frequency of performance. There were positive gains in all 5 leadership practices as measured by other persons selected by the mentee. Largest gains were found with the practice *inspire a shared vision*. Visioning as a leadership practice was emphasized in the curriculum, because mentees in each of the 4 circles selected visioning as an important topic for circle stories and discussion.

Smallest point gains occurred in *enable others to act*. The practice had the highest pre scores (high 40s to 50s). Because a major part of occupational therapy prac-

Table 4.1. Leadership Practices Inventory: 2007 Group Score Averages

Practice	Self Initial	Self Post	Change	Others Initial	Others Post	Change
Model the way	44.5	47.3	+2.8	46.4	50.3	+3.9
Inspire a shared vision	40.7	44.0	+3.3	42.0	48.8	+6.8
Challenge the process	44.3	45.7	+1.4	46.9	50.2	+3.3
Enable others to act	49.1	49.9	+0.8	51.2	51.6	+0.4
Encourage the heart	46.4	47.8	+3.4	47.2	49.3	+2.1

Table 4.2. Leadership Practices Inventory: 2008 Group Score Averages

Practice	Self Initial	Self Post	Change	Others Initial	Others Post	Change
Model the way	43.5	47	+3.5	46.4	50.3	+3.9
Inspire a shared vision	44.8	48.5	+3.7	44.7	48.8	+4.1
Challenge the process	42.8	46.3	+3.5	44.9	48.8	+3.9
Enable others to act	49.4	51.1	+1.7	48.3	50.8	+4.5
Encourage the heart	43.8	43.9	+0.1	46.3	49.1	+2.8

Table 4.3. Leadership Practices Inventory: 2009 Group Score Averages

Practice	Self Initial	Self Post	Change	Others Initial	Others Post	Change
Model the way	39.4	44.3	+4.9	44.4	47.7	+3.3
Inspire a shared vision	34.7	42.0	+7.3	41.0	44.9	+3.9
Challenge the process	38.9	42.8	+3.9	44.9	44.8	+3.9
Enable others to act	45.8	48.6	+2.8	46.9	48.2	+1.3
Encourage the heart	38.5	43.0	+4.5	43.6	46.9	+3.3

Table 4.4. Leadership Practices Inventory: 2010 Group Score Averages

Practice	Self Initial	Self Post	Change	Others Initial	Others Post	Change
Model the way	43.6	47.0	+3.4	45.3	47.1	+1.8
Inspire a shared vision	43.4	44.0	+3.6	43.4	46.6	+3.2
Challenge the process	41.5	46.0	+4.5	44.6	47.2	+2.6
Enable others to act	48.8	51.0	+2.2	47.9	50.0	+2.4
Encourage the heart	44.3	47.0	+2.7	45.3	47.3	+3.3

titioners' work with clients aims to enable them to act, it is not surprising that this practice had the highest pretest scores and thus the smallest point gain.

Mentees who participated in the pre–post measurements were from 47 colleges and universities, representing both faculty and academic administrators in graduate and undergraduate occupational therapy programs, including programs in research institutions to programs in community colleges.

Mentoring Circles were offered in different years, with different topics requested for the mentors' stories. There were two mentors: one for the circles offered

---

> ### *Box 4.1. Leadership Readiness and Performance*
>
> "The LPI has given me a language of leadership that provides a framework for evaluating and reevaluating behavior and outcomes related to leadership activities and helps me communicate to others."
>
> "The Mentoring Circle program has given me knowledge about leadership and the courage to seek for and take risks in leadership roles that are out of my comfort zone but use and build on my strengths."
>
> "The mentoring and support of the group [were] so helpful in enabling me to see how to be a leader, and that some of the things that I had not realized were examples of leadership, in fact, were!"

in 2007 and 2010 and another for circles in 2008 and 2009. Gains and findings were consistent among the groups, despite these differences. Circle methodology, process, and facilitator comprised the only constant variables in each Mentoring Circles. The diversity of people and organizations reflected in this data collection bolster the positive findings about Mentoring Circles' methodology and process.

Leadership Readiness and Performance

Five outcome categories and subcategories that emerged have operational definitions as follows (see Appendix 4.C). The first outcome category evolving from participation in circles was termed *leadership readiness and performance*, defined as willingness and confidence to perform leadership practices that create supportive and productive environments and empower others to translate their strengths and action into common outcomes. Leadership readiness and performance are considered to be basic, important outcomes for ongoing development of leadership and building a leadership culture. The category includes two subcategories, *leadership learning* and *leadership language*. There were frequent remarks in the questionnaires that the LPI provided a leadership language that was useful for understanding and discussing the concept of leadership (see Box 4.1). A common language is essential for building a leadership culture.

Transformation of Self

The second outcome category identified is *transformation of self*, defined as a process of reflecting, developing, modifying, changing, and acquiring self-efficacy and finding the self's voice. It included four subcategories as additional outcomes of circle mentorship programs: (1) *self-awareness,* (2) *self-confidence,* (3) *perceiving self as leader,* and (4) *perceiving self as a mentor*. Like leadership readiness and performance, outcomes of transformation of self and its corresponding subcategories are essential elements in the development of leadership practices and building a leadership culture (see Box 4.2).

Box 4.2. Transformation of Self

"A major value of the Mentoring Circle was the increased insight I have into my strengths and areas for improvement. The strength survey and the mentor's story about identifying and using strengths were defining moments for me. I am much more aware of my own skills, especially around the practice of modeling and enabling others to act."

"I spend more time reflecting on my values and actions. I will do things and approach situations before I start and also [spend] more time reflecting after I am finished. I have a new sense of self that is very positive."

"The circle has given me renewed confidence that I am a competent leader who can maintain a productive environment even when surrounded by adversity."

Engagement, Retention, and Leadership Endeavors

Mentees reported that participation in circle programs increased their engagement, retention and leadership endeavors in the workplace and with their professional associations. *Engagement* is defined as the extent to which people enjoy and believe in what they do and feel valued for their performance. *Retention* is the state of remaining or desire to remain at an organization. *Leadership endeavors* are the undertakings, happenings, and accomplishments achieved for the organization.

Leadership responsibilities assumed by mentees as a result of participating with circle activities and processes, and their decisions regarding retention and increased engagement, show the impact from the circle curriculum and process (see Box 4.3). For an individual, this category indicates his or her feelings of self-worth and commitment to the workplace. The category is important for an organization because it documents the return on investment that an organization receives when it sponsors a mentoring circle program. Subcategories include a *commitment to both the self's development and to the welfare and future of the mentee's organization.*

Box 4.3. Engagement, Retention, and Leadership Endeavors

"I am more engaged with my university community, as I now have the confidence to assert myself and be an active part of the community of scholars."

"I have received so much value from the mentoring circle program. The group validated my experiences from my first few years in academics to the point that I have chosen to remain in academia, and I now view the job with much more enthusiasm and as a positive challenge."

"I am becoming more open to the possibilities of applying for leadership opportunities, both at my college and with our associations."

Box 4.4. Collaboration and Trust

"The contacts with the members of this group are the roots of a network of leaders that will sustain itself over time. I value each person's knowledge and experience and expect to continue to benefit from this."

"Safety and confidentiality of the group is critical to building the network; builds mutually supportive, not competitive, concern for each other's well being – I now have a new network of leaders."

"I know that I can pose a mentoring need to this group and they would be willing to provide stories to support me through situations. I don't have to feel isolated when confronted with seeing challenging situations because I know I can reach out to this group for support and help."

Collaboration and Trust

The power and value of collaboration and trust emerged as the fourth outcome category, with *networking, connections,* and *participating in a safe, trusting environment* subcategories. *Collaboration* is defined as an interconnected group or network of important relationships that enhance leadership performance and goals of the organization. *Trust* is a condition of feeling safe to share the self's experiences, situations, concerns, and issues and having confidence in others. Trust in self and others is an essential element in the success and effectiveness of mentorship. Collaboration and trust are necessary for leadership performance and for building a leadership culture.

Circle Methodology

The fifth outcome category that emerged from analysis of word data was the power of the *circle methodology,* which is includes the methods or underlying principles, process, and words used by the facilitator. Subcategories included *story learning, mentoring from the catalyst mentor,* and *peers and the circle's structured process.* Evaluation comments revealed the circle's methodology promoted self-discovery of strengths and leadership behaviors, knowledge of how to deal with situations, ways to face issues and problems, and ways to solve the problems (see Box 4.5). Storytelling as a mentoring tool was cited as a powerful method to enhance learning and build relationships.

Discussion

Numerical data from the LPI and qualitative data collected from summative evaluation questions substantiate the value of Mentoring Circles as an effective group mentoring process to build leadership capacity. Analysis of comments from circle participants identified benefits or outcomes of the mentorship program. Outcomes include enhanced leadership performance, leadership readiness, transformation

---

Box 4.5. Circle Methodology

"The major value of the program has been the sharing of experiences and the wonderful ideas people have presented for dealing with various leadership issues. Listening to the stories by our mentor and other stories from participants has helped me put my own experience into perspective and to see that these experiences have helped me grow and become even better at what I love to do."

"The program's activities and process were the foundation for learning. [They] gave me knowledge, through stories, of how to deal with situations that I find myself in, and that there are many ways to face issues [and] problems."

"The storytelling process was very powerful in [that I could] see that we are dealing with very similar issues, even if in different roles and contexts. So for me, it's the process more than anything."

---

of self as a leader and mentor, value of collaboration and trust, and retention or engagement with their institution. The value of the process to build collaborative relationships and networks was also noted as a benefit of the Mentoring Circle programs.

Each of the outcome categories is significant for individuals and their institutions of higher education. Discovering the leader within and of self as a mentor positively affects both faculty and students. Likewise, the occupational therapy profession will realize positive social change and emergence of a leadership culture.

The commonality of strengths and domains among the 4 groups of occupational therapists working in higher education is interesting, although the significance has not been determined to date. Some 38% of participants had strengths in the *strategic thinking* domain, 26% had strengths in the *executing* domain, 25% had strengths in the *relationship-building* domain, and only 9% had strengths in the *influencing* domain.

Within the influencing domain, no person had *self-assurance* as one of his or her strengths. This finding supports the importance of the positive gains shown in the LPI self-assessment scores, which showed that occupational therapy leaders in higher education have similar leadership strengths. This means they may need to balance their workplace teams by hiring persons who have strengths in the influencing domain.

Rath and Conchie (2008) noted that individuals should not strive to have strengths in each of the domains; rather, a leader should strive to balance their teams with representation from all domains: "Although individuals need not be well-rounded, teams should be" (p. 21).

Data suggests that Mentoring Circles programs were a transformative experience, a crucible for many participants. Reflection on their own principles, values, and actions and a new sense of self-identity as a competent person with leadership qualities were mentioned by several mentees.

Findings from the online strength-finder surveys and the LPI served as guideposts for the group mentoring session. With each of the groups, the 5 leadership practices were part of the curriculum, "building a leadership community." The mentor shared stories to illustrate the practices and stories provided the platform for reflection and discussion. Story 4.1, "Inspiring a Shared Vision," served as a session topic and shows how one leader inspired a shared vision, changing the occupational therapy education program.

Story 4.1. Inspiring a Shared Vision

I'd like to describe two situations where being able to articulate a vision made a difference. One of these involves a time when I did not have any official role as a leader, but I had a vision and wanted to persuade others. In the second situation, I had an official leadership role, but the work involved working to develop a shared vision with others.

As soon as I joined the faculty and became involved in our doctoral program, I realized that it was not at all like the program from which I had just graduated. My PhD program had followed the apprenticeship model that is more typical of the established sciences, where students worked closely in a faculty mentor's research program. Our doctoral program was course-heavy and research-light, and student research was only loosely connected (if at all) with faculty research. It didn't match my understanding of what kind of experiences were needed to develop strong researchers at all.

This really bothered me because it didn't seem to me that we were doing a very good job of preparing the researchers that I thought our profession needed. I also felt very anxious because, if I had to spend so much time guiding student research projects that weren't connected to my own, I didn't know how I would meet the tenure expectations for productivity. When Mary joined the faculty a year later after graduating from the same program as I, we discovered this was a shared concern. We knew it could be done differently, so we began to work together to try to make a change.

We met over many months to try to articulate why a mentorship model should be considered and how to design a model that would fit with the less developed research context of our department. Then we presented our proposal for discussion by the graduate faculty—we challenged the process.

Two of the senior people were resistant, but we found an ally in Joy, which gave us a majority of three. We began to implement a new program designed around this new vision. We got rid of general comp exams and replaced them with qualifying tasks, each one representing a required competence for research, like submitting a grant and a publication. We started only accepting students who were interested in being involved in a particular faculty member's research program. Now, over a decade later, we really have a mentorship model: Our students are supported for full-time study on faculty grants and are beginning to publish

(Continued)

Story 4.1 Cont.

their work even before they graduate. The new vision gave the graduate faculty a different sense of their relationships [with] and responsibility to the students. Before, it seemed that our mission had just been helping OTs get doctorates, but now we saw our mission as preparing the next generation of OT researchers.

Soon after I became department chairperson, I initiated an entry-program curriculum review. I really felt that there was not a clear or coherent framework for our curriculum; it had evolved more in response to practice patterns and individual faculty preferences than to OT philosophy and principles. It seemed to me that a disproportionate amount of student time was spent on "impairment-level" information and much less on the "whole person."

I wanted to initiate a dialogue about this, but I didn't want to make any individual faculty member feel that I was challenging the courses or subjects in which they had invested so much of their time and energy. I also didn't have a specific alternative model in mind. I just felt that we needed some coherence.

I decided instead to open the discussion around the question "What do *we* collectively believe distinguishes us from other professions but unites us all in spite of our different areas of practice?" This was not a one-time discussion! Over the course of many weeks, it became a lively, collective reflection on who we were and why we did what we did in the way we did it. The role I took on was to facilitate the discussion by identifying unanswered questions, or to pick up a point and ask whether or not it was something we could collectively agree on.

The discussion eventually converged on several key themes that we all agreed would serve us well as our guiding principles. This discussion and the principles we articulated became the guideposts for all our subsequent curriculum activities, including rewriting our vision and mission and completely restructuring the curriculum.

The really wonderful thing is that those principles still influence us and are still experienced as a collective vision that unites us. Whether we are doing a course review, examining our fieldwork placements and evaluation methods, or talking about what continuing education seminars we might offer to our local practitioners, one of the faculty will inevitably bring these key points up to keep us on track. This really became *our* vision, not just mine.

I learned so much from these different experiences over the years. I'll share two that stood out for me. First, I learned how valuable it is to find an ally when you are thinking of challenging the system. A collaborator can help you work out your ideas and think through possible objections or obstacles so that you are really prepared when you present your challenge.

Second, I learned how important it is to be able to capture the group's positive aspirations in order to construct a vision. To do this, you need to gain an understanding of the group members' values and strengths so that you can bring those forward and make them part of the discussion and then part of the vision. I have learned that this process must be given time to really yield a successful result.

Listening to the mentor's stories and telling their own stories became defining opportunities for participants to find their voice for facilitating and leading change. We believe the outcomes that emerged from the data serve as a foundation for building a leadership culture. Part II of this book has additional mentor stories that illustrate the 5 leadership practices.

Summary

Numerical and word data document positive benefits of the mentorship program, Mentoring Circles. Integrating concepts of mentoring, storytelling, leadership, and communication results in mentorship programs that promote discovery of self as leader, facilitate leadership readiness and performance, and contribute to building a leadership culture. Outcomes of quantitative and qualitative data collected from mentees participating in the Mentoring Circles programs substantiate effectiveness of this group mentoring process and demonstrate linking of communication and leadership.

The data used for the evaluation process illustrate effectiveness of programs that use storytelling and mentoring as an innovative approach to leadership development and building a leadership culture within an organization. Results discussed further substantiate the value of using stories as a mentoring tool to facilitate the learning relationships discussed in previous chapters. Analysis of qualitative data from the evaluation questions suggests positive growth in leadership performance and readiness and transformation of self as a leader and as a mentor.

Mentees stated that the circle methodology and process were key factors for building collaborative relationships and networks. Engagement and retention with their organizations were also identified as an outcome of their participation in the circle programs. Results from the evaluation process provide data that validate a positive return on investment, both for participants and their institutions. An important goal was achieved by AOTA and AOTA with their investment in the Mentoring Circles program—developing a leadership culture within the profession.

Although the data indicate strong, positive gains in building leadership capacity and performance, the real impact will be realized in the future, when graduating students become occupational therapy professionals and perform leadership roles within the profession and society.

References

Astin, A. W. & Astin, H. S. (2000). *Leadership reconsidered: Engaging higher education in social change.* Battle Creek, MI: Kellogg Foundation.

Kouzes, J. M., & Posner, B. Z. (1995). *The leadership challenge.* San Francisco: Jossey-Bass.

Kouzes, J. M., & Posner, B. Z. (2003). *Leadership practices inventory* (3rd ed.). San Francisco: Pfeiffer.

Kouzes, J. M., & Posner, B. Z. (2007). *The leadership challenge* (4th ed.). San Francisco: Jossey-Bass.

Rath, T. (2007). *Strength finder 2.0.* New York: Gallup Press.

Rath, T., & Conchie, B. (2008). *Strengths-based leadership.* New York: Gallup Press.

Appendix 4.A.
AOTA/AOTF Mentoring
Circles Program Evaluation Questions

The Mentoring Circle® leadership program, including the Leadership Practice Inventory (Kouzes & Posner, 2003), was designed to help you gain an insight into your leadership strengths and potential. In the space below, please provide examples of how you have deepened your understanding of yourself as a leader and how you have and/or will apply this understanding as a scholar–leader.

1. What has been the major value of the mentoring circle program for you?
2. Provide examples of how you have integrated circle learning in your day-to-day leadership performance in your academic setting.
3. Provide examples of how the Mentoring Circle program has helped you build a network or community of academic leaders within occupational therapy.
4. What new or different academic leadership roles or positions have you taken since the circle began?
5. What new or different professional association leadership roles/positions have you taken since the circle began?
6. Provide examples of how you have and/or will leverage your talent as a mentor to build readiness for leadership in your occupational therapy protégés.
7. Write a brief story about how this mentoring program has been beneficial for you in your role as a program director.
8. Imagine that it's [insert date] … and you recognize yourself as an exemplary leader. What has contributed to your success?
9. Is there anything you wish we had asked about the program or your experience?

Reference

Kouzes, J. M., & Posner, B. Z. (2003). *Leadership practices inventory* (3rd ed.). San Francisco: Pfeiffer.

Appendix 4.B.
Leadership Strengths

**34 Leadership Strengths Organized Into Gallup's 4 Leadership Domains
and Number of Participants Having That Strength**

Executing	Influencing	Relationship Building	Strategic Thinking
Achiever (23)	Activator (9)	Adaptability (6)	Analytical (7)
Arranger (5)	Command (1)	Connectiveness (16)	Context (4)
Belief (3)	Communication (3)	Developer (5)	Futuristic (6)
Consistency (7)	Competition (1)	Empathy (8)	Ideation (15)
Deliberative (8)	Maximizer (6)	Harmony (8)	Input (19)
Discipline (6)	Self Assurance (0)	Includer (2)	Intellection (14)
Focus (4)	Significance (3)	Individualization (9)	Learner (33)
Responsibility (11)	Woo (4)	Positivity (9)	Strategic (9)
Restorative (8)		Relator (9)	

Strength Totals and Percentages in Domain

Executing	Influencing	Relationship Building	Strategic Thinking
75 = 26%	27 = 9%	72 = 25%	107 = 38%

Note. These strengths are organized by Gallup's four leadership domains. The percentages do not add to 100 due to rounding.

Appendix 4.C.
Outcomes of the Mentorship
Programs' Categories and Subcategories

1. Leadership readiness and performance
   Leadership learning and leadership language
2. Transformation of self
   Self-awareness, self-confidence, perceiving self as leader and as a mentor
3. Engagement, retention, and leadership endeavors
   Commitment to self and to the welfare and future of the mentees' organization
4. Collaboration and trust
   Networking, connections, and participation in a safe, trusting environment
5. Circle methodology
   Story learning, mentoring from the mentor and peers, and the structured process.

Part II. Mentoring Through Stories—The Workbook

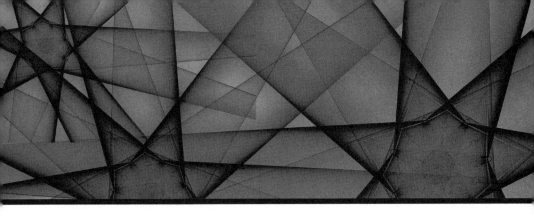

Chapter 5.
Introduction to the Workbook

Tell me and I'll forget, show me and I may remember, involve me and I'll understand.

—Chinese proverb (Thinkexist.com, n.d.)

Introduction

Mentoring relationships are active partnerships where the story engages and connects the mentor and mentee. Storytelling is a uniquely powerful communication tool for mentoring leaders, as stories give substance, voice, and permanence to the abstract and conceptual topic of leadership development. Through stories people can bring tacit knowledge to consciousness, share that knowledge, and then use that knowledge as a basis for action. Through the strong voices of our collective stories we can develop and pass on a culture of leadership that builds our individual and group capacity to lead. This workbook is a collection of mentoring stories to be used as the starting point for sharing our voices and developing our leadership culture. Before each story, activities guide mentors and mentees in learning, considering their own stories, and obtaining additional context and knowledge.

How to Use the Workbook

Simply reading a story does not embody the active partnership and learning of mentoring relationships. One can write or read a story, but the story is meaningless without the relationship between the storyteller and reader that encourages self-reflection, discussion, and ownership of the story. Although you can individually use the workbook, we suggest that you work through the stories with one or more colleagues. Any of the group mentoring approaches discussed in Chapter 3 can be used with a group of coworkers or classmates.

The workbook is primarily aimed at mentees, but it also can be easily used by mentors. Mentees can use the workbook as a self-guided process to leadership development, but again, the experience of the authors suggests that a group experience with a designated mentor is the most powerful use of the workbook. An individual may use the workbook in preparation for becoming a mentor, using the stories and reflective questions as a starting point to assess and develop skills in mentoring and storytelling. Additionally, a mentor working with a single mentee or mentoring groups may use the workbook as an intact collection of stories and exercises or as a guide for self-refection and writing one's own stories.

The stories are grouped in sections that identify the central leadership topic or theme of the stories. You can progress through the stories in any order, but you should start with the first story, Story 6.1, "From Failure to Success: The Power of Self-Reflection," and end with the last one, Story 10.5, "Writing Your Story — The Future of Leadership," in Chapter 10.

All of the stories are written from the perspective of a mentor for the learning benefit of a mentee. Each captures the experience of the mentor within a specific leadership topic or theme. Under each story title, an inspirational quote captures the essence of the story. Next, additional suggestions for reading, questions to consider, and references back to various points of this text will prepare you for the story and enhance learning.

The stories range in length, and you may want to record your reactions, questions, and situations that come to mind as you read or hear the story. Following every story, several questions encourage self-reflection, analysis, and application. These questions are written to guide the self-reflection of mentees and may need to be reframed by mentors who use the stories or who are learning to write their own stories.The questions should prompt mentors to review their own experiences and engage in both emotional and intellectual analyses of those career events.

Getting Started: Preparing to Mentor and Be Mentored

An effective mentee is prepared to be mentored. This means he or she is ready to assume responsibility for his or her learning; willing to invest time, intellect, and emotion in the process; and eager to fully engage in the mentoring relationship (Shea, 1994; Zachary, 2005). At the core of this preparation is the mentee's readiness to participate in honest and objective self-reflection and assessment. Mentors similarly prepare for each new mentoring experience.

Answering the questions in Figure 5.1 is a starting point for the type of self-reflection that is the basis for learning in a mentoring relationship. To develop as a leader or to facilitate the development of mentees, you must begin by understanding how you view leadership that recognizes the people and events that have influenced that view and the values and beliefs that are incorporated into your definition.

Ultimately, leadership is action, and this self-reflective definition must also address how effectively you enact your leadership definition on a day-to-day basis. Take the time now to think about and write your leadership definition. Use the five

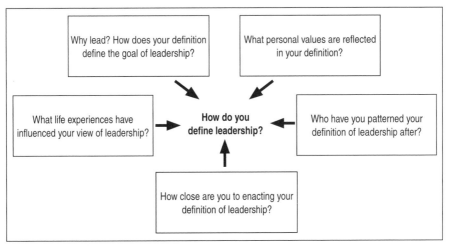

Figure 5.1. Defining leadership.

questions in Figure 5.1 as a guide and add additional questions as you craft your definition. Remember, your definition of leadership is the starting point for continuous self-reflection as you work through the mentoring stories. Your definition will change over time through experience and reflection on your experience, so you'll need to periodically, look at your definition and update it. It's a great indicator of how you are developing as a leader.

The Stories

The mentoring stories in the following chapters are personal narratives of leaders. The context and details may be very different from your situation, but the leadership concepts are universal. You will need to do the work to translate the stories from the mentor's perspective to your own. Focus on the leadership concepts that work for you; don't get hung up or bogged down with details that don't pertain to your situation. The final story will be *your* story—one that you write using the insights and wisdom gained through the power of mentoring with stories. Enjoy reading, reflecting, writing, and becoming a leader!

Chapter 6. Self-Reflection and Growth

The stories in this chapter focus on your individual development as a leader through self-reflection and values clarification.

★ Story 6.1. From Failure to Success: The Power of Self-Reflection
★ Story 6.2. A Slightly Better Version of Myself
★ Story 6.3. Values to Voice to Action: Doing the Right Thing
★ Story 6.4. Accepting My Authenticity
★ Story 6.5. Work–Life Balance.

Chapter 7. Community Building

The stories in this chapter will build your understanding of community in the workplace and provide strategies for community building.
- ★ Story 7.1. The Faculty Who Reads Together Leads Together
- ★ Story 7.2. Building a Community of Scholars Through Living the Shared Vision
- ★ Story 7.3. Research and Leadership
- ★ Story 7.4. Collaboration—The Elegant Solution.

Chapter 8. Enacting Leadership Practices

The stories in this chapter are based on the five leadership practices of Kouzes and Posner (2007). You will learn more about each practice and come away with ideas for how to develop and use the practices in your leadership life.
- ★ Story 8.1. Inspiring a Shared Vision—Lessons From Across My Career
- ★ Story 8.2. Challenging the Process: Finding Your Voice
- ★ Story 8.3. Modeling the Way—From Philosophy to Action
- ★ Story 8.4. My Leadership Achilles Heel—Encouraging the Heart
- ★ Story 8.5. Building a Legacy—Enabling Others to Act
- ★ Story 8.6. Applying the 5 Practices in Faculty Performance Evaluation.

Chapter 9. Building Followership

The stories in this chapter deal with the sometimes difficult challenges leaders face in dealing with the day-to-day issues and problems of the workplace.
- ★ Story 9.1. Problem Employees—Insights and Observations, Not Solutions!
- ★ Story 9.2. Learning to Work Smarter, Not Harder
- ★ Story 9.3. We've Got to Stop Meeting Like This!

Chapter 10. Leading for the Future

In the final chapter, stories focus on the future and the role of leadership in ensuring that change continues to be a positive force within health care professions.
- ★ Story 10.1. Resisting Our Inner Quicksand
- ★ Story 10.2. Leading Change to Design Our Future
- ★ Story 10.3. Leadership in the Curriculum—Our Profession's Future
- ★ Story 10.4. Change Is Inevitable, Growth Is Optional—A Tale of 2 Situations
- ★ Story 10.5. Writing Your Story—The Future of Leadership.

This is a book you should write in! Writing as you read the story and in response to the questions will increase your understanding and serve as a basis for in-depth discussion. The final story is slightly different as you will be guided through the process of writing your own leadership story—a great culminating activity for the work you have done and a foundation for your future development.

References

Kouzes, J. M., & Posner, B. Z. (2007). *The leadership challenge* (4th ed.). San Francisco: Jossey-Bass.

Shea, G. F. (1994). *Mentoring: Helping employees reach their full potential.* New York: American Management Association.

Thinkexist.com. (n.d.). *Chinese proverb.* Retrieved February 1, 2011, from http://thinkexist.com/quotation/tell_me_and_i-ll_forget-show_me_and_i_may/10546.html

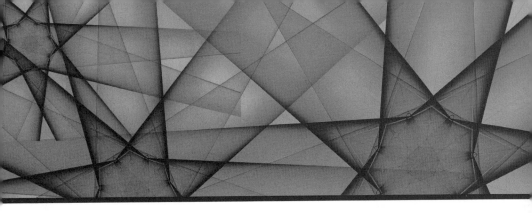

Chapter 6.
Self-Reflection and Growth

Story 6.1. From Failure to Success—The Power of Self-Reflection

I've gone through life believing in the strength and competence of others;
never in my own. Now dazzled, I discover that my capacities are real.
It's like finding a fortune in the lining of an old coat.

—Joan Mills (Getmotivation.com, n.d.)

Before you read this story,

1. Start your process of personal reflection by completing the defining leadership exercise (Figure 5.1) presented in Chapter 5.
2. Re-read "Mentoring With Stories" in Chapter 3 to understand how stories build the mentoring relationship and foster learning for both the mentor and mentee.

My university has two basic divisions: (1) Health Affairs and (2) Academic Affairs. There's a fair amount of competition between the two divisions and not as much cross-campus collaboration as you might think. There are also misperceptions that contribute to the competition and make it harder to collaborate. For example, faculty in Academic Affairs think that all the Health Affairs programs are rich—that's where the money goes, in their minds. In Health Affairs, we think that the academic folks are "snobs"—that they believe they are the true academics, while we over on the health side of campus are glorified trade schools.

When we started to redesign our curriculum and create an occupational science base, we knew that we had to cross the divide, that we needed to work with colleagues in programs such as geography, sociology, and anthropology. But we had few contacts and no tradition of this kind of collaboration, and we had all the misperceptions on both sides to deal with. As the program director, I felt a huge responsibility to start crossing the divide.

I was inducted into the newly formed Academy of Distinguished Teaching Scholars as a charter member. This was personally significant to me because teaching is my love, and the recognition of this honor was awesome. But the possibilities in terms of the responsibility I felt to lead the division across the divide were equally exciting. As a member of the Academy, I was in the same club as the most honored and respected teachers, many of whom were legends on the academic campus.

Because the Academy was just forming, officers and committee chairs were being elected. A friend of mine encouraged me to run for the chair of the Interdisciplinary Committee. This seemed like a natural for me—exactly what I wanted to create for my own program. I ran and was elected, but there was this little voice in the back of my head saying "You're in over your head. What are you thinking? You can't lead these people—they think you have the academic background of a plumber."

I kept trying to ignore that bad little voice and went on to organize a committee and get started. My committee decided to start a campus mentoring project that would have members of the Academy as leaders of mentoring circles that would focus on the development of teaching. Membership would be open to any faculty member with the idea that each circle would have diversity of age, experience, and discipline. It was a really good idea.

Now, I'm going to jump to the end of the story and tell you what happened: We never got a single circle established. It was just a complete failure. And I'm going tell you how I felt: terrible and totally responsible. In my mind, I had proven my little voice right, and I had missed the chance to prove to the campus that someone from Health Affairs had the knowledge and ability to bring the campus together. Of course, I also felt that I'd let down my program colleagues and I hated to admit to them that this project was a failure. This is how I felt for years, in fact—until I started to write this story.

But writing the story was a truly amazing learning process. There is nothing like the power of self-reflection, of revisiting a critical event, of retelling it and arriving at a whole new level of understanding. Telling the story allowed me to reframe what I had seen as a complete failure. First of all, I went to the Academy Web site and saw nothing—still no interdisciplinary programs, no initiatives, nothing. Now, I knew this—I'm still a member of the Academy—but

(Continued)

Story 6.1. Cont.

until I went and really searched the whole site and found nothing, I'd harbored this idea that I had failed while someone else had probably succeeded.

This was my first set of insights: I accept too much individual responsibility when something doesn't work. In reality, communities share successes but also share failures—that's how communities develop. I also see that I allowed the pressure that I felt to succeed to intimidate me to a point that I didn't use the planning skills I have. My committee needed to take more time, to work out the logistics of scheduling, to run a trial, to start small and grow the program—things I know, but, in my need to succeed, didn't honor. Now, initially, this is where my insights stopped. But I've come see some other outcomes.

One of the outcomes I'd hoped for with the Academy experience was to use my skills outside of the comfortable arena of my own program and discipline. Now I realize that after the failure of the teaching circles, I did have positive leadership experiences outside of my comfort zone. I successfully led and participated in university and graduate school committees. My record of successes outnumbers my failures. I gave a lot more power to the failure and because of that really didn't see the connection between what I learned from the Academy experience and subsequent cross-campus activities that were successes.

I did, in fact, gain contacts across the campus and created the precedent and the environment for faculty from my program to seek out and establish relationships with faculty in Academic Affairs. There are now occupational science program faculty with dual appointments in academic departments; there's an ongoing series of scholarly seminars with participants from Academic Affairs. We have crossed the divide. Although I didn't achieve the outcome I'd initially hoped for—the circles did fail—I did achieve very positive outcomes for myself and the program.

The interesting thing about how we learn through stories is how the story evolves and the learning continues. When I initially wrote this story, I was struggling with post-retirement life. I was no longer in my familiar environment and comfort zone and really wasn't sure how to establish myself professionally outside of the university and the profession.

Something very positive happened to me in telling this story and those that followed. I had the privilege of revisiting my career, putting lots of mistakes to rest, and enjoying my accomplishments. My sense of myself and my skills was empowered. But it wasn't just telling my stories that allowed this kind of growth; it was the mentoring process. I came to know mentoring as a uniquely powerful learning relationship for both the mentor and mentee. It is a journey that dissolves boundaries and opens our abilities to learn from one another.

I'd like to end my story with a few summary points about my own learning.

★ Self-reflection is one of my most valued tools, but when it's combined with storytelling and mentoring, the value is exponentially magnified.

★ I always learn from my failures and now know that the learning will continue to unfold and deepen as long as I continue to engage in the process of examination and exploration alone and with trusted colleagues.

★ The skills that I have as an occupational therapist and leader are not only transferable but highly valued.

Mentoring Leaders: The Power of Storytelling for Building Leadership in Health Care and Education

Reflective Questions

1. Why would the mentor share a story about a failure?

_____

_____

_____

_____

_____

2. As you read the story, what were your emotional reactions? What prompted these reactions?

_____

_____

_____

_____

_____

3. Have you had a similar experience? How did you handle it? What would or could you do differently now?

_____

_____

_____

_____

_____

4. What did you discover about yourself from the mentor's story?

_____

_____

_____

_____

Story 6.2. A Slightly Better Version of Myself

> *To exist is to change, to change is to mature,*
> *to mature is to go on creating oneself endlessly.*

> —Henri L. Bergson (Thinkexist.com, n.d.)

Before you read this story,

1. Learn more about the Gallup online assessments Strengths Finder 2.0 and Strengths-Based Leadership at www.strengthsfinder.com.
2. Consider reading the books *Strengths Finder 2.0* (Rath, 2007) and *Strengths-Based Leadership* (Rath & Conchie, 2009).
3. Take one of the online assessments to learn about your strengths.

This story is about my current journey to understand and embrace my strengths. You'll hear what these strengths sound like to me and also how I am working to refine and develop them by looking back at a past situation through the newly acquired lens of these strengths.

When I first took the Strengths Finder (Rath, 2007) assessment a year ago, I have to admit that the list dismayed me. Then, my strengths were

★ Learner
★ Intellection
★ Discipline
★ Achiever
★ Responsibility.

I didn't think these 5 words depicted the kind of person I thought I might be. This person seemed boring, predictable, uninspiring—certainly not the visionary leader I was hoping to see.

Who is this person? I wondered. Surely it was not me, certainly there was a glitch in the system when I took the inventory and I've gotten someone else's results. But as I started to read the Strengths Finder book, a quote caught my eye: "You cannot be anything you want to be—but you can be a lot more of who you already are" (Rath, 2007, p. 9). That stopped me as I suddenly realized that maybe it was time to understand and appreciate who I really am. Maybe I could stop investing energy in my imposter identity and start investing in who I really am, or as my daughter likes to tell me, "Mama, you're really fine. You just need to work on being a slightly better version of yourself."

So, with the goal of becoming a slightly better version of myself, I started learning more about these 5 strengths.

At my core is *intellection*—this is *me*, the critical thinker, the lover of ideas and plans, my mental hum. Closely related is the *learner*, the person for whom education is a lifelong activity, the person who really never left college.

These strengths are where I also found myself as the change leader I am. My drive for change comes from my comfort with the unfamiliar, my willingness to work through what must be revamped, revised, or fixed. Learning and thinking are my rechargeable power supplies. But I need *responsibility* to push me outside of myself, to go beyond the processes of learning and introspection to commit to follow an idea to action.

(Continued)

Story 6.2. Cont.

Discipline is a companion strength. This is the source of my ability to create order, to be thorough and diligent. Lastly, the *achiever*—this is my energy, my strong work ethic, my ability to launch new initiatives, my drive.

I've also recognized the undertones of my discontent in some of these strengths: the discouragement I've often felt when having to admit that what I can actually do is less than what I can conceive of or think, the disappointment at having to admit I'm not perfect, and the many times when my obsession over my work has taken priority over everything else. This was enlightening, sobering, and funny as I recognized myself in many of the stories, quotes, and caveats in *Strengths Finder* (Rath, 2007).

As strongly as I related to these descriptions, I continued to feel a disconnect between these strengths and myself as a leader. I just couldn't quite believe that this list could really be the core of who I was as a leader. I decided to go back and look at a time when I felt most effective as a leader to see if I could recognize these strengths in action.

This is a snapshot story about community building. Specifically, it's about how the process of engaging in strategic planning and then curriculum planning contributed to the development of our occupational science faculty as a community of scholars. This is just one element of our community building that allows me to focus on how I used my strengths.

We undertook a huge planning process that resulted in a complete revamping of every aspect of our life as a faculty: the curriculum, our teaching styles, our admission processes, and ultimately our name and identity as a program. We started out thinking that we were just revising the curriculum, but in reality we were redefining who we were internally as a community as well as externally within our school and university.

I now know that this process of deconstructing ourselves and carefully reconstructing every piece was a powerful component of our development as a community. It was also a process that made us vulnerable individually and as a group. *Deconstructing* meant raising questions and criticizing what had been. *Reconstruction* was equally difficult as we auditioned, evaluated, rejected, and finally accepted many new ideas. We became able to challenge each other and to debate, we learned how to defend our intellectual positions with information, and we came to understand the difference between passion and emotion.

We had disagreements. We had arguments. We had fights. We also had lots of wine, many potluck dinners, and great celebratory moments when we reveled in how smart we were and what good work we were doing. We wrote together about our process and product; we presented in dyads, triads, and groups of 6; we became each other's greatest critics and most avid supporters.

We called my role the "process manager." I provided the order we needed through fairly rigid adherence to a multistage planning model. This was my *discipline* theme. I made my colleagues follow the model, even when one of my most passionate and articulate colleagues persuasively lobbied to jump over several steps and develop courses and syllabi before we had worked through the curriculum framework.

At the same time, the core strength of *intellection* allowed me to fully engage in the intellectual discussions and processes, not to simply be the manager and gatekeeper. I wanted and needed—and the group wanted and needed—me to participate at an intellectual and thinking level.

(Continued)

Story 6.2. Cont.

I see now that it was the *learner* who motivated and inspired the whole change process. I truly was not afraid of this mammoth undertaking. I was charged by the opportunity to create and translate ideas to tangible products, and my belief and enthusiasm energized the group. I also know that several of my colleagues are learners and share my strength in intellection, so we fueled each other's passion for learning and creating. We could approach this huge task as a learning process, and that was the key to tapping into our intellectual energy.

Too many thinkers can be dangerous, however, with lots of great ideas and slow or no action. But that *responsibility* theme allowed me to push ideas to action. I set timelines, I made assignments, and I held myself and everyone else accountable.

Lastly, as an *achiever,* I was totally focused on our accomplishments. Not only did I work hard and set expectations for others, but I could lead the recognition and celebration of what we did. When I look back on this effort, I think we became our best as a community in part because I was at my best as a leader who really pulled from my complementary strengths to inspire and sustain the group.

Before I close the story I want to talk a little bit about my results from taking the inventory a second time. Not surprisingly, I am not a new or different person, although a few different but related skills have emerged. My strengths still cluster in the same two domains: executing and strategic thinking. I have no strengths in either influencing or relationship building (Rath & Conchie, 2009).

When talking about this with my mentor, she said something I think is quite true: My strengths in executing and strategic thinking are inherent while I have worked hard on relationship building. I have strong, positive relationships with those I lead and work with, probably a function of one of my other strengths, achiever.

When I now conceptualize how these strengths fit together, I see the core as *input, intellection,* and *learner* as a leader. I am grounded in my knowledge base, and the second ring includes *responsibility, discipline,* and *arranger* as I thoughtfully work to move beyond just knowing toward action. Finally, the outer ring of *achiever* and *strategic* ensures that the action is the right action.

This story was about developing my understanding of my strengths through a retrospective analysis. I encourage you to each find a way to do a similar process of examining and understanding your strengths.

Here's what I've learned:

★ I am much more accepting that these are my top strengths. I have a positive view of them and can see how the collection of strengths has helped me learn and develop skills in other domains where I don't have inherent strengths.

★ I am more able to see and value these strengths as components of my leadership ability. I don't feel a need to apologize for skills I don't have. I now more clearly understand how important it is to surround myself with individuals whose skills complement mine.

★ The retrospective analysis was critical in developing that more positive view. To see a successful past event through this lens allowed me to analyze and understand my strengths in context. The contextual view gave me irrefutable evidence of my strengths.

(Continued)

Story 6.2. Cont.

★ I am intrigued by the possibility of using these strengths in a more intentional manner. As talked about before, becoming more intentional in our use of the leadership
practices and our strengths can only strengthen our overall leadership ability.

★ Lastly, I am impressed by the consistency of my results from last year to this year,
which provides more evidence that these strengths are, in fact, my strengths. I also
am impressed by the impact of context in bringing skills to the forefront.

Reflective Questions

1. This story is based on the use of a specific instrument to identify strengths. Using
   this same instrument (or another of your choice), list your identified strengths
   and your initial reaction to each strength. Are you in agreement? Surprised? Dismayed?

   _____

   _____

   _____

   _____

   _____

2. The mentor talks about analyzing a past success to understand and appreciate
   leadership strengths. Briefly describe a past success. What happened? How did
   your strengths contribute to the success?

   _____

   _____

   _____

   _____

   _____

3. How can you intentionally develop and use your strengths on a day-to-day basis as a leader?

   _____

   _____

   _____

   _____

   _____

4. How could this type of assessment be used in team or community building? What would the benefits—and risks—be?

_____

_____

_____

_____

_____

Story 6.3. Values to Voice to Action—Doing the Right Thing

In matters of style, swim with the current; in matters of principle, stand like a rock.

—Thomas Jefferson (Brainyquote.com, n.d.)

Before you read this story,

1. Refer to Chapter 1, and consider the relationship among communication, finding voice, and taking action.

This is a story about self as leader, a time when my values gave me voice and the courage to do the right thing. It's about being assertive and acting with integrity because my values were clearly guiding me.

I have a great deal of respect for our professional accreditation process in occupational therapy. I see the need for a rigorous review based on carefully developed standards and have actually enjoyed the process of preparing for and participating in the reviews. We've had successful reviews each time—and by "success" I mean receiving very good reviews, positive feedback, and constructive criticism that often resulted in tangible changes in my resources, improvements in administrative processes, or refinements to the curriculum.

With that said, over the years I also developed a strong understanding for my role as an advocate for my program and faculty both within the university and with external groups. In other words, as much as I respected the accreditation process, I would not simply comply with requests that I felt compromised my program's unique identity and mission within the university or jeopardized the faculty's right to confidentiality. I often found myself weighing competing interests when considering new interpretations of standards or new requests for information.

Several years ago, when a requirement was instituted for a more substantive biennial report, I welcomed this change, thinking that greater accountability between accreditation reviews was essential to the integrity of the accreditation process.

I began the work of compiling the information for the report. I was frustrated at times with the focus on administrative compliance versus compliance in areas of actual curriculum content. I thought that there should be equal emphasis on administrative standards such as credentialing, strategic planning, faculty development, and curriculum content standards. Instead, my perception was that the emphasis on administrative issues was more prescriptive and detailed. The faculty development area was my ultimate frustration. I was asked to send all of the faculty development plans as an appendix to the report.

Initially, in my compliant mode, I spent time pulling all the plans from individual faculty files. In the process, I came to the realization that we viewed these plans as confidential personnel records, and I was not comfortable sending them for external review. I felt a lack of trust. The accrediting agency would not accept a response that the plans were done; they had to see them.

I talked with the faculty and with my chair about my concerns. The faculty agreed with me, as did my chair, and it was decided that I would pursue this with our university attorney. The attorney agreed that this request violated our state personnel act and that sending the reports would jeopardize faculty rights to confidentiality. Together, we drafted a response for

(Continued)

Story 6.3. Cont.

the report in lieu of submitting the faculty development plans. The response outlined the legal issues and included a copy of our faculty development plan format and a schedule of the review meetings I had conducted with each faculty member.

The accrediting agency rejected this, cited the program for a deficiency, and required a plan of correction that said we had to submit the plans. At this point, with further discussion with the attorney, I learned that our chancellor could override the state personnel act if he decided it was in the best interest of the university. He could require me to send the faculty development plans in order to preserve our accreditation status.

After talking with the faculty and again with my chair, we all agreed that we did not want this kind of attention from the chancellor and decided to offer another solution. We drafted a new version of our faculty development plan that omitted the evaluative content that faculty felt was confidential. Each faculty member signed an additional waiver stating that this information could be shared with the accrediting agency, and the attorney drafted a cover letter again outlining the legal issues and presenting the revised format as one that was in compliance with the state personnel act. I sent the revised plans for the year covered by the original request on the biennial report.

What did I get back? A letter stating that we were still noncompliant because we were now in a new year, and I should provide the reports for that year. I was furious. I felt that I was being punished for raising a question and was being asked to provide information that no one else had to provide. What did I do? I sucked it up. I redid the reports for the year requested and sent them in. I then got a letter stating that the deficiency had been removed and we were once again in compliance.

The outcome was a solution that everyone could live with. I learned that I have to take a stand when values that are critically important to me are at stake. I absolutely believe that individual development can only be effective in an environment of complete confidentiality and trust. The faculty had to be able to trust me to keep their performance information in confidence. But everyone—the faculty, my chair, the university—also had the right to expect me to make reasoned decisions and to not capriciously jeopardize the accreditation status of the program. I had to decide when to stop making something an issue and when to create and offer a better solution.

As I look back on this episode, I feel comfortable about what I did at the time and the risk I took. It increased my confidence to be certain of what my values are and to take action based on those values. I was clearly supported by the faculty and my chair and sought out and used the legal resources of the university. It was good for me to be assertive but also to see the line between being assertive and being obstructionist. Because the value of protecting faculty confidentiality was so strong, I was able to continually reflect back on that value in deciding when a compromise was reached that was in line with the value and consistent with my responsibility as program director.

So, here's what I learned:

★ As a leader, knowing my values gave me voice. I never lost sight of the importance of confidentiality and trust.

★ Acting on my values gave me the courage to do the right thing.

★ Doing the right things means acting on my own values but also considering all of the other elements in the situation.

(Continued)

Story 6.3. Cont.
- ★ It's sometimes hard to know what the right thing is, but if I listen to my inner voice and seek out the counsel of others involved, the right thing to do will be apparent.
- ★ The bottom line is that my values gave me the courage and voice to act with integrity.

Reflective Questions

1. What are your core values as a leader?

_____

_____

_____

_____

_____

2. How do you demonstrate these values in voice and action?

_____

_____

_____

_____

_____

3. Identify a time when your values were challenged. Describe the challenge you faced, and critique your response.

_____

_____

_____

_____

_____

4. What will you do differently as leader to strengthen your values–voice–action connection?

_____

_____

_____

_____

_____

Story 6.4. Accepting My Authenticity

> *To contact the deeper truth of who we are, we must engage in some activity or*
> *practice that questions what we assume to be true about ourselves.*

> — A. H. Almaas (Watts, 2010, p. 2)

Before you read this story,

1. Locate and read the article "Managing Authenticity" (Goffee & Jones, 2005).

This story is a response to an article I recently read, "Managing Authenticity" (Goffee & Jones, 2005). Although I'm still not completely comfortable with all of the concepts presented by Rob Goffee and Gareth Jones, two experts on organizational behavior and development, I realize that I don't have to buy into all of them. After all, these two authors start out with the admonition that if you "try to lead like someone else, you will fail" (p. 87). I take that to mean that I shouldn't, don't need to, and won't accept everything in this article. I do, however, see some of their points in my own journey, and I think the journey may have been easier had I had this insight along the way.

All of my life I've struggled with contrasting identities. Was I, am I a . . .

★ Well-behaved southern girl or a nonconventional individualist?

★ Career-driven feminist or a nurturing spirit?

★ Creative, free-thinking visionary or a loyal, organized worker bee?

My conflict was even more extreme once I started to assume leadership roles. Now I had questions about whether these different aspects of my identity could somehow pull together into a cohesive and effective approach to leadership. My conflicting and contrasting identities were no longer just my own neuroses. I was now concerned that I would seem erratic, inconsistent, and manipulative. I did not see being a chameleon as a positive trait for a leader.

When I would decide to base my leadership in just one of these facets of my identity, I knew I was denying my history and shortchanging myself, my colleagues, and my future. When I shifted back and forth between them, I felt fraudulent and manipulative. Over the years I did have a few moments when I felt I'd successfully combined these diverse pieces of myself, and at those times I felt authentic, powerful, and comfortable with the synchrony between my multiple internal and external imagoes. But it's been difficult for me to maintain that sense of authenticity.

I'm going to start this story by sharing one of the moments when I knew I was an authentic leader. Then I'll talk about the challenges of maintaining this image and end with some insights from this last year as I am finally accepting my authenticity.

The thrill of authenticity. I was in my second term as the representative from my state to the American Occupational Therapy Association Representative Assembly (RA). When I was preparing for the RA, I knew that year that a leadership position would be open. I thought about it and decided that I would run for the position.

This decision was my first breakthrough. As a well-behaved southern girl, I always waited for someone else to recognize my talents and invite and encourage me to apply, run for, or take a position. To do otherwise seemed to be bragging and too bold. But the career-driven feminist and creative visionary overruled the good girl, and I put my name on the ballot.

(Continued)

Story 6.4. Cont.

As a candidate, I was required to give a 3-minute speech to the RA, and on the basis of that speech, the representatives would make their decision. I worked very hard on that 3-minute speech and was the third candidate to speak. I remember sitting there feeling a little panicked as I listened to the other two speeches and realized that mine was different. Although my competition detailed their many accomplishments and credentials, I talked about leadership, who I was as a leader and what I would bring to the RA. When I sat down, I thought, "Oh, my God, I didn't tell them the right things; they don't know what I've done; I seem like I don't have the right qualifications for the position."

Well, I won, and two of our profession's leaders came up to me after the election and told me *why* I won. They said to me, "You told them who you are and not what you've done, and it's who you are that matters as a leader." I won the election because I was able to share my sincerity, honesty, and integrity and was successful in the position because I was able to accept, own, and manage the image of myself as a leader I'd projected that day. My RA peers saw and heard who I was as a leader and attributed authenticity to me in their vote. I became a stronger version of myself as a leader because of what others heard and saw in me during that speech, but I was ultimately successful because what I had said reflected genuine aspects of who I was and am. My words and my deeds were consistent.

Goffee and Jones (2005) tell us that *authenticity* is about knowing who you are, appreciating your own diversity, and offering the right pieces of yourself to the right people in the right situation. That leads to why I've had trouble over the years maintaining that wonderful sense of authenticity. I haven't always been able to appreciate and integrate all the facets of my self while simultaneously segregating out and highlighting distinct pieces, depending on the situation. It was hard enough to integrate the disparate parts and value the whole, but to then intentionally pull out one piece and use it in a situation seemed artificial and manipulative.

Over the years, through a great deal of self-reflection, integration became a way of knowing myself, and I came to accept and enjoy the diverse contributions of the southern girl, feminist, caring spirit, visionary, and worker bee. Although I grew to understand and value my diversity, I was very aware of when I actually switched gears and consciously presented a different face to an individual or a group. I wasn't always comfortable doing this. I worried that this variability was seen as a "something for everyone" or "one-size-fits-all" approach to leadership, and thus an unbelievable and amorphous approach. With reflection, I have increasingly come to grips with the "all rightness" of consciously using the diverse facets of my identity at different times, in different situations, and with different people.

My increased comfort grows out of two experiences. The first was the process of leaving my last position and the incredible affirmation I received of my authentic leadership. Although I was afraid my diversity limited my authenticity, my former colleagues let me know that this is what they valued so much about me. I treasure their words and would like to share from two of those people, even though the well-behaved southern girl in me is cringing at the thought of all this bragging.

From one of the staff, "On the serious side, I have always had great admiration for your sense of perspective. You can calm a drama, dry a tear, or de-escalate an angry situation by offering a different view of what is going on while at the same time affirming the person who has sought your counsel. It's a rare gift."

(Continued)

Story 6.4. Cont.

The words of my mentor and supervisor resonate with this article (Goffee & Jones, 2005): "You have a personal style called 'verve.' *Verve* is the special ability or talent to pull something off with panache. It is said that verve comes into one's life when we finally trust our instincts. When we take risks and they pay off. Verve is passion. It's also the secret of personal style. Verve is focused, creative energy, a sense of vitality and zest. You are verve."

I read these words now and I hear the attribution of my authenticity. I wasn't and am not amorphous or manipulative. I am defined by what others see in me because I have carefully developed and shared the pieces of myself that matter most in a situation. It is not manipulative; it's caring, it's wanting the most and the best, it's creating points of connection between myself and others.

The second experience that is increasing my comfort with authenticity is the fact that I, having left my long-term position, must now define myself as a leader not by a position but through my inner sense of who I am. Since leaving, I have had to create points of connection with people by bringing the right piece of myself forward. I no longer have my former role to give shape and continuity to my multifaceted self. Instead, I have to read a situation and decide who to bring forward—the southern girl, the visionary, the career feminist, or the hard worker.

I've learned that sometimes I don't want to lead, and in a funny way, I see that as maturity of my identity as a leader. There are some situations that just aren't right for me a leader. I've also learned that I can lead from any position or no position. At this point, a leader is who I am, not what I do.

Now for the learning—and my paraphrasing and embellishing of Goffee and Jones (2005):

★ Authenticity is painstakingly earned through both self-knowledge and self-disclosure, and it must be carefully managed and safeguarded.

★ Gaining authenticity is a two-part challenge that requires

1. Knowing and valuing the diversity of who you are while understanding the core values that weave all of those diverse facets together, and

2. Knowing what part of yourself to reveal to whom and when. This is not manipulation but true expressions reflecting different aspects of your inner self.

Mentoring Leaders: The Power of Storytelling for Building Leadership in Health Care and Education

Reflective Questions

1. As you read this story, what was your reaction to the mentor's dilemma about contrasting identities?

_____

_____

_____

_____

_____

2. How do you define being an authentic leader?

_____

_____

_____

_____

_____

3. Select a picture that represents you as a leader. Briefly describe why you have chosen this picture and how it represents your authenticity.

_____

_____

_____

_____

_____

4. What are the key experiences and who are the key people who have influenced your growth as an authentic leader?

_____

_____

_____

_____

_____

Story 6.5. Work–Life Balance

Never have we had so little time in which to do so much.

—Franklin D. Roosevelt

Before you read this story,

1. Write out what *work–life balance* means to you.

2. Identify 2 things that you have done to achieve a healthy balance.

3. List 2 things that you want to do to balance your life.

When we identified topics for our mentoring circle, the majority of participants wanted me to discuss how I balanced my work and life. I have to be honest with you, most of my past work life has not honored the importance of balancing work with my other aspects of my life.

For most of my career, I was known as a "workaholic." I thought this was a compliment, as I believed workaholics were energized by their work. I struggled with this for many years and began to feel guilty because I loved my work, and I didn't want to do the things that others and the literature suggested in order to balance life—you know the drill, balancing your work with exercise, eating a healthy diet, and selecting activities to reduce stress. That might be okay for some, but not for me.

I didn't have time for every meal to be healthy, so I sometimes resorted to "fast food" diets. I don't like to exercise, so health clubs were more stressful than helpful, and I struggled to learn how to meditate! I also decided thinking about work–life balance was incorrect and got me on the wrong track. Think about it: Work is a part of life, not something separate from your life. As occupational therapists, we talk about the occupations of our life—work, play, leisure, self-care, rest—so I want to think about the topic as *occupational balance in our lives*.

As I think about my past career and learning how to have a healthy balance with the many facets of my life, I discovered that what we do to achieve occupational balance is not the same for everyone. No recipe works for all. I learned that you can't achieve balance every day but need to think about balancing over a period of time.

Creating occupational balance is different at different times of your life. Balancing all the occupations you encounter is hard to achieve, and sometimes it is out of whack! When that

(Continued)

Story 6.5. Cont.

happens, you can't feel guilty—that is still difficult for me. I haven't discovered the best equation for balancing my life, but I'm beginning to get the "guilt thing" under control!

Let me share some key times in my past and what I discovered that led me toward a healthy occupational balance in my life.

When I started my career, I was also a newlywed and living in a new city. I wanted everything to be perfect, and I would frequently cry to myself because everything couldn't be perfect. My job wasn't the best; I didn't like my supervisor and disagreed with many of the activities she did. I held all my feelings to myself, and things just piled up.

I finally shared my frustrations with my husband and discovered the positive power of sharing and support. The support for us came from each other, and it strengthened our marriage. About my job, my husband said, "quit." Quitting wasn't an option for me because I knew that we needed the money I was earning. Instead, I gained new support from a co-worker as soon as I started sharing my frustrations. Soon my co-worker and I were laughing about the decisions and actions of our supervisor. Humor really helped. I stuck it out for another year and learned a lot about the value of honesty, sharing, and trust with others.

Soon, I found a new career position at a very exciting organization that had just opened. Because we were just starting the business, my coworkers and I formed a strong team and enjoyed each other. My friendships broadened, but I began to work long hours and travel. Fortunately, I had a very understanding and supportive husband who enjoyed my work friends and felt we were stronger together because I was happy and less concerned about having everything right at home. I learned I didn't have to do it all, and I let my husband help. He even started to do his own ironing! The big lesson, sharing feelings and tasks with a support system (family and friends), was a first step for me to relieve stress and achieve some balance with my career and home life.

After a few years I changed jobs and accepted a management position. We soon had a son, and that added to the equation. We had more money to spend, which helped us to hire a nanny who was a Mary Poppins–type nanny. I didn't feel guilt about leaving my son with her. I do have to admit that the first few days were tough, and I would cry all the way to work! As I think about that time, I was achieving some balance with work and family, but I had forgotten a big piece of this balance thing: I had forgotten about myself.

My self-care was horrid. I started gaining weight and had trouble sleeping at night. My husband and I decided to have a date at least twice a month in which we went out to dinner and to a movie or play. These leisure activities were great because we both enjoyed them together; they proved to be a better stress relief for me than exercise!

In a few years, I was promoted to a higher level leadership position, and I had to learn how to balance all my new responsibilities. I was tired most of the time, and the stress began to show. I was not getting the rest I needed because it was hard to go to sleep. After thinking about it and talking with my husband, we discovered the problem: After our son went to bed, my husband would read, and I would answer e-mail and voice mail and plan for the next day. All this activity was getting to my brain, and I couldn't shut down and go to sleep.

I changed my time for emails and voice mail and planning to the morning after my husband had gone to work and the nanny had arrived to care for our son. Organizing my work and home tasks and planning for the next day's activities helped me work smarter. I love crossing off things on my to-do list!

(Continued)

Story 6.5. Cont.

Our son is now in school, and with this new part of our life, we have had to learn to juggle our time to be part of his school and after-school activities. Another variable to juggle was the addition of a dog in our family!

All these new tasks took organization and planning, and sharing the driving and volunteer tasks with my husband, our nanny, and other families became vital. I soon learned that I had to leave work at certain times, and I began to let others know I couldn't stay at work or attend a meeting after 5:00. I was surprised that everyone understood and honored my commitment to my family. In fact, it was good modeling for them! I knew that someday when our son wasn't so dependent on us that I could once again feel free to stay at work, but at this time, participating in our son's life was a priority for both my husband and me.

I started thinking about my weight and our diet and decided that one thing I could do was to stop the fast-food binge and instead bring home prepared foods and salads from Whole Foods. I tried the exercise bit, but I hated it, stopped, and decided to take a walk during the day at work or walk the dog in the evening.

I still had to deal with all the work tasks I had and how to get them all done. I had been a good multitasker and usually could do many things at once, but I found that my multitasking skills weren't working because I had too much on my plate.

When there was a project to be done or my boss asked me to do something, I just said "yes" and put it on list of responsibilities. Someone asked me if everything I did at work was necessary. He said that if you have more than 3 priorities, then you have no priorities, and you just spin your wheels trying to accomplish it all.

So I made a list of all the things I was trying to do in my job and talked with my boss to have him review the list and let me know what were his priorities for me to accomplish. Just admitting to him that I couldn't do it all was a relief. He was very pleased to have the conversation, and together we determined what needed to be done, what could be assigned to others, and what could be dropped or delayed. Our conversation led to me assigning projects and tasks to other people to carry out. This was a great learning experience for me, because bringing others into our day-to-day responsibilities actually empowered them. They knew I trusted them, and I was pleased with the increased engagement with our organization that I saw in them.

Currently, one of my direct reports has resigned, and another is out on an extended medical leave. Our son has turned into quite an athlete, and his activities have increased with some requiring travel. So things are out of whack once again, and talking about creating an occupational balance at this particular time feels a bit ironic!

I just need to remind myself that this is temporary, and I need to keep control over my work tasks and balance it with some leisure and self-care activities. I keep telling myself that this too will pass, and I will survive.

Preparing this story has been good for me, as it has given me the opportunity to learn from my past experiences. I don't even feel guilty about being out of balance because I know that I can achieve it in the near future. In fact, I even feel relaxed about it all.

The key points I want to share about achieving occupational balance include

★ Talk to yourself to discover what *occupational balance* means to you. It is a personal thing.

★ Everyone is different, and balancing your activities and tasks is different at different times in your life.

(Continued)

Story 6.5. Cont.

★ Occupational balance in your life is about your expectations, not someone else's.

★ Build a support system at home and at work.

★ Get help in doing some of the tasks—you don't have to do it all!

★ Use your planning and organizational skills. If multitasking is easy for you, do it as well.

★ Decide what your priorities are, what you can do, and what you can get rid of.

★ Remember yourself, what gives you enjoyment, what is important to you, and what allows you to relax.

★ Don't feel guilty about not achieving balance everyday or not doing the things others tell you to do to balance your life.

★ Laugh a lot. The power of humor to relieve stress is amazing.

★ When you have balance, your quality of life improves. As a result, you are a better leader.

Reflective Questions

1. As you read the story, did you identify with some similar experiences you have had? What did you do to move yourself to better balance?

_____

_____

_____

_____

_____

2. From all the tasks you have to do, list 3 that you believe are priorities to accomplish. What tasks could you assign to another person? What tasks could be discarded?

_____

_____

_____

_____

_____

3. From the mentor's story, what are 3 "take-aways" or valuable learning items for you?

_____

_____

_____

_____

_____

4. Who are your support systems at work and in your life after work? How do you use your support people to help you with balancing your life?

_____

_____

_____

_____

_____

References

Brainyquote.com. (n.d.). *Thomas Jefferson quotes*. Retrieved February 1, 2011, from http://www.brainyquote.com/quotes/quotes/t/thomasjeff121032.html

Getmotivation.com. (n.d.). *Favorite motivational and inspirational quotes*. Retrieved February 1, 2011, from http://getmotivation.com/favorites4.htm

Goffee, R., & Jones, G. (2005). Managing authenticity. *Harvard Business Review, 83*, 87–94.

Rath, T. (2007). *Strengths finder 2.0*. New York: Gallup Press.

Rath, T., & Conchie, B. (2009). *Strengths-based leadership*. New York: Gallup Press.

Thinkexist.com. (n.d.). *Henri Bergson quotes*. Retrieved February 1, 2011, from http://thinkexist.com/quotation/to_exist_is_to_change-to_change_is_to_mature-to/154046.html

Watts, A. (2010). *Authenticity quotes*. Retrieved February 2, 2011, from http://www.thepogostick.com/FileManager/Integro/fafe08a7-4ff0-4f29-ba5f-6fdff9cb3395.PDF

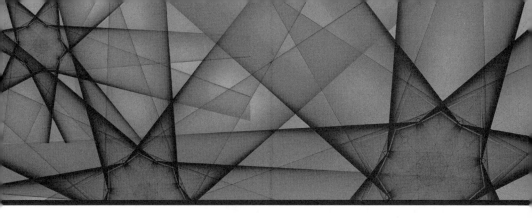

Chapter 7.
Community Building

Story 7.1. The Faculty Who Reads Together Leads Together

The greater the loyalty of a group toward the group, the greater is the motivation among the members to achieve the goals of the group, and the greater the probability that the group will achieve its goals.

— Rensis Likert (as cited in Heathfield, 2011)

Before you read this story,

1. Explore the Web site of Etienne Wenger, author and co-author of seminal books on communities of practice at www.ewenger.com. Wenger's (1998) book *Communities of Practice* is an excellent guide for community building in all types of workplaces.

This story is about community building, with a focus on building community within our faculty groups to build a community of scholars. A focus on community building is important for many reasons.

Community building is one of a leader's most critical roles. It is how you build a strong collegial group; how you recruit, retain, and develop the best faculty for your program; how you all continually learn from one another. And finally, it is a gift to yourself—a chance for you to think beyond your day-to-day operational responsibilities and to participate in and enjoy the intellectual and relationship sides of your faculty. The concept of community building can be a little abstract, so we need to make it more tangible and doable.

This story provides a positive and powerful starting point for a number of related topics: team building, reframing success and failure within the community, dealing with difficult people, conflict resolution.

The activity that I am featuring in this story is a semester-long faculty development seminar where we read 2 biographies and talked about them from an occupational science perspective. In preparing to write this story, I e-mailed the faculty and asked them some questions about our process, what they individually learned, and what they think we gained as a group from this activity.

We read these biographies about 9 years ago. The day I sent the e-mail, I heard back from every single person. To me, this says 2 things worth noting: First, this was a memorable activity—a very positive, valued, significant faculty development activity for us. Second, their quick response speaks to the strength of the community. They responded thoughtfully and quickly, built on each other's responses, disagreed on some points and self-corrected, and elaborated on the learning and impact. In short, they very effectively demonstrated the community in action.

Here's how this came about. Several years after we revamped our curriculum, Karen, a doctoral student from another university, contacted us to see if she could spend a semester doing a cognate (a concentration of coursework within a doctoral program—in this case, occupational science) with us. One of the senior faculty took the responsibility of working with Karen to develop the cognate, and as the plans were shared with us, we were all envious of what Karen would be learning. We knew that we needed to have some kind of structured way of bringing her into our community and realized that learning from and along with her would accomplish this.

Karen came up with the idea of a seminar series in which we would read biographies and talk about them from an occupational science perspective. Rather than reading to understand the person historically or psychologically, we would read to understand the person as an occupational being.

Karen selected two biographies for us to read: (1) Jill Ker Conway's (1989) autobiography *The Road From Coorain* and (2) Mikel Gilmore's (1994) family autobiography *A Shot in the Heart*. Our structure was minimal. We met about every 3 weeks for the semester. Karen let us determine the discussion topics each time and had prompting questions if we came to a point of prolonged silence or didn't have a "core" of conversation. She brought us back on course at times and summarized or pointed out the questions that remained.

(Continued)

Story 7.1. Cont.

We started with *The Road from Coorain* (Conway, 1989). It was a beautiful and inspiring story of her life journey from a sheep farm in Australia to the presidency of Smith College. Her life was rich with influences of culture and context, and profound occupational themes emerged. It was easy for us to read and begin to tease apart her occupational history and nature. The chronology of Jill's life was our structure. Initially we were guided by questions like

★ What were Jill's childhood occupations?

★ How did the environment of the sheep farm—the isolation, hard work, seasonal nature of farming—influence those occupations?

★ What were the family occupations?

★ What co-occupations did Jill share with various family members?

★ What were the family and farm rituals?

As Jill's life and story progressed we talked about how her childhood occupations were expressed as she aged, we looked at how the farm environment and culture continued to influence her. We talked about her adult relationships in terms of shared and co-occupations. We came to know Jill Ker Conway as an occupational being and, in doing so, to know and understand occupation in a more substantive and meaningful way.

Shot in the Heart (Gilmore, 1994) was completely different. We were discouraged and overwhelmed by the dysfunction of the family that produced Gary Gilmore, the first man executed in Utah when the death penalty was reinstated. We used similar questions with this book but had to struggle with a family and context that was so negative and destructive. We had to come to grips not only with the effect of occupational paucity but also with the dark side of occupation and to accept that if we were to embrace the positive aspects of occupation, we had to accept the negative.

I think it's easy to see that this type of activity can be very enjoyable and beneficial while it is occurring. But it's the longer term impact that is more telling about the community building. To get to the heart of this activity as community building, I asked the faculty two questions: (1) What did you learn individually? and (2) What did we gain as a group?

Not surprisingly, the answers overlapped. Sharing their comments adds some length to this story, but I think you'll gain insight into the nature of our community that will be helpful in understanding the concept and appreciating how a simple faculty development activity can have a profound impact.

"In the curriculum, we were already using disability narratives...so the narrative approach was in our thinking, but Karen bringing those particular books into our learning was clarifying and served as grist for what we meant by occupation/occupational science. This process helped me shift from a psychology to an occupation focus. I also I think it helped us a lot with a shift from quantitative ways of knowing to qualitative and narrative thinking."

"Personally, I think it contributed to my realizing what occupation-centered study felt like. The shift for me was from changing a focus on variables like a person's attitude, values, thoughts, and feelings to a person's life in the form of everyday activities. As a group we gained a vocabulary and a shared understanding of occupation as a way of understanding lives, including dysfunctional lives and pathological situations."

(Continued)

Story 7.1. Cont.

"I think one of the outcomes for me was affirming my interest in life stories as occupational stories, whether they were disability related or not. I like hearing people's stories, and this whole discussion gave me a new legitimacy for that, academically and clinically."

"*The Road From Coorain* represented a different way of knowing in a very literal sense in that it was presented that way from the author, as well as our way of studying it representing a different way of coming to know. *Shot in the Heart* led us to deconstruct the notion of occupation as always positive or healthy and to try and understand contexts and routines in which societally [sic] unacceptable occupations develop. The activity confirmed and affirmed our curriculum revision."

My own reaction? I loved not being in charge. This was a time when delegation really worked. I didn't have to organize, plan, and make it happen. I could participate and learn along with everyone else. I loved that we weren't as structured and driven as we often were. This was clearly different from how we usually approached work. It was fun, it was free flowing, it was learning for learning's sake. I remember that it felt a little vague, but I also remember thinking that it was okay, and I didn't step in and take charge. I let it flow, and I let Karen be the leader. Lastly, I loved that everyone took part—clinical, adjunct, and core faculty.

To sum up, this activity was relatively simple, but it had tremendous impact on our community.

★ It gave us language and a way of knowing, studying, and learning together.

★ It shifted the whole group from traditional ways of thinking that were based in other disciplines to thinking in a way that was unique to occupational science.

★ Individuals were reinforced and affirmed while the group shared common reactions and reached new ways of understanding together.

★ This was one of our most powerful community-building activities because we engaged together in an occupation. I hadn't thought of it like that until right now, but we experienced the power of the very concept we were studying, and that had a profound impact on us as an intellectually and emotionally connected community.

Reflective Questions

1. What did you learn about community from the mentor's story?

2. This was a story about using stories (i.e., autobiographies) to build cohesion in a group. Why do you think stories can be such powerful tools for community building?

3. How was the mentor a leader in this story?

4. What did you learn from this story that you can enact as a leader?

Story 7.2. Building a Community of Scholars Through Living a Shared Vision

If you want to build a ship, don't herd people together to collect wood, and don't assign them tasks and work, but rather teach them to long for the endless immensity of the sea.

— Antoine de Saint-Exupery (Leadershipnow.com, 2010)

Before you read this story,

1. Re-read Chapter 1 for an overview of Kouzes and Posner's (2007) 5 leadership practices.
2. Explore Kouzes and Posner's Web site to learn more about their available writings and resources at www.leadershipchallenge.com.
3. Read *The Leadership Challenge, 4th Edition* (Kouzes & Posner, 2007) for an in-depth understanding of this approach to leadership development.

This is a story with many layers. We'll revisit community building, but we'll also review the 5 leadership practices of Kouzes and Posner (2007) as we hear how they how they contributed to community building. We'll see, in particular, how a shared vision inspires the action of a community.

This is a faculty story about a time when we made a conscious decision as a community to gather together and work, study, socialize, and enjoy each other. I will talk about what we did, the immediate and the longer term impacts, and how I see the leadership practices contributing to the story.

The purposes of telling this story are threefold: First, this story is another example of a specific way we nurtured and enhanced our community of scholars. Second, the story provides insights into how all 5 leadership practices can be used in concert to achieve a broader goal. Finally, the story demonstrates a shared vision in action. It is a story that could only take place with a faculty who share a strong vision.

As you read the story, consider all 3 levels. What do you hear about community building? Where are examples of the leadership practices? How was the shared vision enacted, represented, or strengthened? You may want to jot down your ideas for additional reflection at the end of the story.

Retreating Into Pragmatism

Every year in June we had a retreat—a day devoted to a specific project, usually something that we hadn't been able to get to during the academic year. For example, we used this day to review our entry-level curriculum, to jump-start the planning of our doctoral program, or to develop our strategic plan. The day was always task-oriented and focused on bigger projects that needed uninterrupted time and all of the faculty's attention and contributions—pretty typical faculty retreat topics.

(Continued)

Story 7.2. Cont.

These retreats were always low-budget. In the early years, we stayed on campus and brought our own lunches. Eventually, we evolved to meeting at someone's home and sharing a potluck lunch. These days were always enjoyable and very productive, but we reached a point at which, as a community, we needed something more and different from our retreats.

One year, as we approached the end of the semester and started to talk about our annual retreat, there was a real lack of energy and enthusiasm. We couldn't agree on an agenda, not out of controversy but out of boredom.

I decided that because we were not making progress discussing this as a faculty meeting topic, perhaps a smaller group could take on planning the retreat. To make this at least palatable—and hopefully enticing—to a volunteer planning group, I gave the group carte blanche to redesign the retreat. I was comfortable doing this because I knew we were guided by a common mission and vision and shared values of collaborating, blending productivity and creativity and building on our diversity of thought and experience. Three faculty volunteered, a mix of senior and junior, tenure- and nontenure–track faculty. The group got together and started to work on a new retreat plan.

Soon, the group approached me with their first questions. Did I have any items that had to be covered that day? Were there any larger projects from the department or university that we needed to work on? I did have a short list of items that would need some discussion. In the past, we had used the retreat to actually work on this type of project, but with more planning for the coming academic year, I felt that we could use the retreat time differently. I agreed that, prior to the retreat, I would develop a comprehensive schedule for the next academic year that would include all faculty meetings, special work sessions, and faculty development seminars. With this schedule established, I thought that we could use the first hour of the retreat to talk about the work items and then make an initial decision for how we would deal with these issues over the summer and throughout the next academic year. This left the majority of the day free for the retreat planners.

The group went back to planning and next asked the faculty for their input. The questions for the faculty centered on their interest in using the retreat as time for our intellectual regeneration. Would the faculty be interested in identifying a topic, reading articles, and discussing the readings and topic? There would be no task and no expectation of an outcome or product other than our own learning and intellectual enjoyment. The response from the faculty was overwhelming—yes! Everyone loved the idea of a day devoted to exploring a topic in some depth. With that response, the next questions turned to identifying a topic and ultimately selecting the articles to read for the retreat.

Our topic was a unanimous decision: pragmatism and the environment. We had been bothered for years about how to define and develop the interrelated concepts of the human–occupation–environment relationship. We had considered adding an environmental theme to our entry-level curriculum and talked about how to develop a specific "take" on the concept as a core to our doctoral program, but we had not made much progress other than some initial reading and half-hearted attempts to meet and talk.

Using our earlier readings and discussion as a starting point, the planning group identified just 2 articles and presented to the faculty the idea of a full day's discussion of pragmatism

(Continued)

Story 7.2. Cont.

and the environment based on these articles. Again, the response was overwhelming—yes! Everyone agreed the topic and the articles would provide the kind of focused, in-depth discussion that we could all invest in, enjoy, and benefit from.

The group continued planning the logistics of the day. We'd meet at Melinda's home, a great place out in the country, and faculty signed up to bring either breakfast or lunch foods. The planners also decided we would have a post-retreat cookout with our staff and everyone's families joining us. A week before the retreat, the planning group made copies of the 2 articles for each faculty member and distributed them. They planned a very open agenda; other than the first hour for announcements and work planning for the next year, we did not have a timeline, goals, or expectations. The planners decided we would need a facilitator and a recorder and would establish those roles and some rules for the day the morning of the retreat.

The day of the retreat was absolutely beautiful. We spent the morning out on Melinda's porch sitting in rocking chairs, sipping coffee, eating breakfast, and talking. Our rules for the day were simple: Everyone, including the facilitator and recorder, could actively participate in the discussion. Our formal roles were suspended; we would make every attempt to disregard seniority, rank, and formal positions. Everyone was an equal—a scholar interested in the topic of pragmatism. I took on the role of facilitator, and another faculty served as recorder. When I was involved in the discussion, another faculty member would casually assume the facilitator role.

The day was memorable for us. We had time to really think, talk, toss out ideas, and reframe them all without time or performance pressures. We talked, ate, talked, ate, talked… and once our families and staff joined us, we tried to stop talking about pragmatism and the environment and just enjoy the evening. We played killer bocce ball, drank and ate, talked. It was a great end to a great day.

The "retreat when we just talked" became one of those events that we all would refer to, acknowledging how refreshing it was, how this is what we expected academia to be like, how inspired we were to continue to explore the concepts of pragmatism. Short term, our energy was restored after the academic year. We felt ready to start our summer's work and prepare for the next year without feeling bogged down with a lot of task details and follow-up from a working retreat. We still had the work to do, but we had a manageable schedule for getting it done and the energy to start working.

Longer term, there were several key results. This discussion deepened our understanding of the connections between pragmatism and occupational science and therapy, helped us identify the common ways we all looked at the human–occupation–environment, and have shared terminology. We were then able to go back and look at the doctoral program proposal and present a cohesive set of concepts that focused the core seminars of the program. Most significantly, 6 months later we successfully recruited and hired the author of one of the articles we had read at the retreat. Our in-depth exploration of the writing convinced us that this was someone who would substantially add to our intellectual community.

I've loved revisiting this day. I'm remembering all the good feelings that surrounded the day—our intellectual satisfaction, our enjoyment of each other. As a leader, I have some distinct memories. I was pleased at the initial response to my suggestion that a small group of

(Continued)

faculty take on the planning role; it was good to delegate so successfully. Although it seemed a very open-ended delegation, this was a mature group with a long history of working together, and I knew the planning group could work with such open delegation. I was very proud of the work the planning group did. Its approach of independently planning yet checking with key people at the right times was indicative of how well they knew our group.

I know that this day was a reward for my good leadership. In some ways it seemed effort-less—the community did all of the work. Yet I know that our ability to do this work was a result of years of my attention and effort as the leader.

This was a story that was a pleasure to recall and tell. It embodies the true joy of leader-ship. As a summary of what I've learned from the story, I'd like to look back at the story through the lens of the 5 leadership practices (Kouzes & Posner, 2007). For each of the practices, I've selected one thing that I see as representative of the practice.

1. Inspiring a shared vision

Inspiring a shared vision was the essential first step. My comfort in giving the planning group carte blanche was based in my confidence that we already had a shared vision, and any plan they made would be in line with that vision. In the end, our discussion-oriented retreat strengthened and furthered the vision by enhancing the scholarly base.

2. Challenging the process

With the security of that shared vision, it was relatively easy to suspend the old way of doing the retreat and be comfortable knowing that not only would the routine work get done but that having a new type of retreat would energize and reward us.

3. Enabling others to act

The most obvious action here is having the faculty plan the retreat. I honored my initial statement that the group had carte blanche and trusted their decisions and plans. The plan-ning group clearly felt empowered to take on the retreat and was reinforced at every step by me and by their colleagues.

4. Modeling the way

Two things come to mind here: (1) valuing teamwork and (2) valuing our intellectual lives. These values were at the heart of my decision to delegate the retreat to a faculty planning group and to totally support the plan they developed. It was important for me as the leader to act on the value that our work was not just a series of tasks but had to be an intellectually based process.

5. Encouraging the heart

The whole day was a gift to ourselves—time devoted to one topic, the luxury of in-depth dis-cussion, good food, and fun. It was a way of acknowledging our hard work and enjoying our community. The fact that it was an idea generated from within the community heightened the authenticity and the impact.

Reflective Questions

1. What did you learn about community building from this story?

_____

_____

_____

_____

_____

2. How was the shared vision of the group enacted, represented, or strengthened?

_____

_____

_____

_____

_____

3. How did you see the leadership practices carried out?

_____

_____

_____

_____

_____

4. What community-building activities could you propose in your workplace?

_____

_____

_____

_____

_____

Story 7.3. Research and Leadership

Commitment, by its nature, frees us from ourselves and, while it stands us in opposition to some, it joins us with others similarly committed. Commitment moves us from the mirror trap of the self absorbed with the self to the freedom of a community of shared values.

— Michael Lewis (Values.com, n.d.)

Before you read this story,

1. Don't discount this story because it's about research if you are not a researcher or not in a position in which research is part of the organization's mission. Think about any complex task that you face in your setting, such as developing new clinical programs or services, and consider that challenge as you read the story.

The past few weeks I've been thinking about the role that leadership plays in developing a research program in an academic department. It's a topic that has generated lots of questions for me throughout the years I was a program director, particularly in my early years in that role. I am not a researcher; my areas of expertise have been teaching and leadership.

Early on, I struggled with how a nonresearcher could lead and develop a faculty in a research university. Along the way, I realized that leadership was the essential ingredient in building a cohesive research program that allowed individual research interests to develop while also creating a community that valued all research efforts and worked to identify and build interrelated research programs. My story describes how our program grew to become that kind of research community, including how my leadership influenced and directed that growth.

Our university has a strong research emphasis in our mission; some would say at times and in some parts of the university, it is *the* mission. The current reality is that no academic program can survive without strong researchers whose research expertise is recognized within their fields, whose publications are evaluated as making critical contributions to the profession's knowledge base, and whose research programs are supported by external funding.

During the years I was at the university, the emphasis on the research mission intensified along with the impact of that emphasis on every key area in our program: the financial health; hiring, promotion, and tenure decisions; and curriculum design—in short, the overall health of the program.

Today, I would describe the research program as surviving, perhaps thriving, in the university climate. There are some external indicators that support my evaluation. There are 2 streams of funded research in the program, with each stream led by a primary researcher and involving other faculty from the program and other disciplines in some capacity. Each stream is interdisciplinary with a clearly defined, primary occupational therapy/science focus.

In addition to the university-funded faculty and staff positions, there are about 15 additional full- or part-time employees in the funded research programs. The funded grant programs fully or partially support about half of the faculty, significantly decreasing reliance on university funding. Most importantly, the research mission developed simultaneously with the teaching mission so that the missions interrelate and, to a great extent, we avoided creating

(Continued)

Story 7.3. Cont.

a 2-tier faculty with class distinctions between teachers and researchers. It's the integration of the teaching, research, and clinical missions that infuse scholarship into our curricula, uniting the educational programs and creating a unified community of scholars within the faculty.

This was not easy work. As the leader, most of the challenges centered around managing 3 areas of tension:

1. The needs of an individual faculty member vs. the needs of the whole group,
2. The research expectations of the university vs. the state of research in our profession, and
3. The narrow focus and intensity required of a researcher vs. the interactive and broader nature of teaching entry-level professional students.

As the program developed as a research entity, we dealt with these same tensions over and over. The goal became not to resolve the tensions but to use them as both indicators of where we were as a research community and as drivers of change in our development. I'm going to talk about 3 phases of our development as a research community and how the tensions were both status indicators and change drivers.

Phase I. One Size Fits All

In this phase we believed that every faculty member should be on the tenure track conducting an independent research program. We weren't concerned about fundable research but simply investigating areas of interest to the faculty member, publishing articles, and getting tenured. Our curriculum reflected that belief with every student completing an independent thesis.

During this phase, I first introduced the idea of a unified research agenda within the division, an idea that was well received by the faculty because everyone was feeling the stress of trying to manage their own research programs while serving as thesis advisers to as many as 5 different individual students' research projects. Although we weren't really clear on what we meant by a "unified research agenda" or what it would look like or do for us, identifying and integrating the commonalities across our research interests seemed a doable first step that might somehow decrease the burden and increase our productivity.

We met for a special meeting to talk about everyone's research and to identify the common threads. I facilitated and remember standing at the board, taking notes and trying to pull everything together into some kind of representational model. We ended up with something that looked like an umbrella, with each faculty's ideas and projects written on one of the tips. We decided very simplistically that the unifying concept was occupational therapy and left the session feeling frustrated by our inability to create a more sophisticated and helpful model.

As time went by in this phase, we had a number of realizations related to the 3 areas of tension. First, we had to put individual faculty development at the forefront. Forcing a group identity before individual faculty research was sufficiently developed would jeopardize the faculty member's tenure review and career at the university, and our resulting group identity would be artificial and watered down.

Although we held onto the ideal of a unified agenda, I said yes to every faculty member's request for time and resources to independently develop their research agenda. For example, I gave Linda, one faculty member, release time to work clinically and allowed her keep the

(Continued)

Story 7.3. Cont.

income generated from that activity in order to pay for small research projects and books and software needed for her research.

Second, we had to find a way for faculty to meet the university's expectations for sophisticated funded research. This translated into interdisciplinary research, something not really valued in our profession at the time because the prevailing belief was that we needed to strengthen our knowledge base within the field by conducting single-discipline research. However, single-discipline research is rarely fundable, and we had to move into interdisciplinary and collaborative models. Linda used her small individual research projects as an entrée into meeting faculty in other disciplines and developed a collaborative relationship with a faculty member in another school that led to shared projects and publications.

Ultimately, this established the expectation that our faculty would seek out interdisciplinary collaborations and work on larger funded projects as a means of building their research skills and credentials.

Finally, we realized that, with a small faculty of 4 to 5 members, all of us needed to be in the classroom and advising students, but our thesis requirement was counterproductive to faculty research development and productivity. Too much time was spent advising student-selected topics that might not relate to a faculty member's research program, and it was neither necessary nor feasible to educate our students to be independent researchers at the entry level. We redesigned our student research requirement to reflect our growing understanding of collaborative research by creating student research teams and allowing the teams to select a faculty member as an adviser with the understanding that the team and adviser would develop the research question and project. This more closely aligned the research advising process with the faculty's research program and cut the research advising load by a third.

Phase II. Collaboration Evolves

During this phase, we further developed our understanding of and commitment to a collaborative research model. As faculty were hired, we identified existing research groups and projects within the university that fit with faculty members' research interests. The faculty member then had the responsibility for building the relationships and meshing their research with the team's work.

In some instances, this lead to very successful long-term collaborations; in others, our faculty member was never fully incorporated into the team, and we gradually learned when and how to pull out of collaboration that wasn't meeting the individual faculty member's needs.

Jennifer is a great example of a successful collaboration. She came into her faculty position having been at a clinical research program for a year where she had the opportunity to become part of an interdisciplinary research team. She used the results of that work and the relationships she had established to extend her involvement into other interdisciplinary research teams across the university that were investigating the same topic. Her work as a member of several of these interdisciplinary research teams led to submitting her own proposals and ultimately to getting funded projects where she was the principal investigator and leader of the interdisciplinary research team. We didn't actively pursue the idea of a coordinated research agenda for all faculty during this phase, but the work we did during this time to

(Continued)

Story 7.3. Cont.

base our identity in occupational science meant that existing faculty and new hires all had a shared view of the discipline and the profession that was infused into our curriculum and into faculty research programs.

In this phase, as in the first, the 3 areas of tension influenced our attitudes and actions. I realized that investing program resources in individual faculty research programs was essential not only for that one faculty member but for the long-term benefit of the program and the rest of the faculty. Jennifer came to me with an RFP for a project that would fund salaries for research assistants and some supply costs for the project but would not fund either her salary or pay for lab space.

I decided that we would reduce her teaching and advising load to free up her time to devote to the project, even though this meant asking other faculty to pick up additional responsibilities. I also requested and received additional space for her lab and used program money to supplement the costs of up-fitting the lab. These were transparent decisions to the entire faculty as were the decisions to devote support staff time and further reduce Jennifer's program responsibilities when she wrote her first large external grant based on the results of that initial, partially funded project.

Equally transparent was the use of the funds generated from the external grant and all future funded research. It was clear to all faculty that this money was paying for things that benefitted everyone, such as adjunct faculty to pick up teaching and advising activities and money for faculty travel and development.

During this time, we moved away from the model that faculty owned all revenue they generated through research or clinical activities; instead, I negotiated with each faculty member an amount of funds they could access for their own use, and the remainder became part of the program budget. By the end of this phase, there was much closer alignment between the university's expectations for research productivity and the state of research in our profession. However, we were experiencing a variation in the tension in that, increasingly, our faculty research was qualitative in nature, a methodology relatively unknown and, therefore, not always accepted in the school where tenure and promotion decisions were made.

Changes in our student research requirement reflect the third area of tension as, for the first time, we limited faculty who would serve as research advisers to only doctoral faculty with active research programs. This meant that student research teams were still given a choice of advisers, but the questions to be studied were derived by the faculty member and very clearly related to and complemented their own research programs. Although we made progress in individual research programs during this phase and covert progress on a unified research identity, we were also at much greater risk of dividing our community into the elite research tier who generated revenue and had limited contact with the students and the worker-bee tier who did the bulk of classroom teaching, advising, and program administrative activities.

Phase III. Unity Through Diversity

This phase is characterized by our learning through the tensions and our evolution as a community of scholars, not just researchers. As we entered this phase, we recognized the divisive risk we were facing of becoming a 2-tiered faculty. We started to see that our program and our

(Continued)

Story 7.3. Cont.

profession needed a variety of scholarly contributions. We needed externally funded research but also needed to be able to value and support research that was not fundable and scholarly contributions to teaching and clinical practice that may not be research based.

Although we continued to recruit and hire faculty with the potential to become externally funded researchers, we admitted that the program could not survive if everyone was that type of researcher. We needed diversity. Simultaneously, there were positive changes within the school that supported this conclusion when the school revamped the tenure and nontenure tracks, declaring them equal and doing away with the adjectives in front of someone's rank that denoted the track they were on.

At our university, a professor is a professor regardless if they are on a tenure, clinical, or research track. The primary distinguishing expectation of the tenure track is a program of externally funded research; all of the tracks have equivalent expectations for scholarship, disseminating information, and peer review. In our program, most, but not all, of the faculty teach or advise students in the master's program, some teach and advise in both the master's and doctoral programs, and a few only teach and advise in the doctoral program. We do our best to keep communication open and not to create special exclusionary groups. For example, when we started the doctoral program, all faculty met to review and approve the doctoral student handbook as everyone's feedback was needed, and it was important as we added the program that all faculty had a degree of understanding of the program and felt ownership of it.

Our enactment of collaborative research extended to collaboration within the faculty, blending individuals' research skills and programs. Bridget is a co-investigator on one of Julie's research programs; Ellen is a co-investigator on Jeff's grant. Master's and doctoral students are employed as research assistants in both programs, and other faculty provide clinical services to the grants. As we progressed into this phase, I realized that saying yes to all faculty requests was no longer necessary or appropriate. In fact, it could be detrimental. I had to tell Lindsey that she could not be involved gratis in a department project because it was not likely to evolve further and would drain our resources. I had to limit another faculty member's request to work off-campus because that absence was taking away from our whole community's work and time together.

We tweaked our master's students' research requirement once again, retaining the research teams and the assignment to a faculty member's research program but further structuring the process and projects and limiting the choice of adviser as we added the doctoral program to the division. This area of tension will continue to evolve as we have added the doctoral program without adding faculty and must continue to balance teaching responsibility and other interests, now across both programs.

Funded research programs have added to the financial health of the program, but during this phase it was necessary to make transparent that our core state funding, the money that helped establish the research initiatives, was, in fact, money generated through the teaching mission. In addition, we added a supplemental professional school tuition that increased program revenues, again from the teaching mission. This transparency around funding keeps a balance of power within the program that is critical.

(Continued)

Story 7.3. Cont.

We did something one semester that, as it unfolded, took me back to that meeting during our early days when we struggled to create a unified research program. In the planning stages of the doctoral program, we spent weeks of faculty development time hearing presentations of everyone's work and, through discussion, building and clarifying the philosophical base of the doctoral program. There were 2 of us there who had been part of that early meeting, and both of us grasped the significance of this work. We didn't have to create an artificial structure and force everyone's work into it. Although each body of work was unique to the faculty member, it was also apparent that each work also addressed an ecological component, and we all viewed occupation as naturally emanating and evolving from human–environment interaction.

That day, I saw that we had finally reached a level of maturity as a community of scholars, recognizing the need for and value of various types of research; seeing the essential relationship among the research, teaching, and clinical missions; and working with the inevitable tensions.

Here are a few insights specific to leadership:

★ As a leader, I repeatedly called on 2 of our leadership practices—inspiring a shared vision and enabling others to act—to help the group productively use the tensions and move forward as a community.

★ I learned that sometimes inspiring a shared vision is long-term allegiance to an ideal and not necessarily driving the group to immediate action.

★ I understand that sometimes I have to choose between enabling individuals to act vs. enabling the group to move ahead, but unless I have the overall health of the group in mind at all times, both individuals and the group ultimately will suffer.

★ I learned to live with—actually to *value*—certain tensions. The 3 I focused on cannot, and do not need to, be resolved and are important indicators of a group's status and drivers of important change.

Reflective Questions

1. The mentor describes 3 phases of developing a unified research program. Where do you see your program's evolution? As importantly, what is the ultimate goal?

---

2. What leadership practices did you see enacted in this story?

_____

_____

_____

_____

_____

3. What insights has the story prompted for you about a shared vision, community building, or other areas?

_____

_____

_____

_____

_____

4. Although this story was about an evolving research program, different work groups face other developmental issues. What developmental issue is your group facing, and what is your role as the leader in helping the group evolve?

_____

_____

_____

_____

_____

Story 7.4. Collaboration—The Elegant Solution

> *In the long history of human kind (and animal kind, too), those who learned to improvise and collaborate most effectively have prevailed.*
>
> —Charles Darwin

Before you read this story,

1. Write out your definition of collaboration. After you've read the story, return to the definition and see how you might want to add to it.

   _____

   _____

   _____

2. If you can find a copy of *People Skills* by Robert Bolton (1979), we recommend that you read it. The book is a great primer on communication, and Bolton provides many insights into collaboration.

My last story was about how, over time, we developed a unified research program. As I re-read the story, I realized that it was a story about collaboration. Too often we view research as the singular activity of the researcher and fail to see the multiple levels of collaboration that must be in place in order for an individual researcher to be successful. When you add the expectation of creating a research program that unifies a department, collaboration becomes both the solidifying base and the energizing impetus for the development of such a program.

In talking about this with my mentor, we came to realize that true collaboration is at the base of all development activities, not only for research programs but for curriculum and community development as well. Facilitating collaboration is another important leadership skill that is definitely story-worthy. So with this story we'll take a walk though some of my experiences in collaboration.

My story starts with a little book review. When I was a graduate student I took a great course in human resource management, taught by one of my favorite professors. When Bill assigned us the book *People Skills* by Robert Bolton (1979), my initial reaction was disbelief that my esteemed professor would ask us to read a pop psychology book on communication. As I read the book, though, I quickly understood his reason for requiring it. Over the years, this little paperback has been my go-to source when I needed a refresher in any communication area: listening, being assertive, problem solving—and collaborating. I'm going to start my story with how I have learned to view collaboration, thanks to Bolton.

First of all, Bolton says we can collaborate only when emotional and values conflicts have already been sorted out and resolved. The focus can then be on needs, those substantive issues where there are differing needs or different methods of addressing needs.

Bolton then distinguishes collaboration from compromise: *Compromise* is a state of mutual concession where everybody is acutely aware of what they gave up; *collaboration* is a state of generating a novel solution that meets all needs and produces commitment to a

(Continued)

Story 7.4. Cont.

new way of doing things. This is "the elegant solution"—the new, better, unique approach that brings out everyone's best ideas and blends the best into a solution or programs that no one person could have created on their own (Bolton, 1979).

Bolton has a 6-step collaboration process that is pretty much a basic planning process, except for the first 2 very important steps: (1) define the situation in terms of needs and not solutions, and (2) brainstorm possible solutions (Bolton, 1979). His remaining steps describe a basic process of evaluating possible solutions, selecting one and defining a timeline and action plan, and ultimately evaluating the results.

To me, what has been most important as base for collaboration is first of all the pre-collaboration process of clearing the emotional and values conflicts, followed by Bolton's first steps: (1) being very clear about the needs to be addressed and (2) not confusing solutions with needs and allowing plenty of time for the creative process of solution generation to fully evolve.

From Bolton I learned that collaboration produces an integrative solution and gains commitment, but it's not a linear approach with clear answers quickly emerging. Collaboration is a messy process that takes time and energy, but as a friend of mine says, "Out of ambiguity comes clarity … eventually." When I think about it, true collaboration really isn't feasible or necessary all the time. It's a labor- and a time-intensive approach to be brought out to deal with our most complicated challenges.

Building an integrated research program, developing a new clinical program, redesigning a curriculum—these are among the complex challenges we face as leaders that deserve the elegant solution. I've already talked about collaboration as it relates to building a cohesive research program, so this story will deal with the challenges of curriculum development.

For many years, our model of curriculum development was cooperative. Each year we had an annual retreat where we reviewed all of the courses, and often we would have work sessions before the semester began and after it was over to review courses and make changes in course content, assignments, and cross-course connections.

Often we would end up negotiating these changes. If Carol would add more content on clinical reasoning in the fall, then Becky could decrease that content in the spring and add more on treatment planning; if we added a 1-hour course in geriatrics that Julie wanted, then we would cut back content on older adults in Beth's human development course and add more on children. This worked, but we all knew that we were responding to bits and pieces of feedback from the status quo rather than taking charge with a systematic and thoughtful approach that would move us beyond practice "as is" to practice that "could be."

What finally moved us into collaboration was simply talking to each other. We have always been a faculty who shared experiences from our research, clinical work, and professional organization experiences. It eventually became apparent to us, that every one of us was identifying common needs within the profession from our varying perspectives. We saw some of our grads modeling their practice after physical therapy, others becoming jack of all trades who'd do anything and call it OT, and no grads willing to work in mental health. We saw a common lack of core identity across practice areas that frightened us. As we talked this over, we worked through those precollaboration stages of resolving emotional and values conflicts.

(Continued)

Story 7.3. Cont.

Faculty began to drop their territorial hold on a practice area and see the bigger issues of a professional practice that had lost its grounding. Faculty were no longer defensive about their areas of expertise and related courses as our discussion centered on the broader concerns about the core of practice and how that core, *occupation,* should, could, and must be reflected in every practice arena. This was the point where we decided to completely dismantle our curriculum and systematically rebuild it. There was no longer anything to negotiate. Everything was off the table.

Our rebuilding began with Bolton's (1979) first step, identifying the educational needs of the occupational therapist who would practice in the next decade. We described a therapist and a practice—roles, settings, outcomes—that didn't yet exist but that was fully supported by our knowledge of humans as occupational beings and our understanding of the external forces that can affect practice. This first step of collaboration merged visioning and environmental scanning with our existent knowledge base to allow us to write a vision statement, a mission statement, and philosophical statements that would underpin all of the rest of our decisions.

As our discussion continued about what this occupational therapist of the future needed to know, we were able to group those needs into curriculum content areas, to describe the interconnections between those areas, and to ultimately produce both written and diagrammatic representations of our curriculum model. These documents became our point of reflection and resolution as we learned that collaboration is not a linear process. More than once, we cycled back into emotional and values conflicts with arguments over specifics that were based in our original practice allegiances. In the midst of the argument, someone would stop the discussion with the reminder that we needed to look at what we said in our mission statement or curriculum model. We no longer negotiated differences away but would talk though the conflict with our common view of the future of the profession as both the starting and ending point.

For example, our physical rehab faculty came back several times to their concern that our curriculum themes didn't support instruction in anatomy, neuroanatomy, and kinesiology. Rather than jumping into solution mode and compromising by saying, "We'll add a 2-semester sequence in anatomy and neuroanatomy and give up the course on applied research," the group went back to the content areas to rework definitions and clarify the educational outcomes, creating a new, expanded conceptual base that was a more inclusive, better written guide for the development of courses—the next step.

Keep in mind that all of the work described so far was within the first of Bolton's (1979) steps: clarifying needs; building a common understanding of the situation; and creating a framework for the second step, brainstorming solutions.

Solutions for us were the courses, the teaching methods, and the assignments. Interestingly, this is where we used to start our curriculum development work and where, I think, many faculty groups do their curriculum work. But in the world of collaboration, course design is solution generation, and starting there skips over the important precollaboration work of resolving emotional and values conflicts and that first step of building a communal view of the profession and a curriculum design that responds to that communal view.

There were a few times when we were tired of step 1 and begged to jump ahead into course design. The one time I broke down and said okay, one faculty member arrived at the next meeting with an entire 2-year course sequence mapped out for us. The reaction to this

(Continued)

Story 7.3. Cont.

was an indicator of our commitment to collaboration. The group said we weren't ready, that no one person could or should take that responsibility, and we went back to work on step 1.

When we got to Bolton's (1979) step 2, solution generation was fun and fast. Everyone took their favorite content areas and designed courses that would address the outcomes of those themes. We had lots of overlap and lots of courses to consider, merge, reject, or adopt. Once again, though, we saw ourselves recycle back to some conflicts based in practice allegiances. The pediatric faculty were adamant that the core courses we were considering were not age-range inclusive and that pediatric-specific content was insufficient and out of sequence. We didn't deny this and didn't compromise, but we reconsidered how we were interpreting themes and outcomes and ended up resequencing the curriculum and expanding the focus of the core courses—an improvement across the curriculum, not just in pediatric content. The amount of time that we spent on these initial steps enabled us to very quickly work through the rest of the planning process, those logistical steps of implementing the new curriculum and ensuring that we had program evaluation in place.

This process was a true collaboration that we grew into as we learned how to collaborate and began to see the elegant solution emerge. It was exciting and reinforcing to look at a piece of our work and know that it was so much better because of the collective wisdom that went in to creating it. It was a time-consuming process, in part because we were learning how to work this way, but also because collaboration takes time. This first adventure in collaboration took 3 years of working together every Friday morning. As we grew more skilled, we became more adept at recognizing the situations that called for collaboration and could more quickly work through the early steps. It's like any other skill. The first time through is slow and a little painful, but once learned the skill is in the repertoire, it can be efficiently and effectively used.

The results are worth the time and emotional and intellectual energy invested. Leading a collaborative process allows you to bring all of our leadership practices into play simultaneously, challenging the typical process of compromise and negotiation, encouraging the heart through the resolution phases, inspiring a shared vision to build the communal understanding, modeling the way by guiding people through the steps, and empowering the group to think and act outside of the restrictive boundaries of customary thinking.

Once again, I have loved the opportunity to explore a leadership practice through my story. I have learned

★ How much I really like Robert Bolton's (1979) little book *People Skills.*

★ How important the precollaboration stages are. You can't expect a group to come up with an innovative solution if emotions are interfering or values are in conflict.

★ The importance of time spent talking about common needs and working to build the communal understanding of the situation.

★ The strength of the collective view of a situation. Alone we are at risk for short-sighted views that don't accurately represent the situation.

★ How energizing the contagious creativity is that builds from the communal understanding.

★ How much better the end result is when we collaborate rather than negotiate or compromise.

★ How all of our leadership practices are enacted and strengthened when we collaboratively lead.

Reflective Questions

1. Take a look at how you defined *collaboration* before reading the story. Has that definition changed? How?

_____

_____

_____

_____

_____

2. Describe a situation in your workplace that deserves the "elegant solution."

_____

_____

_____

_____

_____

3. What will you do as the leader to guide the group toward collaborating in that situation?

_____

_____

_____

_____

_____

4. What are some specific actions you can take to help the group through the pre-collaboration stages dealing with emotions or conflicting values?

_____

_____

_____

_____

_____

References

Bolton, R. (1979). *People skills*. Englewood Cliffs, NJ: Prentice-Hall.

Conway, J. K. (1989). *The road from Coorain*. New York: Random House.

Gilmore, M. (1994). *Shot in the heart*. New York: Doubleday.

Heathfield, S. M. (2011). *Inspirational quotes for business: Team building*. Retrieved February 2, 2011, from http://humanresources.about.com/od/inspirationalquotations/a/quotes_team.htm

Kouzes, J. M., & Posner, B. Z. (2007). *The leadership challenge* (4th ed.). San Francisco: Jossey-Bass.

Leadershipnow.com. (2010). *Quotes on vision*. Retrieved February 2, 2011, from http://www.leadershipnow.com/visionquotes.html

Values.com. (n.d.). *Commitment*. Retrieved February 2, 2011, from http://www.values.com/inspirational-quotes/3724-Commitment-By-Its-Nature-

Wenger, E. (1998). *Communities of practice: Learning, meaning, and identity*. New York: Cambridge University Press.

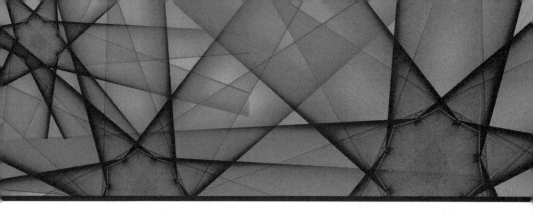

Chapter 8.
Enacting Leadership Practices

Story 8.1. Inspiring a Shared Vision—Lessons From Across My Career

> *A shared vision is not an idea. It is not even an important idea such as freedom. It is, rather, a force in people's hearts, a force of impressive power. It may be inspired by an idea, but once it goes further – if it is compelling enough to acquire the support of more than one person – then it is no longer an abstraction. It is palpable. People begin to see it as if it exists. Few, if any, forces in human affairs are as powerful as shared vision.*

> —Peter Senge (Senge, 2006, p. 192)

Before you read this story,

1. Reread Story 1.2, "Ellen Inspires a Shared Vision," in Chapter 1.
2. If you have a copy of *The Leadership Challenge, 4th Edition* (Kouzes & Posner, 2007), read the section "inspiring a shared vision," which is discussed in depth on pages 103–160.
3. Finally, another book by Kouzes and Posner (2003), *The Leadership Practices Inventory, 3rd Edition, Participants Workbook*, is a practical guide for developing each of the leadership practices.

I have a vision for everyone reading this to become the leader that is within you. I see you in 3 years or 5 years, so excited about your work and our profession. You are leading vibrant faculty or staff groups who are exemplary in teaching, research, and clinical practice; you have exciting curricula and clinical programs that are recognized as models for moving the profession ahead; and your faculty, alums, and staff present at state and national conferences and win recognition for their academic and clinical expertise. You are in a leadership position in our professional association, inspiring the people around you to think and act big. You are sought out in your own institution to lead committees and serve on critical task forces. You are self-confident, unafraid of change, and powerful. People come to you, they learn from you, they work with you, and they are inspired by you.

Now, that's my vision, but it needs to be yours—a vision you own and set out to achieve. Your vision may not exactly be that scenario but may be a closely related one that you have tailored to your unique situation and personal goals.

What I have just done is the first step in inspiring a shared vision: Talk about it with passion, with conviction. Let other people know what your vision is. Be specific, give details, paint a picture with words that someone else can begin to see. Then step back. Allow others to add details, make changes, and own the vision along with you. If we worked together, that's what we'd do. Next, sit down, incorporate your vision with mine, and create that compelling view of the leader you are going to be. That then becomes the guide for what you do and what you don't do, your source of inspiration for when you are discouraged, and your internal benchmark for how far you've come.

Before this becomes a lecture on Visioning 101, I do need to switch to story mode. But I wanted to start with that example of a little mini shared vision to give you a taste of the excitement and inspiration you can create, to give you something to think about as I tell the stories of how I have developed this leadership practice. My story this time is actually a series of short vignettes from across my career that will show how I have worked—and continue to work—on learning the leadership practice of creating a shared vision (Kouzes & Posner, 2007).

Vignette 1. If You Build It, They Will Come—Or Not

Creating the initial vision has always been fun for me. I love the process of acquiring a lot of information and sifting through it to create something new. The first time I did this was as a staff therapist in my first job. I worked in the male admissions unit of a large state psychiatric hospital. The decision was made to close the building that housed admissions and to reopen as a smaller, intensive treatment unit. The move was scheduled to take place over a week, with current patients transferred to longer-term buildings and only emergency admissions scheduled for our unit. With few treatment responsibilities, we had the time to finish packing and to also plan a new program so we could start with it when we opened the doors.

What fun! I spent the week with my 2 colleagues spinning out all kinds of ideas for new programs. By the time we opened the door to the OT clinic in the new building, we had a full schedule of new groups—and no one came. The nursing staff ignored our schedule, the patients wandered in and out but wouldn't stay, and the 3 of us spent many dejected hours alone

(Continued)

Story 8.1. Cont.

trying to figure out what had gone wrong. Now I can look back and understand: We developed our vision and tried to impose it on everyone else. We didn't share the vision, get the ideas and input of our patients or of other staff, and create the program based on the shared vision. We were visionary, but in a vacuum. The initial vision, the treatment program in this case, needed to be a catalyst that invited responses and different ideas. It wasn't the final vision, just a step along the way. Ultimately, we did figure this out and eventually and slowly created a new program and schedule—that our patients came to.

Vignette 2. This Isn't Anything New; It's the Way We've Always Done It

Fortunately, I learn from trial-and-error experience. In fact, trial and error is one of the Leadership Practices Inventory (Kouzes & Posner, 2003) three *Es* of how we learn to lead. This is another story from my clinical days. I was first a staff therapist and then the supervisor of an OT program in an acute inpatient psychiatric unit. I was actually hired because of my success in program development in my first job. The director of the OT department wanted to revamp the psych program, and a key component in successful implementation of a shared vision, the environmental support, was already there.

Over the course of 9 months, I led the OT staff in a process of program development that included a needs assessment of the patients and many meetings with nursing staff, recreation therapists, and our attending psychiatrists—all key players in a successful program.

We implemented the program, and I knew we had been successful when after 6 months of running the new programs, one of the long-term nursing assistants told me she couldn't remember a time when the OT program was any different. Clearly we had created and implemented a shared vision. I learned how to open up the vision, truly share it with others, and through that process gain support and a better vision.

I also learned that when you have success, you need to share it. We presented our program at state and national OT conferences, and the response was incredibly reinforcing. We had such recognition and a sense of shared accomplishment that invigorated and kept the group developing and implementing new ideas. The shared vision became an ongoing source of ideas and energy.

Vignette 3. Sometimes You Have to Work Very Hard Before the Vision Is Really Shared

The next story takes place during my first appointment as an academic program director. I decided, along with my program director colleague at another university, that both programs should sponsor a shared clinical educators meeting. This sounds like a no-brainer, but at that point in time, it was unheard of for our 2 schools to collaborate.

When I first presented the idea to my faculty, I did it in my typical way of describing this fabulous event with all kinds of benefits. It was not well received—just silence, and no amount of my embellishing the vision seemed to work.

(Continued)

Finally, probably to get me to shut up, the faculty agreed to go along with the idea, but it was very clear to me that we'd not reached the point of a shared vision, and it would be up to me to do a lot of work to make this event a success. So, I went into hyper-mode, talking up the event, soliciting support from our clinical educators, working through the faculty concerns, obtaining new money from my chairperson to pay for it, and doing a whole lot of the legwork to make it happen.

As the planning progressed, faculty did take part and, although not enthusiastic, they became more supportive and invested. Finally, they got excited when I announced that Ellie Gilfoyle, then president of AOTA, had agreed to come as our speaker and to spend time with both faculties before the meeting. It was a great event and one that the faculty enjoyed and felt ownership of in the end.

I learned that sharing a vision is more than a sales pitch. True ownership of the vision can take a while to achieve and can require hard work and some risk taking. I also learned not to gloat and to simply act as though everyone had always been 100% behind the idea.

Vignette 4. How Did You Get Your Faculty to Go Along With This?

Much later in my career, I was doing a presentation at a conference about the early stages of our transition to a curriculum based in occupational science. My biggest fear was getting questions about occupational science. I was terrified that I wouldn't be able to answer the questions. I finished the formal part of the presentation with time for questions. I held my breath and asked the audience if they had any questions. The first—and only—question was "How did you get your faculty to go along with this?" referring to the transition and all of the curriculum and program development that accompanied this decision.

I was stunned. I was initially relieved, and then really at a loss for what to say. I look back now and see that this question was really "How do you inspire a shared vision?" I don't remember what I said then, but I do remember how much the faculty and I talked about this after the conference.

By the time of this fourth vignette, collective action and change was a way of life for us as a faculty. I keep trying to tease apart how that happened and can offer a few thoughts on how we came to hold such a strong shared vision. I'm going to focus on my role as the leader but have to say that there were environmental factors as well as the skills and talents of many other faculty that contributed to this phenomenon.

As the leader, I was able to take the support we had within the university to innovate, along with the individual career interests and goals of faculty and the information we were all bringing to the group about environmental trends, and weave all of that together into a story about what we could do, who we could become, and what we could offer the profession. My role was to paint a clear picture of the big possibilities, to speak publicly and passionately about our greater purpose, and to solicit and honor all of the refining ideas that changed my vision into everyone's vision.

(Continued)

Story 8.1. Cont.

My initial story eventually was written as our program's vision statement. I never "got the faculty to go along with me." I captured our collective talents and aspirations into a story that everyone wanted to be a part of—a shared vision.

So, to summarize, here are some of my best lessons from my visionary mistakes and successes:

★ Visions are based on real information. Scan multiple environments, and share the information you gain. You can't be visionary in a vacuum.

★ Visions are genuine expressions of the group's values. You can't use a vision to make people do something that's not right for them.

★ Listen to other people, their values and their information. The leader plays a major role in integrating all of this into a cohesive story.

★ Have fun with the process! Be creative and expansive in your thinking, and encourage this with the group.

★ At some point, take the risk and actually spin out the vision. Be detailed and specific about what could happen. Show your enthusiasm and passion.

★ Remember that your initial vision is a catalyst, not the final vision. Step away and allow other people to shape that initial vision into one that resonates for everyone.

★ Take care of the vision. Do what you can and need to do to make it a reality.

Now, to end where we started, with a shared vision of you as a leader. You can change the future of the profession. You have wonderful ideas for how to nurture faculty and staff, how to bring ideas forward to administration and how to build supportive communities. Creating the vision of yourself as leader is your first step in inspiring the shared vision with your faculty and staff.

Reflective Questions

1. How do you now define a "shared vision?" Why is it important for a group to have a shared vision?

_____

_____

_____

_____

_____

2. Consider all 4 vignettes. What did the mentor do to create the shared vision? Make a list of the actions.

_____

_____

_____

_____

_____

3. What leadership skills do you have that support this leadership practice? What skills do you need to develop? How will you develop them?

_____

_____

_____

_____

_____

4. What is your vision of yourself as a leader in 3 years? 5 years?

_____

_____

_____

_____

_____

Story 8.2. Challenging the Process—Finding Your Voice

It takes a lot of courage to release the familiar and seemingly secure, to embrace the new. But there is no real security in what is no longer meaningful. There is more security in the adventurous and exciting, for in movement there is life, and in change there is power.

– Alan Cohen (CreatingMinds.org, n.d.)

1. Reread Story 1.1, "Anita Challenges the Process," in Chapter 1.
2. If you have a copy of *The Leadership Challenge, 4th Edition* (Kouzes & Posner, 2007), read about this leadership practice, "challenging the process," which is discussed in depth on pages 161–220.
3. Explore *The Leadership Practices Inventory, 3rd Edition—Participants Workbook* (Kouzes & Posner, 2003), which is a practical guide for developing each of the leadership practices.

When I think about the leadership practice of challenging the process, I start by thinking about the end product: the result (Kouzes & Posner, 2007). Challenging the process is a practice that creates change by challenging the status quo. The end result is always change, but the ways I can challenge the process and create change are varied.

Initially I thought that the methods associated with this practice were only overtly assertive actions. This is what the title "Challenging the Process" brings to my mind—a leader who is vocal, questioning, risk taking, and at times aggressive in his or her pursuit of change. But as I read and thought more about this belief, I realized that there are other methods that achieve the same results in a more incremental fashion. I am more likely to approach challenging the process in this second way, being focused, setting goals, pushing myself and faculty to seek out new ideas, piloting innovation, reviewing our progress, quietly fixing what's broken. I have lots of stories about this approach to challenging the process. This is my natural tendency. But the stories that have the most impact for me are about the times when I acted more assertively, took a risk, and became a better leader because I pushed myself to step out of my comfort zone.

This story focuses on my relationship with my chair at a time when an activity, in this instance an accreditation self-study, was a catalyst for overtly challenging a process. This takes place early in my career, during the first accreditation under my direction as the OT program director.

The work of producing the self-study document had gone smoothly. We had divided the standards, and each OT faculty member had several areas of primary responsibility. One of my areas was the review of the standards dealing with physical facilities. At that time, our physical facilities were abysmal—a basement lab with steam pipes overhead, noisy window air conditioners, ancient kitchen appliances, cockroach infestations, inadequate storage—the list goes on. We were embarrassed to take anyone down there and would do so only with the caveat that, despite our terrible facilities, we really were a good program.

(Continued)

Story 8.2. Cont.

When I looked at the standards, I knew that I had to be honest in my evaluation of our lab. I wrote an accurate description and identified the lab as a weakness. At our regular meetings to review progress on the self-study, I talked with the faculty about my evaluation of the facilities, and they knew and were comfortable with identifying the lab as a problem area. We all felt that trying to disguise the inadequacy of the lab on paper would only bring serious problems during the onsite visit. During this same time period, I regularly updated my chair, Stephen, on our progress, including my evaluation of the lab.

I need to insert a note about Stephen. He and I had—and still have—a wonderful relationship. We have always gotten along well, think very similarly about the future and how to get there, and enjoy each other's intellectual and social views. I was always confident of his support.

So we completed our self-study on schedule, and I sent a copy to the chair for his review and signature prior to the document going to the dean of the School of Medicine for his review and signing. I had arranged a meeting with the chair and the faculty to discuss the self-study and our key findings prior to his signing and forwarding the document.

This is a day I will not forget. It was December 21, 10 days before we had to send the document to the accrediting agency. Stephen walked into the conference room, sat down, and said, "You cannot send this document to the dean or to the accrediting agency. I cannot support your evaluation of the physical facilities. You have got to change this."

My first reaction was that he was joking. We had regularly met throughout the fall, and I thought he was in agreement with me on what type of facility evaluation I was going to send forward. When I realized that he was serious, I was stunned. I remember sitting there and thinking, "Okay, you have a choice. You can acquiesce and write something that glosses over the problem, or you can do the right thing and stand up for what you believe in and what the faculty expects of you."

My natural tendency was to do the rewrite and to try to do it in a way that was still accurate but softer. But I couldn't do it. I felt that I had to be assertive, that I had to take the risk and challenge Stephen. So I did. I said I would not change the document and that I wanted it to go forward to the dean and the accrediting agency as it was.

There was silence and there was tension, but Stephen did agree to this. He clearly let me know he did not think it was a good idea, but I believe that our relationship was so strong that he was willing to let me make this decision. He signed the self-study and forwarded it to the dean, warning me that there would be consequences when the dean saw and reacted to the evaluation. The self-study went to the dean over the Christmas holiday.

On that day and over the next few days, I enjoyed the empowered feeling that I had stood up for my beliefs and actively challenged the process, but I did so with the terrible anxiety of one who does not usually act this way. I was sustained and supported by the faculty reaction—they saw me as their leader! They had agreed on the facility evaluation; had witnessed the actual challenge; and felt proud that I had stood up for myself, them, and the program. It was one of those times when I strongly felt my leadership, and I still get that rush of satisfaction and pride in my action.

I came in the day after Christmas to find out that the dean had signed the document without any question or comment. It was in my office ready to be sent to the accrediting agency. The docu-

(Continued)

ment was sent, and the onsite visit occurred. The onsite team acknowledged how bad our facilities were, appreciated our candor in the self-evaluation, and did not cite us. They felt that although our facilities were terrible, they did not affect the quality of the education. We had strong evidence of our student's high levels of academic and fieldwork performance. They also felt that a brick-and-mortar issue was beyond our ability to change within the cycle of correcting a deficiency but that by us acknowledging the situation, we had, in fact, started the process of dealing with the problem.

A month after we received the final written report, I got a call from the associate dean of the school. He congratulated us on a positive accreditation review and asked to come over and tour our lab. I let Stephen know about the call, and he and I both met with the associate dean and toured him around the lab. After the tour I got the news that the school was paying to remodel the teaching lab—a new kitchen, appliances, counters, cabinets, new storage cabinets in the main lab, new table, chairs, air conditioners, paint—everything.

I think you can imagine how it felt to tell the faculty about this. As wonderful as it was to get the lab remodeled, though, the best thing for me was the realization that I had been and would continue to be that assertive leader who actively challenged the status quo. I knew that this was a skill I had added to my leadership repertoire.

Reflecting on this story has reinforced my understanding that this leadership practice is about pushing toward excellence, making sure that the work that is done is the right work. This is about being focused on the mission, vision, and goals of an organization and ensuring that your work and the work of your faculty will move the organization forward in the right direction. But it is also about acting on what you believe in and making sure that there's alignment between your beliefs and actions and the goals and activities of the organization.

In writing this story, I came to understand that I was able to be assertive in this situation because I was standing up for my beliefs and acting in a way that was in line with my own values and goals and also with the values and goals of the faculty and the university. These experiences were instrumental in building my confidence as well as my skill repertoire. I know that I don't have to actively challenge all of the processes all of the time. I need to know when and how to challenge the process and to select the best way so that I have congruence between my personal and organizational beliefs, values, and goals.

To summarize, I learned that

★ Risk taking is anxiety producing but that the anxiety is lessened when my conviction is strong and the support is there.

★ Knowing my values gives me voice. I never lost sight of the importance of honesty, confidentiality, and trust.

★ Acting on my values gave me the courage to do the right thing.

★ Doing the right things means acting on my own values but also considering all of the other elements to the situation.

★ It's sometimes hard to know what the right thing is, but if I listen to my inner voice and seek out the counsel of others involved, the right thing to do will be apparent.

★ The bottom line is that my values gave me the courage and voice to act with integrity.

★ I learned that using this leadership practice isn't about constantly challenging and questioning; it's about standing up at the right time in the right way for the right issues.

Mentoring Leaders: The Power of Storytelling for Building Leadership in Health Care and Education

Reflective Questions

1. Why does a leader need to challenge the process?

_____

_____

_____

_____

_____

2. Challenging, being assertive, and taking a risk are some of the most difficult actions for many leaders. How do you see yourself in relation to this practice? What are your skills and strengths, and what are your fears and weaknesses?

_____

_____

_____

_____

_____

3. What have you taken away from the story that will help you use your strengths, deal with your fears, and develop new skills?

_____

_____

_____

_____

_____

4. Consider a situation in which you needed to challenge the process. Think about how you felt, what you did, and the outcome. Having read this story, what would you have done differently? What would you have done the same? How do you feel about the situation now?

_____

_____

_____

_____

_____

Story 8.3. Modeling the Way—From Philosophy to Action

> *If your actions inspire others to dream more, learn more,*
> *do more and become more, you are a leader.*

—John Quincy Adams (as cited in Heathfield, 2011b)

Before you read this story,

1. Reread the story on modeling the way, Story 1.4, "Jean's Values," in Chapter 1.
2. Read pages 45–54 in *The Leadership Challenge, 4th Edition* (Kouzes & Posner, 2007).
3. Examine *The Leadership Practices Inventory: Participants Workbook, 3rd Edition* (Kouzes & Posner, 2003), a practical guide for developing each of the leadership practices.

I love when I inadvertently discover something from my past that is a clear example of one of Kouzes and Posner's (2003, 2007) leadership practices. This is what happened as I started my initial work on the story on "modeling the way." I got out my copy of Kouzes and Posner (2007) and read through the section "Modeling the Way," taking notes on the various ways we can develop this practice. There are a series of related suggestions that all talk about writing out your leadership philosophy. As I read these, I remembered that that I'd actually done this and decided that I needed to find my written leadership philosophy. I found the statement I was looking for, printed it, and, as I read it, I was taken back to the time when I wrote it and then to a slightly earlier time....

In spring 2000 I was getting ready to take on the role of OT program director for a second time. Initially, I had been very enthusiastic about being the director again, but as the time grew closer I was increasingly unhappy. I really wasn't sure I wanted to be director again, and I was afraid of what I was getting into, the way my time would be spent, the problems, the stress, and the feelings of inadequacy. I knew that I could go talk with Stephen, my chair, but I also knew he was getting ready to retire and really didn't want to hear me panicking and whining. So I made myself settle down and think hard about why I wanted to take this role on again, what it meant to me to be a leader, what was important to me, how I could be positive and remain that way. I sat at my computer the afternoon of May 11, 2000, and wrote a guide for myself.

First, I made some categories like my thoughts about people and their work, the role of the leader, and developing people and programs. Then I wrote down some of my strongest values and beliefs in each category. I included statements like

★ I believe that all positions in the division are equally necessary and contribute to the overall mission of the division.
★ I believe that every person wants to do their best individually and to contribute to the greater good.
★ I think that a major component of the director's job is to encourage those individual abilities and to help access the resources for individuals to do their work.

(Continued)

Story 8.3. Cont.

★ I think the director needs to point out the greater good and help everyone to see the bigger picture to which they contribute and to create opportunities for everyone to contribute and see their contributions.

★ I think that everyone can and wants to be challenged and excited by their work. Supervising, mentoring, and developing are primary interests of mine and need to be given priority but tailored for each person.

★ I think the leader's role is to inspire and energize the division.

I also wrote a brief self-analysis of my skills and a list of the challenges I knew I would face. I was comforted by doing this. I remember feeling my anxiety start to diminish and my excitement return. Now I know what I did for myself that day: I wrote down the outline, the essence of my leadership philosophy and how my values, my beliefs, and my skills would allow me to enact those beliefs. The acts of thinking through this and writing it out gave me clarity again of who I was as a leader and provided a base for taking on the role of director with confidence and excitement.

Over the next several years, I would periodically find that document again. Sometimes I'd go looking for it when things weren't going too well. Other times, I'd just happen upon it when I was looking for something else. Every time I found it, I'd regain that sense of comfort and reinforcement of who I am and why I do what I do.

In 2002, I was preparing my portfolio for a promotion review and was being reviewed under 2 categories: teaching and leadership. I was the first associate professor in our department to be considered for promotion to professor with leadership as one of my categories. I was uneasy. I knew I looked different than the typical scholar–researcher, and at times I was terrified that I would be reviewed and denied promotion.

As first to be reviewed as a leader, I didn't have a model to follow and really had to model the way for myself and faculty who would come after me. One day, I realized that the natural starting point was to write my philosophy of leadership. Then I remembered the guide that I had written 2 years earlier and used that as the basis for writing my leadership philosophy and reflective statement for my portfolio and review.

As part of this story I want to share that statement with you.

Leadership Philosophy and Reflective Statement

Just as my teaching philosophy has guided my role as a teacher, my roles as leader and administrator are guided by my philosophy of leadership and followership. My values and beliefs as a leader have developed over a long period of time as I assumed both formal and voluntary leadership roles early in my career. As a result of taking on those early leadership positions from a somewhat uninformed and unprepared state, I learned to engage in a continuous process of self-reflection and growth. That process has led me to honor my instincts and learn from experience but to also back those instincts with formal study and formal evaluation. At this point in my life and career, I find that the introspection and study have coalesced into a working philosophy and view of myself as a leader that is not attributable to any single influence. I also find that after 25 years in leadership, it is who I am, not a separate role I assume.

(Continued)

Story 8.3. Cont.

I have identified 2 sets of skills that exist in a dynamic relationship and flow and contribute equally to the actualization of leadership. These skill sets are administrative and political. These skills exist in a reciprocal relationship with my values and beliefs of leadership and shape my identity, behavior, and actions as a leader. To further understand this reciprocal and dynamic relationship, I offer my operational definitions of leadership, administration, and politics:

★ *Leadership:* The state of inspiring the beliefs, visions, and actions of others to achieve a state of greater good individually and collectively

★ *Administration:* The process of obtaining, analyzing, organizing, and using information for decision making, planning, and action

★ *Politics:* The interactive process of environmental scanning and interpersonal relationship building to gather information and take strategic action.

Finally, I believe that this complex relationship of skills, beliefs, and actions must be based in core personal values of honesty and humility. Similar to my views about teaching, I see leadership as a powerful and influential role that must be treated and enacted with respect, care, and objectivity.

That's the end of my formal written leadership philosophy. In my portfolio, I included my guide with the introductory statement that philosophy is only relevant when it actually serves as a guide for daily action. I talked about how often I'd referred to the document during the previous months and had really come to see it as the translation of my values and beliefs into my day-to-day actions. I finished assembling my portfolio, went through the review, and was promoted. But that's not quite the end of the story.

When I was writing the story, what excited me as I read my philosophy and the guide was the idea that by sharing this I was modeling the way. Kouzes and Posner (2007) suggest that to develop this practice we write out our leadership philosophy, map the specific ways we can enact the philosophy day to day, and make that philosophy public. You've read my philosophy and a little bit of my behavioral guide, and you know that my written philosophy was made public in my review portfolio as well as in this story. Several years ago, I also included a more concise version on my Web site.

All 3 of these activities make my philosophy authentic for me—the writing, the translation to everyday behaviors, and the public sharing. I hope that my story is a model for you to write your philosophy, to enact those beliefs, and to enjoy the affirmation that comes from knowing who you are and what you believe in as a leader.

To summarize this leadership practice, I learned that

★ Although "modeling the way" seems to be about behavior and action, it's really about clarifying my philosophy and values and beliefs and using that insight to consistently guide my behavior.

(Continued)

Story 8.3. Cont.

★ All of the leadership practices are equally complex. Each appears to be initially simple, yet the more you think, you see not only the complexity of a particular practice but also how the practices integrate.

★ Self-reflection and analysis is the starting point for developing any of the leadership practices.

★ Taking the time to write out my philosophy was an important part of the process of understanding who I am as a leader and gaining clarity on what is important to me and why.

★ Publicly sharing my philosophy statement, values, and beliefs gives me 2 levels of accountability for enacting that philosophy for the (1) people I work with and (2) myself. They are equally important.

★ Sharing this with you in story form is yet another public affirmation of what I believe in and who I am as a leader.

Reflective Questions

1. At the beginning of Part II, you were asked to write your personal definition of leadership. This is a good time to refer to that definition and update it with the values and beliefs you hold that underlie that definition. In this way, your leadership definition will begin to represent and reflect your philosophy of leadership. How did your definition change?

_____

_____

_____

_____

_____

2. Why is it important to base modeling the way on your leadership philosophy?

_____

_____

_____

_____

_____

3. What can you do day to day to enact your leadership philosophy and make that philosophy public?

_____

_____

_____

_____

_____

4. In the story, the mentor modeled the way by sharing her leadership philosophy. What other applications of the practice came to mind as you read the story? How have you modeled the way?

_____

_____

_____

_____

_____

Story 8.4. My Leadership Achilles Heel—Encouraging the Heart

We should seize every opportunity to give encouragement. It is oxygen to the soul.

—George M. Adams (as cited in Morris, 2009)

Before you read this story,

1. Reread Story 1.5, "Ellen—Encouraging the Heart," in Chapter 1.
2. If you have a copy of *The Leadership Challenge, 4th Edition* (Kouzes & Posner, 2007), read the section on encouraging the heart (pp. 279–336).
3. Explore *The Leadership Practices Inventory: Participants' Workbook, 3rd Edition* (Kouzes & Posner, 2003), which is a practical guide for developing each of the leadership practices.

This has been a hard story for me to write. I have to start out by acknowledging this and talking a little bit about why it's been so hard. "Encouraging the heart" is not my strong suit because my expectations exceed what I actually put into practice day to day. This is the Achilles heel of my leadership practice. I can imagine so many things I could do, but I just don't do them because of no time, no energy.

A related challenge was dealing with my self-expectation that I should excel in every one of the leadership practices. I have had to come to grips with the reality that after all these years, I still harbor the notion that I should be perfect.

Finally, I realized that the shared challenge of this practice is that it is often trivialized, postponed, or overlooked. Although it is an area of ongoing development for me, certainly part of the difficulty is that this practice is not well understood overall and may not be as highly valued as some of the other leadership practices.

As I thought about all of this, I realized the crux of mentoring: to grow in our understanding of the leadership practices and then to use that understanding to realistically assess where we each excel and where we each need to continue to develop. The mentoring relationship is a learning relationship. There's not an expectation that I am perfect or that anyone else is perfect. Mentoring supports learning through self-reflection, sharing stories, and learning from each other.

Writing this story has definitely been a process of self-reflection. I'll share the process I used as well as insights I gained about myself and about the leadership practice of encouraging the heart.

I started to write this story exactly as I've approached the other stories based on the leadership practices: by reading about the practice in Kouzes and Posner (2007). I've always found inspiration in the book and been able to readily identify a situation to weave together with the learning points. That didn't happen this time. The learning points struck me as too ordinary or even silly or trivial. I was disappointed in what I read.

(Continued)

Story 8.4. Cont.

I decided to do more research. I Googled "encouraging the heart" and found a chapter by Kouzes and Posner that went into more depth by offering a framework for understanding the practice and offering many suggestions for developing the skills that underpin the practice (Kouzes & Posner, n.d.). I want to share several of the insights I gained from that chapter that shaped how I now understand this practice.

1. Encouraging the heart should be joyous, fun, and creative. I can't allow my expectation of perfection to limit my joy.
2. We each have a style of encouraging the heart that is uniquely ours. I can work on understanding and developing my own style by acknowledging and valuing what I naturally do and by pushing myself to try some new things.
3. Encouragement comes in many packages. I had a narrow definition of encouraging the heart that didn't allow me to acknowledge many of the things I do every day. I was seeing this practice as an ALL CAPS CELEBRATION. It does include that, but it's also listening to people, observing what they do, and immediately giving specific and relevant feedback and genuine thanks.
4. Encouraging the heart is based on the same values as the other leadership practices. I went back and reread my other stories and was struck by the continuity of my values across them. I suddenly realized that these very same values have guided this practice and that realization increased my understanding of the practice and my appreciation of my style and my performance.

With these insights in mind, I could identify 2 leaders who influenced me in this practice and, finally, 2 little stories of how I have put this practice into action.

Encouraging the heart has been on my mind for a long time. As I thought about the practice, I recalled an incident from my first year of work when a psychiatrist I admired and respected made the offhand comment, "As we get older, we just don't need positive feedback and encouragement any more." That comment has bothered me for years. I really thought that we shared similar values about people and their work, but I discovered a world of difference in that one comment. I vowed then to make encouragement part of my practice. From very early on I've felt the importance of this practice and a heightened expectation to act on it, which is probably why it's my Achilles heel.

I was on the AOTA Executive Board during the last year of Ann Grady's presidency. I learned many lessons from Ann during that year, particularly about encouraging the heart. Ann has a way of quietly acknowledging your contributions in both private conversations and group situations. Her comments were always carefully based on her actual knowledge of what I had done and were genuine and authentic. Ann also understood the need for the group to celebrate and enjoy each other. Two of my favorite memories are of a Board dinner at one of Ann's favorite restaurants and a very fun evening at a Capitol Steps' performance. From Ann I learned that encouraging the heart is truly a reflection of your values and that everyone has a unique repertoire of ways to encourage.

The difference between my experience with the psychiatrist and with Ann helps me to understand why encouraging the heart is so important. I clearly remember being so disillusioned with the psychiatrist and so uplifted by Ann.

(Continued)

Story 8.4. Cont.

My little stories represent times when I believe that my expectations and actions matched. I was able to be the uplifting and encouraging leader who I think is so important.

Laura

Laura's story is about encouraging the heart by personalizing recognition and celebrating together. Laura was an administrative staff member. Over the years there were some very good times when she and I were clearly partners. There were other times when Laura required my "tough love"—difficult situations when her personal problems took over and her work suffered. Sometimes the faculty was very understanding of Laura's problems; at other times their frustration with her and with me peaked. Yet, there were still more times when her work was on target and everyone was satisfied.

Throughout the years she worked with me, her goal—and mine—was for her to finish her associate's degree and move to a better job to start a career. She finally reached the point where she had only a few courses left to take and made the decision to leave her job and concentrate on finishing her degree.

By this time, we were all ready for her to move on. Although her performance ups and downs had smoothed out, there was always a little fear that she would backslide. It would have been very easy to simply take her out to lunch, give her a gift card, and say good-bye and good luck, but I wanted all of us to reconnect and celebrate her contributions and the good work she had done. I wanted to send her off to finish her degree and start a career knowing that she had been important to us.

The faculty talked about this and decided that we needed to give her a gift symbolic of our caring that would be both beautiful and practical. One of the faculty suggested a quilt, and she and I worked together to make Laura a quilt. We purchased beautiful fabrics and in less than 2 weeks had crafted a wonderful quilt. In the border we included Laura's favorite inspirational quote and every faculty member's signature. The quilt made an impact on everyone. It was a symbol of the good work Laura had done and our caring for her. Her leaving became a very personal celebration that uplifted all of us.

Maggie

Maggie's story is about encouraging the heart by paying attention, expecting the best, and believing in someone. Maggie is a graduate of our program. Although her application had some weaknesses, her essays and interview spoke to us at a heart-and-soul level.

During her first year she had a few problems, but nothing that alarmed us. In other ways, she was the star we thought she would be. She was both the formal and informal leader of her class, and her leadership was innovative and energetic. Her kindness and her natural grasp of OT made her a treasure.

Then she went out on her first fieldwork and crashed and burned. She completed the fieldwork, but she did so with a grade so low that she was academically ineligible to stay in the program. We were stunned, and she was embarrassed and angry, blaming us for not preparing her for fieldwork. She considered not petitioning for reinstatement, but finally, with encouragement, reentered the program in a part-time capacity.

(Continued)

Story 8.4. Cont.

As a part-time student, Maggie became my advisee. Maggie talked and I listened and learned about what had happened during fieldwork and why she had failed. Together we figured out what problems were social- or support-related and which were academic. We met every other week for 2 hours all year long with two goals: (1) teach her how to assess and appropriately respond to the demands of clinical situations and (2) help her to see the treasure that she was.

Throughout that whole year my theme was "You can do this. I believe in you." I realized that simply telling Maggie that she was great wasn't enough. We had done this during her first year and in doing so had overlooked some of her academic difficulties. Maggie could only believe that message if she saw it in her performance. So, I set expectations, gave her assignments, and believed that she could do the work. She did the hard work and ultimately grew to believe in herself again but with greater substance and conviction. Encouraging Maggie was an investment of my time and attention that continues to give me the greatest satisfaction. Whenever I think of her or hear from her, I have the best feeling. I know that I saw her potential and made the time to encourage not just her performance but her belief in herself.

We all have a leadership Achilles heel. It's painful to acknowledge, but doing so is a necessary part of growing into ourselves as leaders. Writing this story has been a journey. I think I understand more now about why this is my Achilles heel, but I also have a better understanding of the practice and kinder view of my performance.

One of the points that Kouzes and Posner make is that encouraging the heart includes taking care of yourself and your own needs for support. You need to be able to talk about your "grandest hopes and worst fears … your greatest achievements and biggest flops" (Kouzes & Posner, n.d.). The process of writing the story, the self-reflection, and reading have allowed me to do that and has put to rest some of my doubts. I am amazed and grateful for all I've learned.

My hope is that you'll have the same experience with your Achilles heel.

I want to end by sharing my insights about encouraging the heart.

★ Be joyous and creative. Have fun with this practice.

★ Don't be intimidated by environments or people who devalue this practice. As occupational therapists, this is a leadership practice that we are inherently good at, and we should celebrate this ability!

★ Develop your own style and repertoire for encouraging the heart. Know that it includes many different actions, activities, and approaches, and continue to explore and find the ones that work for you.

★ Encouraging the heart is another opportunity to act on your values. When you thank people, provide recognition, and celebrate in ways that reflect your values, you will be genuine and authentic.

★ Go online and look up *150 Ways to Encourage the Heart* (Kouzes & Posner, n.d.). I hope that each of you will see the many ways you already encourage the heart and find your own insights and inspiration for this practice.

★ Encouraging the heart isn't trivial; it isn't something to do only when we have the time; it's not something people grow out of needing. It's a joyous and creative aspect of leadership.

Reflective Questions

1. Make a list of specific ideas that came to you as you read the story that will shape your practice of encouraging the heart.

    _____

    _____

    _____

    _____

    _____

2. What are the ways you can encourage the heart that are consistent with your values as a leader?

    _____

    _____

    _____

    _____

    _____

3. Are you in an organization that supports encouraging the heart? If you are, how can you continue to build on this? If you are not, how can you put this practice in place with your colleagues?

    _____

    _____

    _____

    _____

    _____

4. Encouraging the heart includes taking care of yourself and your own needs for support. How have you done this? What will you do more of in the future? What will you do differently?

    _____

    _____

    _____

    _____

    _____

Story 8.5. Building a Legacy—Enabling Others to Act

To lead people, walk beside them . . . . As for the best leaders, the people do not notice their existence. The next best, the people honor and praise. The next, the people fear, and the next the people hate . . . . When the best leader's work is done, the people say, "We did it ourselves!"

—Lao-tsu (Josephson Institute, 2011)

Before you read this story,

1. Reread Story 1.3, "Lou Shannon—Enabling Others To Act" in Chapter 1.
2. If you have a copy of *The Leadership Challenge, 4th Edition* (Kouzes & Posner, 2007), read the section on enabling others to act (pp. 221–278).
3. Explore *The Leadership Practices Inventory: Participants' Workbook, 3rd Edition* (Kouzes & Posner, 2003), which is a practical guide for developing each of the leadership practices.

This has been another difficult story for me to write. As I looked through the section of the Kouzes and Posner (2007) on enabling others to act, I kept saying to myself "yes, I do this" or "yes, that was a regular part of how I approached being the program director." I saw myself and my approach to leadership in almost every specific strategy for developing this practice. The difficulty I faced was in pulling out a single event that was "story-worthy."

I suspect that many of you would have this same difficulty, because enabling others to act is a strength that many of us share. Developing the abilities of those around us is part of what brought us into the occupational therapy profession; it's integral to our identities as therapists. It's also something that I think makes OTs exceptional leaders and a practice that we should all bring to a greater level of awareness.

As I thought through my daily life as a program director, I tried to think of times when I intentionally used this practice. I came up with several situations and realized that in each instance the staff or faculty member looked like someone who didn't need assistance in taking action; each was already a highly successful employee. I realized that we are likely to overlook people like this because our attention is very often pulled to the faculty or staff member in crisis or with chronic problems. Employees with problems test us as leaders, but the individuals I have decided to focus on in this story present unique challenges when using this leadership practice because they *don't* have problems. How can we find the time and the resources to fix something that's not broken? How can we provide support, recognition, and challenges that are meaningful to high-performing individuals?

I realized that there were multiple reasons for investing in these people, such as their development, my own satisfaction, and the development of our community. As a leader, I feel good when I deal with and resolve problems, but I feel equally—maybe more—satisfied when I build on the positives that are already there.

(Continued)

Story 8.5. Cont.

Diane

We were delighted when we successfully recruited Diane, a senior-level faculty member. Although it's challenging to bring any new faculty member into a well-established group, an experienced person brings unique challenges. We hired Diane because of her experience, expertise, and confidence, and now we needed to be sure that she was genuinely welcomed into the group and that we provided legitimate opportunities for her to contribute.

In preparing for Diane's arrival, during her first year, and for the years we worked together after, I took a very intentional approach to creating experiences for and working with her, identifying and designing opportunities for her to achieve the goals she had in mind when taking her position with us. I'll share 2 strategies: (1) Diane's orientation and (2) her role as international liaison.

Orientation

With the faculty, I designed a formal orientation that had several goals. A primary one was to provide Diane with the information she needed about life at our university, from the division to the community level.

Equally important was the goal that she would begin to know and develop relationships with the faculty. To achieve this, each faculty and staff member assumed a role in Diane's orientation. The content area to be covered was specific, but how the orientation was done was up to the individual faculty or staff. This allowed each individual to share information they were comfortable with or an expert at while also giving Diane one-on-one time with everyone.

An additional concern was that although Diane knew the senior faculty through professional activities, she did not know the junior faculty. I felt it was important for the community that equally strong relationships were established with all faculty, so along with the orientation assignments, each junior faculty had an additional role. I assigned Diane 2 mentors for 6 months: (1) a research mentor and (2) a general mentor. At the same time, I assigned her to co-teach one of our core clinical courses in her second semester with a third junior faculty member.

All of these individuals were junior faculty members whom Diane did not already know and did not share research, clinical, or professional interests. I specifically wanted opportunities for Diane and the junior to faculty to get to know each other because their interests and responsibilities would not create natural opportunities to work together. The idea was that these would be mutually beneficial relationships as Diane gained information and relationships, and the junior faculty assumed new roles and shared their expertise.

When I think about this orientation, I can see how our leadership practice of enabling others to act was enacted at multiple levels. Rather than seeing the orientation of a new faculty member as my singular responsibility, I saw and designed it as a group responsibility. This highlighted each person's expertise and provided substantive ways for getting to know each other.

Having a solid information base from the beginning was certainly central to Diane's ability to quickly assume her responsibilities. By very strategically involving everyone and, particularly, the junior faculty, relationships formed more quickly with mutual knowledge of and respect for one another. Two of the relationships with junior faculty became particularly strong. Diane introduced a qualitative component into her research mentor's research program and is

(Continued)

Story 8.5. Cont.

now partially funded through one of her grants. She nominated her co-teacher for a prestigious university teaching award and continues to co-teach with her because they both enjoy the course and each other.

International Liaison

The orientation laid the groundwork at both the information and relationship levels for Diane to contribute to the group. As she gained basic comfort and familiarity with us, she and I began to consider what roles she wanted to develop or assume. I really wanted to find a way for Diane to develop as a new faculty member while still acknowledging her senior status and expertise. I want to share an example of something we developed together that specifically represents this leadership practice.

I agreed to host an international visitor, an OT who was part of a faculty group touring universities in our state to establish relationships with programs in this country. After lunch and conversation with the entire faculty, we agreed that we'd like to pursue the relationship. My only hesitation was my lack of international experience. I was concerned that I wouldn't have the time or the expertise to develop the relationship. As Diane and I talked more about this, it became obvious to both of us that this would be a perfect role for her. She would use her administrative skills, build on her international experience and interest, and be able to create a new initiative for the division.

Over a period of time we created the role of international liaison. In this role, Diane wrote a proposal for funding, and we received money for all of the faculty to travel to Europe for a week. The following year, she received funding to support our international colleagues' visit to our university.

Ultimately, Diane's role grew to include developing sabbaticals for international visiting scholars, encouraging faculty to present internationally, and providing the incentive for developing international fieldwork. This is such a good example of how enabling a person to act has resonating effects. Diane excelled in a challenging and interesting role that she enjoyed. She received recognition from the faculty, the international office, and the department. The community building for our faculty was significant because we all grew from the experience of traveling together and developing international relationships. Individual faculty and students were also supported in their international interests and projects. By enabling a faculty member to act in a role that was exciting, rewarding, and challenging, the community benefitted and others were encouraged to act as well.

In telling this story, I learned that

- ★ Enabling others to act is about understanding each individual and working with him or her to understand how he or she wants to grow and finding the just-right challenge and just-right support for that growth to occur.
- ★ This practice most definitely relates to your leadership philosophy. It's the opportunity to enact your beliefs on a day-to-day basis.
- ★ This practice also ties in with our therapist roots because it's part of our philosophy to build on someone's strengths, create environments for success, and develop the just-right challenge.

(Continued)

Story 8.5. Cont.

★ Enabling others to act really makes occupational therapy practitioners natural leaders. We need to intentionally use this practice to realize the full potential of how it can affect others. We can't take this skill for granted. Enabling others to act is an inherent part of who we are—it is our inner voice—and we need to own it.

★ A dynamic relationship exists between investing in an individual and reaping the benefits at multiple levels. The individual benefits, but so do the leader and the community. This practice is a critical aspect of community building. A resonating effect takes place when one person is empowered to act to their potential.

★ When I think back on this story, I realize that I created a human infrastructure within the division that ensured sustainable individual and group development. When you invest in others and enable them to act, you are building your legacy. This is how your strengths multiply and get passed on to new generations of leaders.

Reflective Questions

1. One way that we learn to use the practice of enabling others to act is to experience it ourselves. Identify a time in your career when you were enabled to act. Who supported you? What did you gain?

_____

_____

_____

_____

_____

2. Enabling others to act is more than delegation. How is it different?

_____

_____

_____

_____

_____

3. What are the benefits of investing in the leadership practice of enabling others to act? What are the risks?

_____

_____

_____

_____

_____

4. How can you be more intentional in your use of this practice? Be specific about people with whom you currently work.

_____

_____

_____

_____

_____

Story 8.6. Applying the 5 Practices in Faculty Performance Evaluation

An empowered organization is one in which individuals have the knowledge,
skill, desire, and opportunity to personally succeed in a way that leads
to collective organizational success.

—Stephen R. Covey (as cited in Heathfield, 2011a)

Before you read this story,

1. Reread the section, "A Framework for Leadership: The Leadership Practices" in Chapter 1 to review the 5 leadership practices of Kouzes and Posner (2007).
2. Read the previous 5 stories based on the 5 leadership practices, and work through the reflective questions to ensure that you understand how the practices can be applied.

The ability to effectively deal with challenging faculty and problem situations that have gotten out of hand is one of the most difficult tasks facing a program director. One key tool that we have available is the faculty performance evaluation. This may be one of the very few tools we have to try to effect changes in faculty behavior, especially with tenured faculty.

As I gained experience as a chair and program director, I learned how important it was to effectively use performance evaluations. When I learned about the 5 leadership practices, I realized that all of them play an important role in this process, so my story is about some of the things I've learned—sometimes the hard way.

First, I need to tell you how we do faculty performance evaluations at my university, so you understand the context in which the stories I share took place. We have no cost-of-living raises here; the raises are all merit raises. A merit pool is distributed to the dean each spring that is a certain percentage (usually around 3%) of faculty salaries in the college. The chairs then recommend the amount of merit for each faculty member in their departments and must provide a justification on the basis of the faculty performance evaluation.

The process for this evaluation has evolved over the years. There are multiple pieces to be integrated: components required by the university, components that I have put in place in OT, and the ACOTE [Accreditation Council for Occupational Therapy Education] Professional Development Plan. It starts with each faculty member completing a required university report, a just-the-facts summary of teaching assignments, number of student advisees, service responsibilities, publications, presentations, grants, involvement in special centers or programs, and so on.

The university report is generic and nonevaluative, so it is supplemented with a department form that asks the faculty member to highlight his or her meaningful contributions in each area of responsibility (e.g., creating a new module in a course, involving a group of

(Continued)

undergraduates in their research lab, taking on a leadership role in a professional group). In each area the faculty member is also asked to provide an overall self-evaluation of his or her performance in the area, including specific indicators where possible such as course evaluation ratings, student comments, or improved student outcomes. At the same time they are asked to update their ACOTE Professional Development Plan, updating the outcomes of their goals from the previous years and identifying potential goals for the upcoming year (linked to the department strategic plan).

After I get all of this material, I schedule an individual meeting with the faculty members to discuss his or her performance and review goals together. The last step is that I prepare a written chair's report, which goes to the faculty member, and an abbreviated version goes to the dean as justification for the merit recommendation. These last steps are when it gets interesting.

The first year I was in charge of this process, one my tenured faculty submitted a goal of "submit 2 research papers." This was a long-time faculty member who had consistently received high merit raises simply based on the fact that she published. However, she had only published in occupational therapy journals, so her work had limited recognition outside our professional arena, and she did not have any external funding for her research. This was not in keeping with the current strategic goals of the college, nor did it help strengthen the scholarly reputation of our department, either within the university or elsewhere.

I asked her to explain what she was planning to publish and where and, most importantly, how those choices would further her research development. We then had an interesting and valuable discussion about her need to develop a long-term research agenda, the steps involved in achieving successful funding, and publication as a means of establishing credibility. I then asked her to revise her research goals to reflect specific steps to accomplishing her research agenda.

In another program where I serve an interim leadership role, I inherited a headache—a tenured faculty member who simply refuses to get with the program. For years he complained that it was not his fault that he had not gotten a more extensively funded research program (as would be expected with his rank) because the university or department doesn't support him properly (e.g., his load is too heavy, he doesn't have his own lab). The reality was that he had had a lighter load than most faculty for years because, when given something he didn't like or want to do (e.g., help in a lab), he made such a half-hearted effort that the other faculty member refused to work with him again.

He repeated his complaints again in his self-evaluation as an explanation for why he didn't bother listing any goals related to securing funding. This faculty member needed the situation reframed for him, and the performance evaluation meeting was an ideal place to do it. In this private context, I could very directly say to him, "Get over it. Yes, it's true that expectations have changed since you were hired, but this is the way it is now. If, as you say, you want its rewards like merit raises, promotion, or release time from teaching, you're going to have to meet those expectations. It's your choice."

I felt that this conversation (and my written chair's report) was crucial to defining a different dialogue between us. He obviously knew that I was not asking more of him than I expected of myself. He knew that I wasn't going to listen to any more complaints, and he knew that the

(Continued)

Story 8.6. Cont.

"ball was now in his court." This was not a situation that I was supposed to try to remedy; he had a choice to make, and the consequences were clear.

But performance evaluation doesn't help with only "challenging" faculty. I have found them to be a wonderful context to help inspire faculty to take on new challenges or set more tempered expectations for themselves (a problem in my overachieving group). It is a great context for mentoring, as long as the discussion around goals is not just focused on the immediate value of the activity but rather on the long-term personal plan that the faculty member aspires to accomplish.

Performance evaluations provide a great context for collaborative reflection: Why was this group of students such a challenge in class this year? What might have prompted this negative feedback on your course evaluations? What might change that experience both for the faculty member and the students? Which of your faulty peers could you ask to do an observation and give your suggestions?

Performance evaluations create a context in which we can discuss what is important to keep the quality of our department and its programs high and how to align faculty's professional activities and goals with that vision. Should they serve on an AOTA committee? It would certainly help the profession, but would it also help them and the department? Which of two possible commitments is the better one to accept? How do you gracefully say no when you really need to? Is it okay to say no? If we agree you should say yes, are there supports we could provide to help you?

Performance evaluations are also a great place to encourage the heart, especially for people who do not like a lot of public attention. They have given me the opportunity to say to a faculty member, "Thanks for always having such a 'can-do' response to new curriculum initiatives. I really appreciate the support" or "You put enormous time into helping Amy improve her clinical reasoning. I know she was challenging to work with, and not everyone could have done what you did."

I cannot say that I find this process easy, especially with the challenging faculty, but I believe it is so important that I have to keep trying. And when you start using the 5 leadership practices right, it can be a powerful tool for positive faculty development.

So what about those practices? Here's how I have learned to apply them:

First, *inspire a shared vision.* I have learned that organizing the conversation around our department's vision helps keep the discussion focused on why particular goals, activities, or achievements are important. This helps clarify that, although some of the standards being applied in the performance evaluation are derived from the institution's expectations, they are uniquely tailored to help us achieve our vision.

Next, *model the way.* I know that I cannot justifiably ask my faculty to do something that I wouldn't do myself. I'm only credible to the extent that I am also pursuing goals that I share with my colleagues, reflecting openly on how well I am doing, and being realistic when there is a need to adjust or adapt to changing conditions in the institution.

Sometimes it is important to *challenge the process* to make the process work properly. For example, I really hate the format of the ACOTE Professional Development Plan. It just doesn't work well for us. On the other hand, I don't want to make faculty do *2* plans—the whole performance evaluation is complex enough as it is. So I have tried to work within the ACOTE

(Continued)

Story 8.6. Cont.

template and give guidelines to my faculty about how to complete it so that it meets ACOTE requirements but also provides the information that will be meaningful for us in our process. I also created the supplemental form to the university report because I didn't like being limited to quantitative factual information (e.g., how many articles, how many advisees) as a basis for evaluation.

The ideal outcome of a good performance evaluation process should be *enabling others to act*. Ideally, faculty perceive the goals they set as personally meaningful and they are excited to work on at least one of them. Ideally, they feel that they can continue the conversation with their program director as they work on these goals, or they have identified other supports that will facilitate getting where they want to go.

Finally, even if challenges were a major focus during the evaluation discussion, it is important for faculty to feel that the program director has *encouraged his or her heart*. I know my "headache" faculty member did not get what he wanted from me, but hopefully he did not feel berated or disrespected. And if he was listening carefully, he heard that I believe he was capable of making the necessary changes to be successful.

Reflective Questions

1. Consider one of your current employees, challenging or not. How can you re-frame his or her performance issues using the mentor's examples as a guide? If you don't currently supervise employees, use an example from the past when you gave a performance review, or use a performance review you have received.

_____

_____

_____

_____

_____

2. What are the strengths and shortcomings of your organization's approach to performance review? Can changes be made? How?

_____

_____

_____

_____

_____

Mentoring Leaders: The Power of Storytelling for Building Leadership in Health Care and Education

3. Performance reviews can be difficult interactions. How can your values help you to overcome apprehension around a potentially difficult responsibility?

_____

_____

_____

_____

_____

4. How can you develop your individual approach to performance evaluation to incorporate the 5 leadership practices?

_____

_____

_____

_____

_____

References

CreatingMinds.org. (n.d.). *Creative quotes and quotations: Courage.* Retrieved February 2, 2011, from http://creatingminds.org/quotes/courage.htm

Heathfield, S. M. (2011a). *Inspirational quotes for business and work: Empowerment and delegation.* Retrieved February 2, 2011, from http://humanresources.about.com/od/workrelationships/a/quotes_empower.htm

Heathfield, S. M. (2011b). *Inspirational quotes for business and work: Leadership.* Retrieved February 2, 2011, from http://humanresources.about.com/od/workrelationships/a/quotes_leaders.htm

Josephson Institute. (2011). *Quotations: Business and management ethics.* Retrieved February 2, 2011, from http://josephsoninstitute.org/quotes/business-management.html

Kouzes, J. M., & Posner, B. Z. (n.d.). 150 ways to encourage the heart. *Encouraging the heart: A leader's guide to rewarding and recognizing others.* Retrieved December 2, 2009, from http://media.wiley.com/product_data/excerpt/40/07879418/0787941840-1.pdf

Kouzes, J. M., & Posner, B. Z. (2003). *The Leadership Practices Inventory: Participants workbook* (3rd ed.). San Francisco: Pfeiffer.

Kouzes, J. M., & Posner, B. Z. (2007). *The leadership challenge* (4th ed.). San Francisco: Jossey-Bass.

Morris, D. H. (2009). *Encouragement: Oxygen to the soul.* Retrieved February 8, 2011, from http://ezinearticles.com/?Encouragement---Oxygen-to-the-Soul&id=2933542

Senge, P. M. (2006). *The fifth discipline: The art and practice of the learning organization* (rev. ed.). New York: Doubleday.

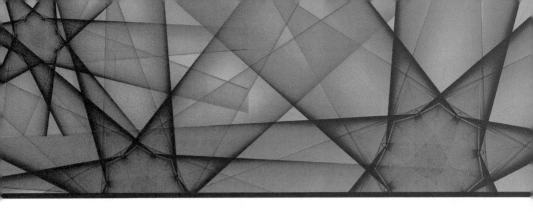

Chapter 9.
Building Followership

Story 9.1. Problem Employees—Insights and Observations, Not Solutions!

Start with good people, lay out the rules, communicate with your employees, motivate them, and reward them. If you do all of those things effectively, you can't miss.
— Lee Iacocca (as cited in Abrahams, n.d.)

Before you read this story,

1. Refer to Chapter 1, "Leadership and Communication," for the discussion on finding voice and the relationship between leadership and communication. Successfully dealing with problem employees brings together all of your communication and relationship-building skills.
2. Read *People Skills* by Robert Bolton (1979). It is a great primer on communication, and Bolton has many insights for working with difficult people.

I've been thinking a lot about difficult employees. I know that in my own experience, the employee stories that haunt me are the ones involving thorny relationships. Talking about these stories can increase our repertoire of possible actions and resolutions.

As I said, these thorny relationships haunt me. I decided to analytically approach my past and try to get a more objective understanding of how I have dealt with problem employees. I made a list of the names of all the employees who somehow qualified as difficult. I ended up with 15 names of people who ranged from mildly and occasionally troublesome to those who made a career out of being disruptive and problematic. I realized that I could easily generate a list many times longer of exceptional people I've worked with; these 15 people are definitely in the minority. They just occupied a lot more of my conscious thought and effort while I worked with them and have historically taken on more importance as a result.

This led to my first learning point:

★ I give negative situations with people far too much power. I need to practice encapsulating them, dealing with them, and not allowing these minority problem situations to assume epic proportions, neither while they are occurring, nor in my memory.

This is easy to say but hard to do. I think I need a mix of wise council from someone with whom I can confidentially discuss the situation, diversion so that I can focus on positive people and events, and thoughtful and timely action.

I then looked at my list and came up with 3 additional insights. First of all, although some of these problem employees were inherited, I was responsible for others because I had hired the person. As I thought about this, I realized that, without exception, each of these times I had actually had a nagging doubt about the person that I ignored, and I had gone ahead and hired that person anyway. I always thought I had a good reason for overriding my own reservations, but now I can see in my second learning point:

★ I need to trust my gut reactions. I have good instincts about the match between someone and the position and the rest of the group, and need to honor my instincts. I don't think that I can be right about this 100% of the time, but certainly thinking through my concerns and paying attention to little red flags is a necessity. I have plenty of examples of not making a hiring decision because I didn't think the match was right, of waiting for the right person to come along, and of hiring excellent people in the end. I need to remember those times and not be seduced into making a decision simply to fill the position.

Some of my problem situations were intensified when I followed the advice of someone with a much more aggressive approach than I would have taken. I think I did this because I was afraid of appearing too passive and reluctant to deal with a problem head on, but generally the outcome created a different problem because the aggressive action didn't match what I had been doing and seemed too severe and out of character. So my third learning point emerged:

★ I have to be comfortable with and own any action I take. When I seek out counsel, I need to process the feedback and incorporate it into my approach and style or appreciate the point of view as different from my own and discard the advice. If someone superior to me isn't comfortable with this approach, we need to discuss it and come up with a compromise before I deal with the problem employee. This is

(Continued)

Story 9.1. Cont.

particularly hard for me because I do have a tendency to avoid taking action. I need to work on being more assertive earlier on when I first see a problem, but I need to remember that I own the problem and the solution and that I am only comfortable being assertive and not aggressive.

Lastly, I realized that I confounded many of these situations by tolerating too much for too long. This caused the employee to be blissfully unaware of the existence or severity of a problem, and the problem would intensify. I would reach the end of my tolerance and patience, and this was when I was at risk for overreacting or taking someone else's advice without thinking through it. I would appear to have a completely outrageous reaction to some seemingly minor event, when I was really reacting to a series of events that had been welling up for me over a long period of time. Thus, I came to my fourth learning point:

★ Avoidance only makes a problem worse. Avoidance is when I am haunted by situations, and I need to act on my knowledge that quickly dealing with a problem means that problems are less likely to grow. If I act efficiently and thoughtfully, I will not continue to be tormented by either the problem or my lack of action. Doing so involves trusting my gut reactions and analysis of a situation, but it also involves pushing myself beyond my comfort zone to confront a problem.

Now I will tell you about 3 situations and emphasize how my insights and learning points played out each time. In this first situation, listen for at least these 2 of my learning points: the need to trust my gut reactions and the importance of using resources and advice but in a way that I own and am comfortable with any action I take.

Jill

Jill was first employed as a work-study student in the department. She was wonderful—attentive to detail, readily assumed responsibility, developed new approaches to the work, and we all personally enjoyed her. She was a great addition to our team. As graduation approached and a permanent position became available, I encouraged Jill to apply for it.

She was very excited about working for us in a permanent position and submitted her application in the weeks before graduation. Before I interviewed Jill, I went on vacation. I came back to find out that during the time I was away, Jill had disappeared for several days. She didn't come in, call, or answer repeated calls from the staff.

She showed up the day I returned, offering a convoluted explanation about an illness and family problems. She was quite apologetic and remorseful about her disappearance. The red flag was waving at me, and the nagging concerns were there. Did I pay attention? No! I went ahead interviewed and hired Jill with an informal warning that this couldn't happen again. I was confident in her ability to do the work and would overlook the problem this time.

We had about one good week after she took the position, and then the pattern of her disappearing for a few days and returning remorseful and begging forgiveness returned. Jill's behavior had such a negative impact on the entire program that I had to immediately confront the problem. She was still on probation, so I had a 3-month window in which I could terminate

(Continued)

Story 9.1. Cont.

her employment without going through a formal disciplinary procedure. I talked this over with our human resources manager and came up with an approach that I could comfortably enact.

I did not have to counsel her, but I chose to do so in an abbreviated fashion because I was not comfortable with simply terminating her without trying to first understand and resolve the problem. When it became clear that she could not work with me, I terminated her employment. I hated to do it. I liked Jill and wanted her to be successful, but I had a greater commitment to the health of my program and to good working relationships with my other staff.

Jill was a good lesson in why I need to follow my gut reactions as well as understanding that I could be supportive and work with employees to resolve problems. I could also quickly and decisively act once it was clear that developmental resolution wasn't possible. As painful as it was to deal with Jill, the pain was short lived because I acted assertively.

Joel

In this next situation, listen for at least 2 learning points: (1) quickly taking action vs. avoiding potentially difficult interactions and (2) disallowing negative people to assume too much power over me.

Joel was an inherited problem, a senior staff member in the department when I took a position as clinical director. Prior to taking the position, I'd been informed of a number of staff problems, some of which involved Joel. After taking the position, I spent a little time getting to know everyone better and gaining firsthand understanding of the problems.

I had opinions and impressions of what the problems were, but now I had to put that aside and work on acquiring an objective and current understanding of the situation. I had heard rumors of Joel's inappropriate interactions with female staff, but no formal complaints had been filed, and no action of any type had been taken. I knew that I could have no tolerance for any sexual harassment; I could not legally or personally overlook it.

After the very first complaint from a female staff member about a comment Joel had made to her, I talked with my supervisor, read through the sexual harassment resources, formulated a plan, and called Joel into my office. We had a brief conversation that focused on clarifying what he had said, instructing him about what constituted sexual harassment, and giving him a clear verbal warning that any further infraction would be handled as a formal sexual harassment charge.

I was firm and serious but not angry or disrespectful. This served as another reminder to me that quickly and decisively acting is best, and that it is possible to honor my values of treating people with respect and seeking to understand while also meeting my legal and institutional responsibilities. I did not give Joel too much power over me; I didn't have angst or worry about confronting him. I did what I needed to do. There was never another problem of this type with Joel.

Ellen

My last story is about Ellen, a coworker in a hospital department where I was first a staff member and then a supervisor. With this story, listen for these 2 points: (1) how avoidance only

(Continued)

Story 9.1. Cont.

makes a problem worse and (2) how avoidance intensifies the power that negative situations can have.

Ellen was hired as a staff member right after I was hired. We worked together for 5 years, first as coworkers and later I was her supervisor. When I first became her supervisor, I found out that Ellen's performance reviews were erratic, varying from very strong in some areas to among the lowest in the department in other areas. As I started to pay more attention, I saw that, in general, Ellen's clinical skills were excellent but her communication skills were problematic. This was the source of most of her problems as well as her inconsistent relationships with coworkers and clients. She had difficulty clearly explaining and presenting herself. In her frustration, she frequently made insensitive comments to clients and coworkers.

I really didn't want to deal with her. I was a young, inexperienced supervisor, and Ellen had been my coworker. Also, I was conflicted, because although Ellen had these problems, we all still enjoyed her sense of humor, intellect, and many contributions to the department. I now look back on this situation with more than 20 years of retrospective insight and realize that I was not decisive enough, early enough. For the most part, I tolerated, overlooked, and made excuses for Ellen. I felt a responsibility to deal with her performance issues, but I was indirect and inconsistent.

Ultimately, I did take action. I counseled Ellen on her communication skills, and she voluntarily sought outside assistance through our employee assistance program. One of the most positive and creative strategies we did was to set up a peer mentoring relationship between Ellen and Carol, a junior coworker who shared Ellen's' clinical interests. Carol added a very clear communication style and ability to translate Ellen's ideas to innovative co-treatment applications. This ended up being a very positive and productive relationship for both women as well as their clients.

Ellen eventually left the department to take a position in another hospital, but during the last year we worked together, I decided that it was time to stop being indirect about the communication and relationship issues and I started to confront situations as they occurred. Remarkably, I was able to do this without overreacting and letting out all of the accumulated emotion. It was effective. When I would immediately point out comments that were offensive to me or the staff, Ellen would apologize and improve her behavior. I also felt much better—more adult, more responsible. Ellen and I maintained a good relationship; confronting her did not lead to greater conflict and more problems as I had feared it would. I do believe that had I acted earlier, the outcome could have been better for me, for Ellen, for the rest of our coworkers.

My final learning focuses around my need to practice *informed assertiveness*, meaning that

★ I need to work to understand a situation, including the person's perspective and any institutional and legal parameters and responsibilities that exist.

★ I need to seek advice and use resources, but I must make information my own by thinking through what I'm told so that I am consistent with any parameters that exist but also honor my values.

(Continued)

Mentoring Leaders: The Power of Storytelling for Building Leadership in Health Care and Education

---

Story 9.1. Cont.

★ I need to take all of that insight, advice, and information and act. Assertiveness feels good; problems are less likely to metastasize, and I am less tormented by my fears and perceived inadequacies when I am direct and decisive and act in a timely manner.

It's always helpful for me to write these reflective stories. I better understand my successes and my failures. I can see the consistency of my actions over the years as well as ways to lessen the anxiety and distress I can feel over employee problems.

Reflective Questions

1. The mentor prepared for this story by writing out an objective review of her history with difficult employees. Take the time now to chronicle your own history and to look for patterns of success and failure.

_____

_____

_____

_____

_____

2. The mentor identified 4 learning points from her objective review. In looking at your review and analysis, what are your key learning points?

_____

_____

_____

_____

_____

3. The emotional costs of dealing with problem employees are frequently the biggest barrier to overcome. What can you do ensure that you have adequate support?

_____

_____

_____

_____

_____

4. The mentor uses the term *informed assertiveness* as her final learning point. How can you use informed assertiveness in your own leadership practice?

_____

_____

_____

_____

_____

Story 9.2. Learning to Work Smarter, Not Harder

Effective leadership is a relationship rooted in community. Successful leaders embody their group's most precious values and beliefs. Their ability to lead emerges from the strength and sustenance of those around them.

— Terrence Deal (as cited in Bolman & Deal, 1996, p. 56)

Before you read this story,

1. Reread Story 1.3, "Lou Shannon — Enabling Others To Act," in Chapter 1 to remind yourself of the power of involving others.
2. Think about your work responsibilities. Are there some changes you could make to work smarter?

For the past year, I have been working as a first-level manager of a large unit. I have 15 direct reports, and our unit is responsible for marketing important products in our organizations. During the past year, I seemed to gather more and more responsibilities, and I found myself working very hard. I began experiencing stress and had some health issues from my work responsibilities, and it showed. I was beginning to be cranky and irritated with others. Some of my staff asked me what was wrong. They said that I wasn't my old, positive self and that I looked so tired. They let me know that they valued my leadership and wanted to work together to become a stronger team. I appreciated their concerns but told them I was okay. I was trying to accomplish all my responsibilities, and it seemed additional ones got added. I was working very long hours and taking work home in the evenings and on weekends.

One day, my immediate supervisor called me to her office and asked me about my change in attitude and if I was having health problems. I cried and said I was just very tired and frustrated as I couldn't get all my work done. I was embarrassed that I cried, but it did feel good! She told me I needed to get some help, but unfortunately there wasn't money to hire someone as an assistant. She suggested I look at the people in my group of 15 people and decide if any of them could take over some of my responsibilities. She also told me there was no money to add to their current salaries.

My first reaction was a negative one. I just didn't see how this was going to work, and I resented my supervisor saying I had to get some help, but there was no money to hire an assistant. I didn't think I should add responsibilities to others without some form of added compensation. I knew that all of them were busy, and I didn't see how adding work to their schedules would be a positive move for our unit. I was concerned that those who might be able to do the tasks would resent being asked to add work without compensation. I was concerned I might lose some of my people.

I shared my frustrations with one of my peer managers, and he was supportive as well as helpful. He told me a story about a similar time in his past and what he did. I listened and got some great ideas that I felt would be positive actions for me and our group.

So, what did I do? First, I made a list of my responsibilities and tasks that needed to be accomplished. I then met with my supervisor to review the list and identify those tasks that

(Continued)

Story 9.2. Cont.

were highest priorities for her and our department. We also looked at realistic dates for completing the tasks. She even identified 2 tasks that she said could be dropped! She also stated how surprised she was that the list was so long. She had no idea I had so much on my plate. At this meeting, we determined that I would think about the tasks and come up with a plan, bringing it back to her when I felt it was completed.

My first step was to review the list and think about the conversation with my supervisor. I was more positive toward her as I realized she was concerned about me and wanted to help, not criticize. I think we both gained some respect for each other. I decided that the tasks she identified as priorities for her were the ones I should continue to carry out.

Next, I identified a group of tasks that I thought others could accomplish. Rather than assign others the tasks, I decided to meet with my group and share my story. I told them about my conversation with my supervisor and the plan to assign additional tasks to them. I shared the list with all the people in our unit and asked them to review the tasks and let me know if there was something they thought they would like to do. We talked about the positive aspects of taking over some of the tasks or responsibilities. I shared that there were not funds to add to their salaries, but I felt they would gain experiences that would be helpful in the future and that I had an underlying goal of involving them in the leadership and management of the unit.

The process worked great! Each person in our unit, professionals and staff, took on new tasks. I was pleased that each of them knew their skills and goals and selected tasks that would help them gain new skills and for which they felt competent to handle. I worked with each person individually to develop their plan of action. We then met as a group to share these with each other. The sharing was like a peer mentoring session as people gained new ideas that would be helpful to them.

When we had completed our plan, I met with my supervisor to present it. She was most pleased with the process and asked to meet with us to share her thanks and compliments with our group. I soon began to realize what was happening: The group was becoming committed to our unit and enjoying working together, and I saw pride in their work. When someone completed a task or a project was completed, our group would have some kind of celebration, like going out to lunch together or taking time for a group event. One time we all went to the local car racing track that offered parties for workgroups, which included the opportunity for us to drive the cars. I even drove one—NASCAR isn't for me! I realized we were becoming a stronger team. No one ever complained about no additional salary!

As I look back on my "old ways" and perceptions, I couldn't have been more misguided. I now realize I was trying to do it all, and I needed to let go of some of the tasks and trust that others could do the work as well as me. The priority for my group was to participate in tasks that would provide valuable experience for them.

What I learned by having to share my work was the power of empowering others. It resulted in their professional growth and my becoming more of a leader than a manager. Additional key learning included

★ Working hard isn't the best approach; one needs to learn to work smart!

★ Don't suffer by yourself. Let others know your difficulties because people do care and want to help.

(Continued)

Story 9.2. Cont.

★ It is important to plan with your supervisor and let this person know everything that is on your plate to identify the priorities to be accomplished.

★ Involving others in determining a course of action is an uplifting experience that brings creative solutions to situations.

★ Trust others to be able to carry out assigned responsibilities.

★ People don't just work for salary. People also want to improve their skills, enjoy their work, and work together as a team.

★ Celebrating accomplishments is a powerful action.

★ Having the title of *manager* doesn't mean you just manage; you also lead your group by sharing in the goals of the unit, enabling them to act and gain new skills, and honor the team's accomplishments.

★ A negative event or situation can at first seem impossible, but it can afford an opportunity for growth and a positive outcome.

Reflective Questions

1. What are the major lessons you learned from the story?

_____

_____

_____

_____

_____

2. How will you use your learning to help you work smarter?

_____

_____

_____

_____

_____

3. Why would the mentor share some of her negative feelings about the situation?

_____

_____

_____

_____

_____

4. Have you had a similar experience at work? How did you handle it? After reading the story and reflecting on the situation shared, would you do anything differently in your situation?

_____

_____

_____

_____

_____

Story 9.3. We've Got to Stop Meeting Like This!

Whoever invented meetings must have had Hollywood in mind. I think they should consider giving Oscars for meetings: Best Meeting of the Year, Best Supporting Meeting, Best Meeting Based on Material from Another Meeting.

—William Goldman (Marfdrat.com, 2010)

Before you read this story,

1. Think about the most recent meeting you attended or led. What was accomplished? How did you feel at the beginning of the meeting? How did you feel at the end?

   _____

   _____

   _____

2. Think about the best meeting you ever attended, and identify what made this meeting so positive.

   _____

   _____

   _____

Some people with whom I have worked seem to think that every decision requires a meeting. Other people act as though asking them to attend a meeting is giving them a death sentence. The two likely go together: The groans, moans, and rolling of eyes probably reflect experiences with very bad meetings.

If you're in a leadership position, like it or not, you end up running meetings. This was one of the things I most dreaded when I become the chairperson, and I was determined to run better meetings than the ones I had been attending. So, I had to ask, "What makes a really bad meeting, and what makes a good—or at least effective, if not enjoyable—meeting?"

One thing that helped me was the feedback the faculty gave me when they came to try to persuade me to take the chairperson's position. They told me some things they valued about my leadership that I hadn't really recognized. One of them said, "You listen and listen, and then when you finally say something, I know it's going to be valuable. It will help clarify the issues or suggest a good solution." Another said, "You are able to stay really balanced when things get emotional and not take sides." It was nice to step into the role knowing that the faculty liked the kind of leadership I showed in meetings. There were some other things I had learned from attending bad meetings.

I hate going to meetings when the first 20 minutes are spent giving announcements that I will not remember because they should have been written down. You're wasting my time. If you want me to remember something, give it to me in writing (preferably on the agenda), and then move on. Assuming (egocentrically) that everyone is like me, I always put announce-

(Continued)

ments on the agenda that is handed out at the start of our faculty meeting, and I don't spend time reading them aloud. (We e-mail the agenda ahead of time, but almost everyone forgets to bring it with them to the meeting.) In another department, the administrative assistant started sending out a weekly e-mail newsletter in which anyone, not just the chairperson, can include an announcement.

I also *hate* meetings in which 12 people are being asked to make a decision that 2 or 3 people could more easily make. In my very active faculty, everyone feels obliged to contribute to any discussion—sometimes at great length—so the decision takes forever, and there's lots of quibbling over small details. I quickly discovered that if small task groups were asked to do a preliminary review of an issue and draw up recommendations to present to the faculty, their recommendations were usually sound and readily accepted. Now, instead of meeting weekly, we have faculty meetings every other week. The alternate time is reserved for ad hoc task groups to meet as necessary.

The third kind of meeting is one where the leader is not crystal clear about what outcome she or he wants from the discussion and why that is important. This causes several problems. First, the discussion meanders because no one is quite sure where it should go. Or someone "takes over" and pushes his or her own agenda into the void. And then maybe some people simply opt out (mentally or physically) because they are bored. Then maybe some people start getting angry at the leader or at the person who has taken over. In the end, nothing is accomplished, so another meeting has to be called.

When I first became chairperson, I started to get caught in this trap. I think it was because I didn't want to seem too "pushy" or authoritarian, but I realized I was going to go crazy if things stayed that way *and* that my job was going to be harder because of all the unfinished business. I had to learn to take charge in a way that worked for me and for the group.

Probably the most important thing I've done is to always make sure at the start of any discussion that we are all clear what decision or outcome needs to be achieved. Sometimes I even set time limits: "We have 2 important items that need to be discussed today, so I'm going to allocate a half-hour to each, and we need to have a decision by the end of that period." Of course, I'm often the one who has to keep track of the time and issue the reminders, and sometimes people get annoyed with me if they want to make "just 1 more point." But at least the work gets done now, and I have realized that that's important: People need to count on being heard, but they also need to count on something getting done, otherwise there's no sense of closure, and people just feel frustrated over what feels like wasted time.

Over time, we created a humorous metaphor that we could use when the group was getting out of control. One day I said to the faculty, "You know some people talk about how hard it is to herd cats. Well, I think running this meeting is like trying to herd fish. You are all wonderful, colorful, and unique tropical fish, but would you please just try to swim *together* in a school?" That metaphor really worked and it stuck with us. Now when things are getting wild, I or someone else calls out "fish, fish, fish!" and everyone laughs and starts to settle down. I especially like it when someone else calls out "fish," because it affirms that the group perceives that getting the work done is everyone's job, and not just mine. Those moments confirm that we really are a collective, at least for the moment. I also have a collection of fish pictures, fish magnets, fish notepads, and fish mobiles adorning my office—from the faculty.

(Continued)

Story 9.3. Cont.

In the past few years, I have participated in more and more meetings via technology—phone conference calls or via the Internet. This has brought some new challenges as well as some old challenges in a new form. For example, the fact that you don't have to get everyone in the same room together can sometimes lead to *more* meetings—why not? It seems so much easier now. But I find that some of the same principles about good and bad meetings still apply. People still need to know what the ground rules are and what the purpose of the meeting is.

For many meetings, especially one-time meetings, I find it really makes a difference if someone sends out an agenda ahead of time that includes preparatory steps or materials and an outline of what issues will be addressed or what decisions will need to be made. This is how we run our weekly research meetings with my project team, some of whom are in my office, one of whom is across town, and another group of whom are out of the country.

This past fall I participated in a grant review meeting conducted via conference call. It was the first such experience with this particular type of grant for several of the participants. The panel leader, who was more experienced with this type of grant and in conducting meetings via teleconference, started by laying out a structure that he had found really helped organize this complex discussion and then guided us through step by step. It was a very long and tiring conference, but I felt like the time was well spent because we knew what we were supposed to do.

Like all other meetings, I find it is also important to send out minutes. Even if you hope that everyone is attentive and taking their own individual notes, it is really easy for something important to be overlooked. The more complex the discussion, the more important it is to have such a follow-up report. If I run the meeting, I try to identify someone else to do this because it's hard for me to pay attention to leading and recording at the same time.

Over time, I have learned that it's important that even something as mundane as running a meeting be guided by my values. I really don't need all or even most program decisions to come from me. It's much more important for a decision to be one that everyone in the group feels fits for the group, for who we are and who we want to become. I see my role as being much more like a guide to articulate the decisions that are needed and maybe some of the options, to synthesize ideas and maybe try to keep us on track, and make sure we are moving forward. The very best meetings for me are those in which we all feel satisfaction in what was accomplished and no one quite remembers where all the parts of the solution came from.

Reflective Questions

1. What makes a really bad meeting and what makes a good — or at least effective, if not enjoyable — meeting?

   _____

   _____

   _____

   _____

   _____

2. This story includes a great example of how meetings can build community ("fish, fish, fish!"). Although this was spontaneous and unplanned, what have you learned about leading meetings that you can use to build this type of *esprit de corps?*

   _____

   _____

   _____

   _____

   _____

3. Think about the most recent meeting you attended. What could you have done to improve it?

   _____

   _____

   _____

   _____

   _____

4. What leadership skills will you use in the future when planning and running meetings to improve participation and results?

   _____

   _____

   _____

   _____

   _____

References

Abrahams, J. A. (n.d.). *The importance of effective communication in the translation business.* Retrieved February 7, 2011, from http://www.translationdirectory.com/articles/article1409.php

Bolman, L. G., & Deal, T. E. (1996). *Leading with soul: An uncommon journey of spirit.* San Francisco: Jossey-Bass.

Bolton, R. (1979). *People skills.* Englewood Cliffs, NJ: Prentice-Hall.

Marfdrat.com. (2010). *On meetings and committees.* Retrieved February 7, 2011, from http://www.marfdrat.net/2010/11/17/on-meetings-and-committees

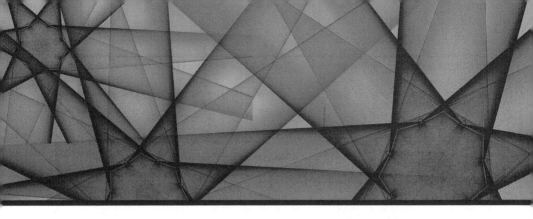

Chapter 10.
Leading for the Future

Story 10.1. Resisting Our Inner Quicksand

The almost insoluble task is to let neither the power of others,
nor our own powerlessness, stupefy us.

— Theodor Adorno (as cited in Ayer & O'Grady, 1994, p. 3)

Before you read this story,

1. It's time for honest self-reflection about the health care professions and their internal cultures. How would you describe your professional culture? What are the positives, and what are the limitations?

   _____

   _____

   _____

2. When have you felt most powerful and valued as a professional? When have you felt apologetic, angry, or disappointed?

   _____

   _____

   _____

Let me start by saying that I am passionate about occupational therapy. I cannot imagine any path I could have followed that would have been more meaningful to me than becoming an occupational therapist. I also believe deeply in the importance of the values and core ideas of occupational therapy.

Having said that, I need to add that I have often felt I have a love–hate relationship with the occupational therapy profession. Why is that? It is because I often feel that one of the biggest barriers to our success as leaders in health care is our own professional culture. To the extent that that culture is embedded in me, I feel I have also to struggle to overcome those negative forces to work more successfully toward my own goals. This story is about those experiences. I am telling it because I believe that developing our leadership means we need to address some of those barriers in our inner culture.

I first became aware of the cultural struggles within occupational therapy when I wasn't even an occupational therapy professional yet, just an aide in an occupational therapy department in an inpatient psychiatric hospital, which also happened to be a prominent university teaching hospital. I supervised an activity room on the unit that was also a work placement in the hospital's predischarge program. Because of this role, I had valuable information to contribute to patient reviews about the person's functioning in this closer-to-real-life context.

At some point, early in my time in the department, my occupational therapy supervisor made an emphatic point at one of our staff meetings. She said, "I don't *ever* want to walk into a unit case review and see one of my OTs sitting at the back of the room. You sit at the conference table or in the front row. Your information and expertise is just as valuable as the resident's, and that's where you belong." I didn't realize it at the time, but she had just steered me away from one of the huge temptations of our profession: to see ourselves as less valuable and less powerful than our professional colleagues. She had also given me an incredibly useful piece of advice: Don't wait for an invitation; assert your rightful place.

Why would such a reminder be needed in the first place? Even then I understood. We were all women with bachelor's degrees in a teaching hospital where all the senior psychiatrists were men, where the first few female residents were just now being accepted, where the dominant model was psychoanalytic. *They* were doctors, *they* were "in charge" of the patient's care. There was a certain aura about their knowledge and a definite sense of power in their interactions with others. In that context, it would be so easy to gradually retreat to the back of the room and thereby define ourselves as less important.

A second "aha!" moment comes to mind. It took place at an annual dinner at the AOTA Annual Conference, which has always been a great gathering for storytelling. I was sitting with a group of occupational therapy scholars, and we got to telling stories about rebellion. The story settings varied from the dorm at OT school to a first fieldwork placement to academia, but the theme was the same: Each of them had challenged some aspect of a system they thought was wrong and unfair and managed to get away with it, to their great delight. Unfortunately, the system they were challenging was the OT culture itself, which had imposed ridiculous restrictions on what they should say and what they should do—on what was "acceptable" as an OT. In each instance, what was deemed acceptable put someone else in control.

(Continued)

Story 10.1. Cont.

Although these stories are set in a time when the medical model was still dominant, I feel that we still struggle with that uncertainty about our value and power. I feel it every time I go to the AOTA Conference and listen to someone in a plenary session tell us how great we are, usually to enthusiastic applause. Why do we need to do that? I don't imagine doctors spend part of their professional conference time telling each other how great and important they are. I also feel that struggle in the AOTA Program Directors' meetings when someone gets up to anxiously talk about how physical therapy is going to take over the world. Are we so powerless?

Perhaps it is anxiety, or perhaps it is our strong desire for harmony that also makes us so uncomfortable with the differences among OTs. At the same time that we talk about the importance of respect for diversity, the Program Directors' group is uncomfortable acknowledging that different types of institutions may face different kinds of challenges, whether they must accept any student who applies, or the impact of stringent tenure requirements on faculty advancement. If the research universities ask for time to talk in a small group about their unique challenges, someone will voice a concern about "elitism." If someone suggests that OTA programs might need some time to talk about their specific issues, someone will worry doing so will create a split between the OTA and OT programs.

Sometimes, to get a better perspective on your culture, you need to step outside of it. When I was a full-time PhD student, I was immersed in another profession's culture for several years, and it provided some really important lessons. One of the things I learned was the language of scholarly dispute. In that world, you could say, "I think your idea is totally wrong," and if you could back up your point with appropriate evidence or logic, you earned respect.

In occupational therapy, we seem uncomfortable with that kind of challenge. We work so hard for consensus that sometimes I think we end important debate much too soon. Or, if the debate continues, it sometimes becomes personal and the opponents stop speaking to each other. On the other hand, if someone outside the profession criticizes our ideas or our science, we become defensive, as if challenging our ideas is challenging our existence. How can we grow without active debate?

I have had to work *hard* to silence my self-doubt and anxiety and to resist my inner urge to "sit at the back of the room." Last year I was invited to serve on an advisory committee of the national Institute of Medicine to advise the Social Security Administration on the disability determination process. My first reaction was to feel flattered. My second reaction, which almost immediately followed, was to think that perhaps they had made a mistake. I called to check, to make sure they understood I was a pediatric OT and a measurement specialist. They said yes, they knew that, and they thought that perspective would be very useful. Still, I went to the first meeting full of trepidation, wondering what on earth I would have to contribute. As it turned out, I had quite a bit to contribute, not the least of which was a deep understanding of function and a language with which to talk about it. It turned out to be a wonderful group to be part of. However, last week as the committee was planning a symposium session and suggested I might be one of the people from the committee to present, I quickly backed away and suggested another member might be better suited.

(Continued)

Story 10.1. Cont.

Building self-assurance often feels like building a new culture. Perhaps in some ways it is. I started by acting *as if* I had confidence. I copied others who seemed to know how to do this. I still watch colleagues or other professionals at meetings to learn strategies that might "fit" for me. I have worked hard on learning the language of scholarly discussion and on being able to hear opposing views without feeling impelled to "make everything nice."

The intent of sharing this story was not to launch a critique of the profession but to stimulate some reflection about the ways in which our profession's culture does or does not support us to become effective leaders, not only of our programs but of the larger academic and professional worlds. It seemed to me that if we want to move into new territory, we need to make sure we know where some of the pitfalls lie. When the pitfalls are within us, I have found that overcoming pitfalls takes a lot of hard work and a lot of support.

Reflective Questions

1. Why would the mentor share this story?

2. What is your reaction to the mentor's admission of her love–hate relationship with occupational therapy?

3. Reflect on the mentor's position that the occupational therapy profession's culture may not support becoming effective leaders. Defend your position with evidence and logic.

_____

_____

_____

_____

_____

4. What did you discover about yourself and the profession from the mentor's story?

_____

_____

_____

_____

_____

Story 10.2. Leading Change to Design Our Future

> *Life never stops teaching about change. As leaders, hopefully we can be gentle*
> *guides and coaches so that people discover their own life's wisdom.*
>
> —Margaret Wheatley (Wheatley, 2002)

Before you read this story,

1. Reread the section in Chapter 1, "Inspiring a Shared Vision."
2. Think about the department or division in which you work. Do it have a vision statement? Were you involved in developing the statement? Do you use it when planning for the future?

   _____

   _____

   _____

3. Read the article the mentor talks about in the story, "Vision Revisited: Telling the Story of the Future" (Lewis, 2009).

Our academic program has been experiencing a period of numerous changes. The changes were directed by our academic vice president and have required our department to change almost everything we do: discontinuing our undergraduate program, admitting more graduate students, doing more research, and increasing grant funding. Some faculty left, we added 2 new hires, and 2 more will be added next year.

Both the faculty and clinical staff seemed so *fearful.* They were worried about the future, especially requirements to conduct more research and the need to obtain grant funding. As a group, we felt negative about the university. The administration as well as our department seemed to be in chaos. At this time, I was the head of our department and knew I had to provide the best in leadership.

Our college dean shared an article about visioning with all the department heads. The article by Ira Lewis (2009) gave me ideas for a process to develop a vision, to have hope for our future, and to change our attitudes from negative and fearful to positive and hope. The article was timely, and it helped me become a better leader for change.

Using some of the ideas in the article, I decided to begin a process of change by focusing on my dream or vision for our future. At the beginning of the academic year, we always had a retreat to plan for the year. At the start of our meeting, I shared my story about how I envisioned our department 5 years in the future. My story spoke to our people, activities, philosophy, and relationships. The story depicted our department through the activities we were doing and roles each of us were carrying out. Then I pulled from the story some ideas that reflected my dream or vision of what our department might be in the future.

I stressed that what I most wanted was for us to develop the vision together so our future would be an outcome of all our ideas. My story was to serve as a beginning for us; it was not the final product. During the meeting, we worked together in pairs and shared each other's vi-

(Continued)

Story 10.2. Cont.

sion for our department. Then each pair reviewed their ideas, synthesized them, and prepared a written document about what they envisioned for our department. There was no structure to how the document was to be written. It didn't have to be a story like the one I presented, nor a text or bullets; the final product was their choice. A few wrote a story, some prepared a list of ideas, and some wrote a vision statement. The process took longer than I thought it would, but it proved to be valuable for us. People were sharing, laughing, and obviously having a good time being creative and having positive ideas about sharing dreams for the future.

Following the meeting, we copied all the documents and distributed them to everyone in the department with the assignment to read them and come to the next meeting with opinions and ideas about the content shared. This was a lively meeting, and people shared openly with thoughts both pro and against some of the ideas for the future. We captured the discussion on flip charts for our use to begin planning a vision statement that would describe our direction, values, and priorities for the future.

The next step was to appoint a group of 5 people to review the flip-chart notes of our discussion and draft a suggested vision statement or a story about our future. This group worked together for a month, interviewing the other department members to help guide them as they prepared the statement. Their document was also posted on our Web site for clarification and comments from our clinical staff, students, alumni, and others.

The next step was to finalize the vision. The draft document was a vision story created by the committee of 5. We were able to edit the story; the document from the committee wasn't changed too much. The edited version was distributed to our department faculty and staff for review and also published on our Web site. I scheduled another retreat for the end of the semester to finalize our vision story. Because we had worked together over several months to develop our ideas, the finalization of our future direction came easily. I was pleased; the ideas presented in my initial vision story were certainly there, but the final vision story was much improved from my original vision.

I believe the story and process inspired others to dream and share their ideas about our future. The process brought us together, and we became more positive. I am a true believer that a shared vision story is the best direction for our future. As I reflect on the process, I discovered the joy of being a leader and working with my group to define what we want for the future.

Reflective Questions

1. What did you discover about the process to develop a vision for the future that might be helpful for you as a leader?

_____

_____

_____

_____

_____

2. This was a story about using a story and collaborative process to develop a vision statement. Why do you think stories can be such powerful tools for visioning and building a culture for the future of a unit?

_____

_____

_____

_____

_____

3. What are some specific actions you will take to develop a shared vision?

_____

_____

_____

_____

_____

4. What other leadership practices (Kouzes & Posner, 2007) will you use when creating and enacting a shared vision?

_____

_____

_____

_____

_____

Story 10.3. Leadership in the Curriculum—Our Profession's Future

Leadership cannot really be taught. It can only be learned.

– Harold Geneen (Thinkexist.com, n.d.)

Before you read this story,

1. Read *The Three C's in Developing Leaders* (Blunt, 2005), an online article about developing leaders in the public sector. Look for the parallels to your profession and the role of mentoring.
2. As you read the following this story, keep in mind that developing future leaders is a responsibility shared across your profession.

This story takes a look at leadership from a different perspective: How do we, as leaders in occupational therapy education, need to consider the development of the next generation of leaders in our profession, and how do we create more definitive leadership experiences for our students? I've been thinking about how we defined leadership at our university and how we infused leadership into the curriculum. In this story, I offer our experience as an example that I expect will prompt you to share your own examples of experiences within the curriculum as well in practice. I think that sharing this story can inspire us to create new educational approaches to leadership development so that we can be the impetus for the profession to look systematically at leadership development for students.

Leadership is an area that we have always considered a strength of our program. We prided ourselves on educating sophisticated therapists who understood systems of care, grasped the bigger picture of health care delivery, and could assume leadership positions early in their careers. For many years, we were like the majority of entry-level programs and had one course that was clearly labeled a leadership course. That course followed the accreditation standards for content that addressed the administrative and management aspects of practice. We were weak in formally evaluating leadership outcomes. The only real evidence that supported our claim that leadership was a strength of our program was our students' performances on the certification exam. Consistently, our students scored significantly above the average score in the practice management areas of the exam. Other than the exam scores, some anecdotes, and a belief that our grads were leaders, we had no real support for considering leadership a strength in our program.

When we undertook our last comprehensive curriculum redesign, we decided that we needed to take a more systematic approach to defining leadership and intentionally infusing leadership across the curriculum. I'm going to tell you a little about the curriculum development process we used and some of the specifics we developed related to leadership. Then I'll share 2 examples of opportunities created for the students to enact leadership.

Our curriculum redesign began with restating our mission and philosophy statement to ensure that leadership was addressed at that level. Within our mission statement, we state our

(Continued)

intention to pursue our university's tradition of producing state and national leaders by producing scientists, practitioners, scholars, and researchers who would be leaders in our profession and discipline.

In our educational philosophy statement we again addressed the concept of leadership by stating that each student would have a strong identity as a leader positioned to lead in clinical settings as well in broader professional arenas. We defined the role, emphasizing the use of evidence and reflection to challenge the status quo, develop new ways of doing things, and anticipate and direct change at professional and external levels.

Writing the mission and philosophy statements led to the identification of curriculum concentration areas, one of which focused on leadership. We also identified distinct professional roles we prepared students to assume: consultant, program planner, clinician, administrator, researcher, and educator, and we stated the clear expectation that our graduates would function as leaders in each of these roles.

Our next actions were to define the concentration area, to delineate an overarching goal for our graduates, and to set curriculum goals to guide instruction in the theme area. With this completed, we were then ready to design courses that would have a primary emphasis on educating students in leadership. We ended up with a 3-course sequence with a primary emphasis on the leadership area: Course 1 in the fall semester of the first year, Course 2 in the fall of the second year, and Course 3 in the spring of the second year. Course 1 introduces the students to various practice settings and the regulatory and funding mechanisms of each setting, Course 2 is a survey of administration and leadership, and Course 3 involves program development. I taught both of the courses in the second year of the program.

In these courses the didactic instruction is focused on leadership and the technical skills of administration and service management as well as on the change process and change agent role. I am not going to talk about those courses but instead will share 2 examples of cross-course experiences that provided opportunities for students to enact leadership skills.

Lucy's Class

My first example demonstrates the value of curriculum design that emphasizes leadership content so that all faculty understand what, when, and how the content is taught. This example also shows that curriculum structure is also a base for flexibility and recognizing an opportunity to teach and experience the theme outside of the primary courses.

Lucy teaches the first course in the leadership concentration area in the fall of our students' first year. In the second semester of Year 1, we don't have a course in the sequence, but all faculty consistently relate student experiences in the clinical courses back to the bigger system picture they gained in the fall semester. In the spring, Lucy teaches a course in geriatric practice. One year, she had a guest speaker early in the semester from a local senior center. Unexpectedly, the speaker talked about her need to develop more programs for the seniors and her frustration of not having time to do this.

After the class session, Lucy came to me with an emerging idea she had to introduce the first-year students to program development in order to respond to her guest speaker's need for more programs. As Lucy and I talked, we decided that we could rethink her current course

(Continued)

and my program development course the following year, going ahead to introduce program development content and an assignment in Lucy's geriatric class.

I did several mini-lectures on program development and needs assessment, and we designed an assignment in which teams of students conducted literature reviews and community-level data gathering to describe the perceived needs of the senior population, address potential program areas, and identify funding sources.

This information was assembled and presented to the senior center director. I then followed up by offering elective courses in the second year to students who would take the class needs assessment, refine it, and develop and implement a program at the senior center. Also, having introduced the program development process and needs assessment in the first year, I re-structured the required second-year course and was able to move the class more quickly into the program development process in Year 2.

The students who took the elective developed and implemented a very innovative Crafts Exploration Program for the senior center that not only addressed the director's immediate need for a new program but also provided her with a model for future program development. In addition to serving as consultants to the senior center director, these 2 students also assumed leadership and instructional roles with their classmates, as I had them serve as class mentors in the required program development course. In evaluating their experiences, the students talked about the confidence they gained through dealing with real-life administrative and leadership problems with the support of a faculty member. They also felt that enacting their program at the senior center gave them a better understanding of what it means to be a change agent and to professionally function in multiple roles: clinician, consultant, program developer, and administrator.

Fieldwork–II

My second example is about a Fieldwork–II we designed to simultaneously develop students' clinical skills and administrative and leadership skills in mental health settings. Although we often had Fieldwork–II experiences designed to incorporate clinical, program development, and leadership roles, these experiences had typically involved second-year students who had completed the 3-course leadership sequence. In this example, we decided to develop the experience for first-year students who had completed only the first course in the sequence. We did this knowing from the previous example that it was possible to successfully introduce students to the change agent content earlier in the curriculum.

One fall we received an internal grant notice for programs that would increase the number of allied health practitioners in our state. We decided to focus a proposal on preparing occupational therapists to assume leadership roles in community mental health programs. We chose this focus for several reasons: Mental health reform is a critical concern in the state, with inadequate numbers of programs and providers, and we have had very few of our grads elect to go into mental health positions, particularly in the community. We decided that a program that allowed students to develop clinical skills while also developing administrative skills would position our grads with a better skill mix for a wider array of community mental health positions.

(Continued)

Story 10.3. Cont.

We received funding and formed a 3–faculty member planning group: Lucy, the fieldwork coordinator; Eliza, who taught mental health content; and me. Our roles were to design and structure the fieldwork, develop the supervisory model, identify the community mental health sites, and monitor the experience. We placed 2 teams of 2 students in local programs. Each team had an onsite supervisor, who was the program administrator, and an off-site supervisor, who was an OT practicing in mental health.

We wrote learning objectives for the experience on the basis of our curriculum objectives for the leadership area and the input of our occupational therapy supervisors. As part of the structure of the fieldwork program, we sponsored several workshops for the students and supervisors on both clinical skills and leadership skills and required several leadership assignments as part of the fieldwork. Each student had to develop a professional portfolio that guided their learning along with the fieldwork objectives, had to conduct a needs assessment for his or her site and work through the logistics of purchasing supplies to address the identified program needs, and had numerous clinical and administrative assignments generated by their supervisors. We pushed the students to see that their clinical and leadership roles could merge.

One of the teams had very successful outcomes where they appreciated, enjoyed, and valued the experience of blending those roles. One of those students pursued and obtained a competitive position for a mental health fellowship. The other team had individual and team issues that seemed to relate to their discomfort with innovation and the team's inability to work together. In the end, we considered this only a partial success and continued to analyze what happened to understand more about the divergent results.

In both of my examples, I have tried to demonstrate our approach to infusing leadership that is based on a very structured curriculum design that emphasizes leadership development but also allows the flexibility to respond to an opportunity. Each example also shows that even though we had courses with primary emphasis on developing leadership content, there were other courses that either had a secondary emphasis or that provided the right context for enacting the skills. We couldn't isolate the leadership content in discrete courses and expect students to have the confidence to use the skills in a variety of roles. We had to provide experiences across the curriculum that allowed students to see the relevance of the leadership in clinical applications. Finally, each example demonstrates the blending of administrative and clinical skills into a leadership role. It is the contextual learning in each experience that resulted in a more powerful experience.

I learned that

★ We have made progress didactically by defining what leadership means in our curriculum, by increasing the focused instruction in leadership in our 3-course sequence, and by infusing the content more broadly across the curriculum. We have also been able to introduce this bigger picture thinking early in the curriculum and know that it is also possible to introduce other leadership skills earlier.

★ It's very frustrating to have to admit that we still haven't figured out how to systematically provide leadership experiences for our students. Although we have a few examples of students enacting leadership, the majority of our students do not have this opportunity. Most students take our 3 courses and have the didactic content but not the applied experience.

(Continued)

Story 10.3. Cont.
> ★ Leadership, like clinical content, has to be infused across several courses *as well as* into practical application and experiences. Book learning alone isn't sufficient.
> ★ This type of comprehensive applied learning required a great deal of faculty time and external resources. We can't duplicate these experiences for all of our students, but maybe by analyzing these "mega examples," we can create more realistic opportunities for more students.
>
> This is my hope that we can collectively use our expertise to design leadership experiences for our students that are both practical and meaningful.

Reflective Questions

1. The mentor talked about how curriculum design must clearly support the outcome of developing the next generation of leaders. In what ways does your curriculum design address leadership? How does this direct leadership learning activities?

_____

_____

_____

_____

_____

2. The mentor also talks about the need to go beyond the classroom to provide applied leadership experiences. What does this mean to you? What are the challenges in doing this?

_____

_____

_____

_____

_____

3. If you had all the resources you needed — without limit — what would you do to develop the next generation of leaders?

_____

_____

_____

_____

_____

4. What are 3 things you can do now to begin to address leadership development in students and new therapists?

_____

_____

_____

_____

_____

Story 10.4. Change Is Inevitable, Growth Is Optional— A Tale of 2 Situations

> *Life is change. Growth is optional. Choose wisely.*
>
> —Karen Kaiser Clark (as cited in Dominguez, 2003, p. 97)

Before you read this story,

1. Think about your personal reactions to change, both emotionally and intellectually. What factors are influencing your response to change?

   _____

   _____

   _____

During a conversation, one of my mentors shared a quote that struck us as so unfortunately true that it just had to become the theme for this story: "Change is inevitable, growth is optional." We had to laugh about this quote because we could recall too many times in our careers when something changed, but nothing happened. There was no learning, no progress. We can all tell stories about our institutions that bear out the truth of this quote—times when change was eagerly anticipated, yet the results just didn't measure up to the expectations, or times when change was imposed on us, and the results ranged from revolt to passive–aggressive compliance to giving up or in. Clearly, change and growth are not synonymous. A relationship exists between both that is very complex. As leaders, the more we can understand about the relationship, the more likely we are to be sure that the change will be positive, be productive, and will flourish.

This story is about different responses to change as well as my own leadership history with 2 different programs in the same university. It was helpful to me to review my history with both programs, as I have puzzled over why I was so successful in one situation yet not in the other. Until I wrote the story and really thought about it, I had attributed my failure almost exclusively to my leadership efforts and didn't have any other way of considering and understanding the situation. This is another instance of storytelling leading to retrospective analysis, and it gave me both a higher level of leadership self-esteem and peace with a difficult time in my professional life.

Situation 1. Change and Growth—Inevitable and Achievable

Our program was in a state of chaos. The director had been asked to step down after the faculty and students had a vote of no confidence and demanded that the dean take immediate action. The dean acted quickly and asked both the program director and the chair of allied health to step down, believing that the leadership problems were at both levels. All of the occupational therapy faculty, except for the former director, left in the late spring and summer. Two new, novice faculty members were hired, and an acting director (a non-OT) was appointed.

(Continued)

Story 10.4. Cont.

One week before the new class started, the faculty learned that someone (a second-year student? a former faculty member? No one knows who) had sent postcards to the new class, warning them not to come to the program, that administration was not behind the program, that the faculty were inexperienced and not prepared to teach, and that entering the program would be disastrous.

Fast forward 25 years...

The program is considered one of the top programs in the country. There is a stable senior faculty who are productive researchers, highly regarded authors, and excellent teachers. There are 6 full-time, university-funded faculty positions and additional positions that are affiliated with the program through grants, contracts, and clinical programs. The transition from a long-time director to a new director went smoothly. This year, as every year, there was a waiting list for admission to the entry-level program, with the top students in the applicant pool electing to attend the program. A doctoral program has been established and is now at full capacity. Both master's and doctoral students are recognized by the university as among the top students receiving coveted merit assistantships and doctoral fellowships.

Situation 2. Change and Growth—Inevitable and Unattainable

Another program in the same department was in a state of chaos. The director had been asked to step down after a vote of no confidence by the students and faculty. Student enrollment had been consistently below capacity for years, with students admitted who were below the academic average of the graduate school. Senior faculty fought among themselves and undermined the success of junior faculty. As a result, there was a revolving door for junior faculty with regular turnover in the junior positions.

There was conflict at all levels: between faculty and faculty, faculty and students, and students and students. Accusations about harassment and discrimination were common, and the chair had to frequently intervene to resolve both day-to-day problems and very serious infractions of university policy. A recent accreditation visit had resulted in re-accreditation but with a list of 10 critical deficiencies that had to be addressed.

Fast forward 25 years...

The program continues to struggle. Faculty are raising questions about the competency of the director and coming to the chair with their concerns. Enrollment has remained under capacity, with a slight improvement in the overall academic credentials for admitted students. Although there is no longer overt conflict and tension across the faculty, there also is not collegial collaboration or support for each other's work. A recent accreditation visit was successful, but faculty relationships were noted as an area of ongoing concern. When a funding crisis loomed for the department, the program was informally identified as the program that could be cut should the financial situation worsen.

(Continued)

Story 10.4. Cont.

Here are 2 programs in the same department in very similar situations at the beginning of each story. Early on, both programs faced disastrous events that almost caused the programs to be closed. Leaders were forced to step down, faculty left, and the caliber of the educational program was compromised. Yet one program was able to rebuild, and the other continued to struggle. Each program underwent change—that's the inevitable part—but the results were very different. In Situation 1, change prompted learning and a positive cycle of change and growth evolved. In Situation 2, change has not driven the same level of learning, and that positive cycle of change and growth has yet to evolve. To understand why this happened, I want to look at the intervening years in each situation and talk about 4 elements that I think are critical to the change–learning relationship: (1) leadership, (2) resources, (3) followership, and (4) context.

Leadership

I think we can all agree that the leader's response to change is fundamental to the group's response. A leader who is energized by change and who manages all types of change well creates a positive climate within the work group. Learning is more likely to occur.

- ★ *Situation 1.* During the 25 years, 4 transitions in leadership took place. I was the leader for a majority of the years and part of each one of the transitions.
- ★ *Situation 2.* During the 25 years, 5 transitions in leadership took place. I was the leader for a majority of the years and part of all but one of the transitions.

I have thought a lot about this! Why was I so successful in leading and transitioning to and from leadership in one situation but not the other? Was I the same caliber of leader in both situations? What did I do differently in both situations? In all honesty, I have to say that I was a better leader in Situation 1, my own professional program. My commitment to my profession was stronger and a real driving force for pushing my development as a leader and our growth as a program.

I tried very hard in the other program and brought my skills and my dedication to the university into the situation. I never had the passion for the group or for their problems that drove me to the level of persistence and pursuit of excellence that I had in my program, but I was passionate abut creating a successful program for the university. Additionally, in my program, there was always a leader following me who had the skills and the passion and made the transition work. In the other program, the leaders who transitioned from me did not have the necessary skills and, in some instances, also lacked the passion for their profession. I feel that the critical element of leadership that pushes learning to the forefront in a change situation is passion, closely followed by skill.

Resources

However, leadership is only 1 of 4 elements. In a changing situation, it certainly is important to have the resources to deal with the change, to fund increased demands, to support innovation, and to reward progress. It must be easier to learn and grow in an enriched environment, right?

(Continued)

Story 10.4. Cont.

★ *Situation 1.* During the initial years that I was the director, I had a static budget and went through a recession. During the last years, I enjoyed an increased budget that my predecessor had received as a result of legislated increases to support mandatory enrollment growth but also lived through another recession and severe budget cuts.

★ *Situation 2.* During my first stint as director, I had additional funds from the chair to bring in consultants and to pay adjuncts to pick up teaching responsibilities so that faculty could work on curriculum revision and accreditation issues. During my second stint as director, I arrived as the recession hit, and we made the decision to close the program. However, soon after we made the decision to close the program, in the midst of the recession, we received additional annual funding from the state legislature to reinstate the program.

Hmmm. Maybe an enriched environment and more resources are not quite the catalysts for change and learning that we might think, or maybe there are more important resources than the obvious fiscal ones.

Followership

Let's consider the third element, followership, as another type of resource. The leader is influential in creating an environment for change and learning, but the followers may be even more important because they either need to be willing to learn and change or willing to leave and allow change and learning to proceed.

★ *Situation 1.* The day that we first heard about the postcard that had been sent to our new students was the day we looked at each other and said we would make this work. The 2 novice faculty (that included me), the former director, and the acting director sat down and made a vow that we would support each other, we would deal openly with the students about the situation, and that we would start rebuilding the program from that point. Within a year, we had hired another faculty member who also embraced those values of honesty, trust, and integrity, and we had the core group to re-build the program. Over the years, faculty came and went, sometimes because of life circumstances but sometimes because the changes we were contemplating were not consistent with their career interests and needs. Our operating values of trust, honesty, integrity, and respect never wavered and saw us through a whole spectrum of change, from those we initiated to those that were imposed on us. We were able to learn throughout all of them. The most important resource in the program has always been the faculty.

★ *Situation 2.* As the leader, I was never able to instill the same values of trust, honesty, integrity, and mutual respect within the faculty. Behavioral patterns were so deeply ingrained in the group from destructive senior faculty that patterns continued, even after those faculty left.

Faculty are the most important resource a program has and can be either positive or negative contributors to growth and learning, depending on their individual make up and the relative strength of the group. I have seen how much negative impact 1 or 2 people can have on

(Continued)

Story 10.4. Cont.

a vulnerable group and how difficult it is for a leader to counteract either the overtly destructive forces or the legacy of destructiveness. A group can not change, learn, and grow when negativity and destructiveness are more deeply rooted than honesty, truth, and integrity.

Context

The last element that I think promotes learning in a changing situation is the context—several different aspects of context: in fact, the environment of the university as well as the external environment of the profession.

In both situations, the immediate context was and is the same: same department, same departmental leadership, same school, same university. At all levels, change was and is promoted as opportunity, innovation is valued, and change and learning are directly linked. So, if learning occurred in one division but not in the other, then the differences must be in the more specific professional environments.

★ *Situation 1.* From the point at which we looked at each other and said we would make things work, we had the support of our professional community. Our clinical community and alumni were alarmed and afraid when it looked like the program was faltering. Our clinical community supported us by continuing to take students for fieldwork, coming to clinical council meetings, and giving us invaluable suggestions. Our alumni encouraged students to apply to the program, they called and visited us, they gave guest lectures, and they served as fieldwork educators. In those very early days, everyone asked what they could do, and they did it. We also had a strong professional association to turn to, and AOTA gave us critical support. Over the years we used so many resources from AOTA and AOTF to rebuild. We simply would not have accomplished what we did without the overall strength and support of the occupational therapy community.

★ *Situation 2.* The context could not have been more different. First, reinstating the program was not sought out by the university but instead was imposed on the university by the legislature, with mandated specialty tracks. This external mandate constrained the natural development of the faculty and curriculum and is an excellent example of the type of external contextual constraints that public universities can face. In addition, faculty and previous leadership in the division had decided to actively distance themselves from the traditional professional organizations and clinical practice areas of the profession. Clearly, alienating yourself from your profession and colleagues is not the way to create change and learning. For this program, doing this meant that when they spiraled down, no one cared, and it was almost too late to ask for help. As an outsider to the profession, I also thought that there were no professional organizations as strong as AOTA and AOTF. The profession itself did not or could not provide the caliber of support that was available in occupational therapy.

Through my tale of 2 situations I hope that we have some insights into what promotes learning when change inevitably occurs. There is a dynamic, powerful, and unique relationship

(Continued)

Story 10.4. Cont.

among the leader, the followers, the resources, and the context that influences the degree, quality, and amount of learning that takes place.

To summarize my learning, I want to share a little more of my thoughts on leadership and resources and explore followership and external context more thoroughly.

My most obvious realization is that the skill of *leadership* alone is not enough. When I went to Situation 2, I had 15 years of administrative experience in both clinical and academic programs, lots of experience in leadership in professional organizations, and a degree in administration and policy. I had the knowledge and the skills. I had the track record that said I knew how to use the skills. But I didn't have the passion for my work. It was an assignment, an obligation.

I took the position to repay a debt for my program. I strongly felt that in our days of trouble and turmoil, the department and school invested in the program, sent us a strong interim director, and saved the program. When asked to take on a similar situation, I saw the opportunity and the obligation to repay that debt. Now I see the difference between obligation and passion. *Obligation* gave me a degree of objectivity that enabled me to make very difficult decisions and to enforce academic standards; it didn't enable me to inspire faculty and create vision and hope. That required *passion.*

I have also come to realize that I did not have the right level of emotional support from my chair in Situation 2. I guess he too was operating out of obligation and not passion. Without passionate support, I just could not withstand the bad behavior of faculty and the lack of community. Ultimately, what I learned about leadership and change is that I must be passionate to be fully committed and to use my full range of skills, but I also see that in a difficult situation, I need the inspired support of an impassioned leader above me.

I have to next talk about *followership* because in telling the story, I realized that developing followership is equally important to developing leadership. Both are linked. I've thought a lot about this because it's so easy to make a statement like that but so hard to know what to do to build that strong follower group. I have tried to think about a few key pieces of advice I've given myself along the way:

★ *Hire the right person.* Look beyond the content area or skill to be sure this person is a philosophical and social fit. The philosophical fit is the hardest because you (and whoever is there with you) have to know, agree on, and articulate what that philosophy is. It needs to be written out and clearly visible to everyone: the faculty, the students, your administration, and potential hires. I had a situation in which a candidate had exactly the right content background and we really liked her—the social fit was there. My chair wanted me to hire this person, but the faculty felt that something wasn't quite right. We went back to our philosophy statements, talked with the candidate about our beliefs of where the profession should be headed, and we all agreed that this was not a philosophical fit for her. What made the strongest impression on my chair was when the *candidate* explained to her why she wasn't philosophically right for the position.

★ *Always have team building on your personal leadership agenda.* Every faculty meeting, every retreat, and every conversation in the hallway is a chance to reinforce

(Continued)

Story 10.4. Cont.

who we are as a team and what we believe in and value. Team building means lots of different things. To me, it's all based on open, continuous conversation so you all get to know each other, appreciate each other, and can see how to work together.

★ *Confront problems, but choose your timing and your battles.* Over the years I did plenty of soul searching about when to confront someone's negative behaviors and when to tolerate and guide them out of negativity. I followed two rules: (1) If the behavior was destructive to the group or another individual, I forced myself to immediately confront the behavior with the goal of eliminating it; (2) if I found myself nagged by a problem (repeatedly needing to vent about the behavior, particularly at home), I would take time to purge my anger or fear, do some rehearsal, refresh my people skills, and go in with a goal of not just extinguishing the behavior but working to developing a positive behavior.

★ *Recognize when it's time for someone to go.* It might be you, or it might be a faculty member. This was a lesson from my earliest administrative days. Helping someone see it's time to go is not as hard as it seems. My experience is that if you know it, so does the other person, and the act of courage to bring the topic up is a relief and a starting point for positive decision making.

Now, final words about *resources*. It's so easy to think that if only we had more money, everything would be okay. This was probably best lesson I learned from this story. Money only makes things better if you can work together, have a common vision, and share values.

Once again, retrospection has brought clarity and insight into a situation from my past. This story has allowed me to see that change and learning are not the responsibility of the leader alone—there are so many other factors that influence the situation.

I was able to identify 4 of those factors: leadership, resources, followership, and context. I think there are others. Each change situation is unique, and understanding the process and the outcomes requires looking for those unique factors. I hope that my framework can be a starting point for you to see the factors that affect your leadership.

Reflective Questions

1. The best way to understand the change–growth relationship is to identify a situation in your work life when there was significant change and to honestly describe what happened: the precipitating causes, the reactions, and the results. You may have been the leader, or not. What was the situation? What happened?

_____

_____

_____

_____

_____

2. Consider the situation you described in the previous question. Did growth occur as a result of the change process, or did change not produce a positive response and growth? Use the mentor's 4 factors—leadership, followership, resources, context—to gain a better understanding of what happened and why.

_____

_____

_____

_____

_____

3. Are there other factors that you think influenced this situation?

_____

_____

_____

_____

_____

4. As a leader, what will you do to promote a positive change–growth relationship?

_____

_____

_____

_____

_____

Story 10.5. Writing Your Story—The Future of Leadership

You must do the thing you think you cannot do.

—Eleanor Roosevelt (as cited in Maxwell, 1999, p. 42)

By now you should be convinced that stories are a powerful tool for the development of your leadership capacity! You've learned by reading the text and the mentoring stories, reflecting on those stories, and discussing the stories with colleagues to share ideas and reactions. The process of writing a story is one of the greatest benefits to the mentor. Story-writing creates extraordinary opportunities for in-depth self-reflection and insightful analysis.

Writing your story can allow you to revisit the past and understand your successes and failures with greater clarity. Writing your story can provide objectivity and guidance for current challenges. Writing your story can describe a future that is so compelling that you must take action and make it your reality. The next step in your learning is to write your own story and learn from the reflection and analysis that are natural outcomes of the storytelling process.

Before you write your story,

1. Take another look at your definition of leadership, and consider how it has changed.
2. Review the leadership practice stories, and think about your strengths as well as the skills you need to develop.
3. Create a career timeline detailing not only what you have done but when you were most satisfied and *why*.
4. Reread the story that most affected you to understand why and how that story affected you.
5. Identify a past event, a present challenge, or a future vision as the core of your story and learning.

To write your story,

1. Think about the challenges, issues, or opportunities you have, or those you will or would like to face as a leader.
2. What action did you take, could you take, or will you take? Who else was or could be involved? What are your feelings and thought processes?
3. What were the results or outcomes, actual or anticipated?
4. What are the key lessons from this story?

(The Mentoring Company, 2007, p. 13)

As with all stories, the full power is realized in the *telling* of the story and the relationships that develop through sharing it. We hope that you will continue the process of mentoring with stories and will share your story with your mentor, your peers, and your future mentees in this next phase of your emerging leadership.

References

Ayer, A. J., & O'Grady, J. (Eds.). (1994). *A dictionary of philosophical quotations.* Oxford, UK: Blackwell.

Blunt, R. (2005). *The three C's in developing leaders.* Retrieved December 2, 2009, from http://govleaders.org/chronos.htm

Dominguez, L. (2003). *How to shine at work.* New York: McGraw-Hill.

Kouzes, J. M., & Posner, B. Z. (2007). *The leadership challenge* (4th ed.). San Francisco: Jossey-Bass.

Lewis, I. (2009). Vision revisited: Telling the story of the future. *Journal of Applied Behavioral Science, 36*(1), 91–107.

Maxwell, J. C. (1999). *The 21 indispensable qualities of a leader: Becoming the person others will want to follow.* Nashville, TN: Thomas Nelson.

The Mentoring Company. (2007). *Mentoring Circles: Mentoring orientation manual.* Loveland, CO: Author.

Thinkexist.com. (n.d.). *Harold S. Geneen quotes.* Retrieved February 9, 2011, from http://thinkexist.com/quotation/leadership_cannot_really_be_taught-it_can_only_be/209068.html

Wheatley, M. J. (2002). *Leadership in turbulent times is spiritual.* Retrieved February 10, 2011, from http://www.margaretwheatley.com/articles/turbulenttimes.html

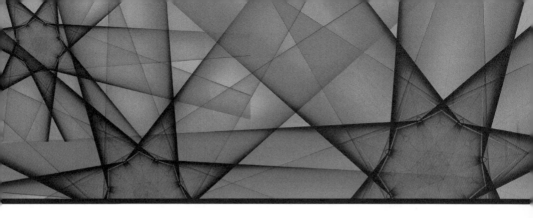

Glossary

Adaptive capacity. Ability to grasp the context of a situation and its value to constituents.

Bias toward action. Ability to act quickly and effectively in creating change.

Challenging the process. Experimenting and taking risks by constantly generating small wins and learning from mistakes.

Craft knowledge. Critical lessons learned that inform practices and promote discovery and learning.

Collaboration. Interconnected group or network of important relationships that enhance leadership performance and goals of the organization.

Communication. Connecting aspect of leadership.

Corporate culture. Concerns the conditions and forms in which meaning and value are configured and communicated; the soul or essence of an organization; a social energy that moves people to action.

Creative reflection. Introspective dialogue carried on in thought and narrative form. Reflection is the essential element for self-discovery and learning.

Crucible. Transformative experience through which a person comes to a new or altered sense of identity.

Crucibles of leadership. Ways in which individuals use crucible experiences that seem negative to develop leadership opportunities.

Defining opportunity. Event or experience that changes a person's life course in a significant way.

Education of All Handicapped Children of 1975 (P.L. 94-142). Federal legislation designed to promote inclusion of all children in typical education settings.

Enabling others to act. Fosters working together by promoting collaborative goals and building trust.

Encouraging the heart. Recognizes contributions of others by showing appreciation for individual excellence.

Engagement. Extent to which people enjoy and believe in what they do and feel valued for their performance.

Finding voice. Instances in which voice is used to speak out, articulate values, or lead change.

Inspiring shared vision. Envisioning the future by imagining exciting and ennobling possibilities.

Leadership. Art of mobilizing others to want to struggle for shared aspirations.

Leadership culture. Organization's strategies and development of leaders; values, style, character, informal rules, and the way of doing things are grounded in leadership and the development of leaders to empower people, break down the barriers of hierarchy, and distribute leadership throughout the organization.

Leadership Practices Inventory (LPI). Standardized instrument developed by Kouzes and Posner (2003) and designed to measure leadership performance, providing an assessment of self compared to an assessment by others in 5 leadership practices: (1) modeling the way, (2) inspiring a shared vision, (3) challenging the process, (4) enabling others to act, and (5) encouraging the heart.

Leadership readiness. Willingness and confidence to perform leadership practices that create supportive and productive environments and empower others to translate their strengths and action into common outcomes.

Learning context of stories. Environment for a deeper and more permanent level of learning created through immersion of the mentee in the values, emotions, details, and suggested actions of the mentoring story.

Mentee. Person who is mentored; a partner in a learning relationship; a protégée who receives guidance, training, knowledge, and support from someone who has more experience or influence.

Mentor. Partner in a vibrant, evolving learning relationship focused on sharing and discovering knowledge to build upon the mentees' capacities and vitality; a loyal and trusted counselor or teacher.

Mentoring. Communication and learning process to influence thoughts, voice, and discovery of ideas and action; process occurs through a transformative relationship with a mentor and mentee(s) and includes critical reflection and application of ideas to creative actions.

Mentoring Circles®. Facilitated group mentoring process developed by The Mentoring Company (2008) that involves a group of people who use storytelling to foster safe, trusting communities to transfer best leadership practices.

Mentorship. Transformational process that encompasses mentoring as its practice, mentor and mentee(s) as its people, storytelling–listening as its communication tools, and applied learning as its outcome.

Mentor's story. Narrative account that weaves detail, character, and emotional content with a personal event or leadership experience; most notably, it includes outcomes and key leanings that are woven into the story.

Modeling the way. Setting examples by aligning action with shared values.

Narrative. Organizational scheme expressed in story form.

On-boarding. Organization's process and activities to assist new employees or members to adapt to and understand the organization and its systems.

Once born. Describes people whose sense of self comes from an orderly sense of events in their environment.

Reflective backtalk. Relationship with a trusted individual who openly responds to requests for feedback on ideas or actions.

Story. True or fictional narrative account that weaves detail, character, and event into a meaningful and memorable tale that is vivid and emotionally stimulating.

Storytelling. Creative conversation or narrative method that puts together a personal tale about experiences relevant for an individual's everyday work or activities; knowledge sharing; the essence of influence, entertainment, communication, understanding, and sharing of self.

Transactional leadership. Process related to management role in which individuals are engaged on the basis of exchanged relationships, mostly reward or punishments.

Transformative co-journey. Cycle of self-reflection leading to self-awareness and self-understanding that organically evolves organically through the mentoring process for both mentor and mentee.

Transformational leadership. Process in which leaders recognize existing need in potential followers and engage followers on the basis of the need.

Spoken language. Communication through verbal expression of thoughts or ideas.

Strengths Finder: Online survey developed by Gallup and designed to identify an individual's leadership strengths (Rath, 2007).

Tacit knowledge. Implicit, inferred knowledge; the wisdom hidden within a story.

Temporal learning. Integrating past experience, present situation, and future action through storytelling and listening.

Twice born. Describes people whose life experiences are marked by a struggle to achieve a sense of order in their environment.

Unspoken language. Communicating through gestures, body movements, or space utilization.

Vulnerable. State in which one is open to others' ideas.

Self-directed learning. Process of setting learning goals and accepting the significant emphasis on self-reflection and self-analysis inherent in learning through stories.

Learning mechanism. Specific ways learning occurs in story-based mentoring; includes listening, self-reflection, and writing.

Transformation of self. Process of reflecting, developing, modifying, and changing; acquiring self-efficacy and finding the self's voice.

Retention. Remaining or desiring to remain at an organization.

Leadership endeavors. Undertakings, happenings, and accomplishments achieved as a leader.

Trust. Condition of feeling safe to share self's experiences, situations, concerns, and issues and having confidence in others.

References

Education of All Handicapped Children of 1975, Pub. L. 94-142.

Kouzes, J. M., & Posner, B. Z. (2003). *The Leadership Practice Inventory* (3rd ed.). San Francisco: Pfeiffer.

The Mentoring Company. (2008). *Mentor orientation manual.* Loveland, CO: Author.

Rath, T. (2007). *Strengths finder 2.0.* New York: Gallup Press.

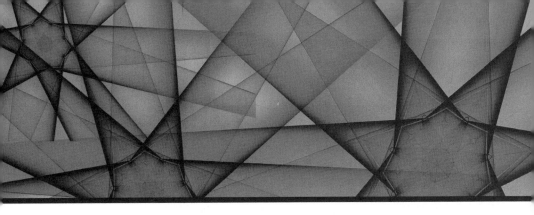

Index